# THE
# Sewing
## ANSWER BOOK

*Solutions to Every Problem You'll Ever Face*

*Answers to Every Question You'll Ever Ask*

BARBARA WEILAND TALBERT

Storey Publishing

*The mission of Storey Publishing is to serve our customers by
publishing practical information that encourages
personal independence in harmony with the environment.*

Edited by Deborah Balmuth and Nancy D. Wood
Art direction and book design by Jessica Armstrong
Text production by Jennifer Jepson Smith

Cover photograph by Mars Vilaubi
Floral pattern, back cover and interior, by iStockphoto/
   ©Joachim Angeltun
Illustrations by Missy Shepler, Shepler Studios
Indexed by Catherine Goddard

**Storey Publishing**
210 MASS MoCA Way
North Adams, MA 01247
*www.storey.com*

Printed in China by Regent Publishing Services
10  9  8  7  6  5  4  3  2  1

LIBRARY OF CONGRESS CATALOGING-IN-PUBLICATION DATA

Talbert, Barbara Weiland, 1947–
   The sewing answer book / by Barbara Weiland Talbert.
      p. cm.
   Includes index.
   ISBN 978-1-60342-543-8 (flexibind with cloth spine : alk. paper)
   1. Machine sewing. 2. Serging. I. Title.
TT713.T35 2010
646.2'044—dc22
                                        2010007170

*This book is dedicated to the strong and beautiful women who taught me to sew. I owe them my profound thanks for influencing the direction of my life and livelihood:*

- ♥ Big Grandma, Emma Gamble Nelson
- ♥ Grandma Tina (Sorenson)
- ♥ Grandma (Mary) Weiland
- ♥ My sweet mother, Eloise S. Weiland

# Contents

## ACKNOWLEDGMENTS

There are many to thank for their support during my lifetime sewing career — especially my mother and grandmothers. In addition, I have been supported and influenced by two very special women: Susan Foster (Pletsch) and Pati Palmer. Traveling and teaching sewing seminars for them expanded my knowledge of sewing and of the world.

I have had many opportunities, including stints as editor of two sewing magazines and as editor-in-chief at That Patchwork Place. Special thanks to Linda Turner Griepentrog, former editor of *Sew News*. Her faith in my ability to sew just about anything she could dream up encouraged my problem-solving, writing, and creative skills for 21-plus years.

I have had the opportunity to interact with many talented sewers and quilters. I was privileged to edit the work of many, while expanding my own bank of creative knowledge. Blessings to all!

Thank you to Storey Publishing for the opportunity to write this book, and to my editor, Nancy Wood.

Special thanks to Bernina USA for the opportunity to act as a National Artisan for Bernina and to interact with others in the same role. It's been wonderful to sew on Berninas during most of my sewing career and to explore machine embroidery on their artista machines.

Most importantly, I owe much gratitude to my sweet husband, Stan. His love and his support in everything I do is a blessing. His daily admonition, "Time to call it quits," brings balance to my life. Thank you, Sweetie!

# Introduction

The gift of learning to sew is one of the best legacies you can pass on to children. I did my first hand sewing at the knee of my "Big (great) Grandma." Together, we made a dress and bonnet for my best doll by cutting a pattern from newspaper and the pieces out of scraps from Grandma's Sunday dress. I still have it — a treasured memento of my childhood. Both grandmothers, and especially my dear mother, encouraged and instructed me as I grew; my love of sewing turned into sewing for 4-H and Make it Yourself With Wool competitions, then a college degree, and a lifelong career of sewing and teaching, and writing about it.

In the intervening years, I've learned so much — and so much has changed. Although computerized machines are now the most desired option, you can sew just as beautifully on a standard mechanical model, if that's what's available to you. New books, tools, and wonderful notions have turned sewing "chores" into rewarding, even exciting, experiences. Relaxation of some of the old sewing rules, by which my 4-H projects were judged, means you can use a machine for just about any sewing technique (hems included) and relegate hand sewing to mending chores and places where you *do* need a hand sewing needle and thread for sewing strength or invisible stitching. I love the rhythm of hand sewing, but I do substitute machine sewing when time is of the essence. "Doing it right" when it comes to basic techniques such as cutting, marking, and stitching will ensure the projects you make will be ones that you are proud to wear or use in your home. This book will help you master the essential steps for planning and sewing garments and basic home-decor items.

Sewing is a treasured creative skill that soothes and satisfies my creative soul. In the pages of this book, you will find answers to many of the most basic sewing questions. The field is so broad that I found it necessary to home in on basic techniques that every sewer needs to guarantee success. And I've included many that vary from the standard directions you'll find in sewing-pattern guide sheets, those that will make your sewing easier and the resulting project more professional looking.

There's so much more to sewing: Be sure to check out my favorite references in Resources for more great reading and problem-solving — and to help you build your own sewing library. As you delve into the pages that follow, I hope you'll consider my "rules for satisfying sewing" that follow:

## Get Ready

* **Choose fabric you love.** Don't waste your time sewing with something that's not perfect for you and your project.
* **Be sure to preshrink fabrics and notions** that require it before you begin.
* **Make sure you have everything you need for the project.** There's nothing more likely to dampen the creative spirit than needing to stop midway in a project to go to the fabric store, especially if you are a sewing night owl.
* **Clean up your sewing room/space before you start.** Vacuum the floor to pick up lint and scraps. A clean sewing room just begs for some creativity and will give yours a jump start.
* **Tape paper bags to the edge of your sewing/serging tables, cutting table, and ironing board to catch**

**threads as you clip.** Use a lint roller to clean off work surfaces and even to pick up threads from the floor.

## Get Set

* **Make any pattern adjustments to fit your figure *before* you cut anything.** Don't plan on marking them on the fabric as you pin the pieces. It's too easy to forget them or to mark them and then follow the original pattern edges when you cut.
* **Cut and mark as you go to ensure accuracy!** When you're ready to cut out your project, allow enough time to cut out everything and transfer construction markings before you must stop. That way, when you're ready to sew, you're *really* ready to sew.

## Sew!

* **Make two.** You can almost make two of the same thing or two coordinating garments in about the same time it takes to make one. Plan ahead!
* **Forget the rules sometimes and follow your creative instincts.** Even if it doesn't work, it's worth the lesson(s) you learn from trying something different.
* **If you cannot see it from a galloping horse, don't bother to redo it.** Some "mistakes" simply are not worth correcting, but if it really bothers you, fix it or you won't be comfortable with the finished item.
* **Don't do it if it's not fun!** If your project continues to present sewing challenges, take a break — or perhaps ditch the project entirely. Yes, it really is okay to ditch a project.

Before you do, determine why it's not successful so you won't be faced with the same challenges in future projects. Is it the fabric, the pattern, or the combination of the two? Are you in over your head with the skill level? Did you make test samples first? Save the fabric to use in other projects, but if the sight of the project makes you tired, angry, or frustrated, get rid of it and move on to something that will restore your good mood and result in a finished project that you will truly enjoy making and wearing or using.

See you at the fabric store!

CHAPTER ONE

# Setting Up Your Sewing Room

The quality of the tools and equipment you use affects the final results. The top three essentials are: a sewing machine with an array of basic presser feet, a good iron, and an adjustable ironing board. Many sewers would also recommend a serger as essential. Good lighting and a comfortable cutting surface are also necessary. After these major expenses are covered, adding special tools for special functions as your budget allows will make your sewing experience more fun and enjoyable.

# Sewing-Machine Primer

For starters, you need a sewing machine in good working order. If in doubt about what to buy, check with a respected sewing teacher or expert at your local fabric store for his or her recommendations.

---

**Q** I learned on my grandmother's machine, and I'm ready to buy my own. What should I look for in a sewing machine?

**A** Today's machines are not like your grandma's or even your mother's first machine. Built-in decorative and utilitarian stitches, an array of automatic buttonholes, automatic needle threaders and thread cutters, sensors that let you know when the bobbin thread is running low — these are just a few of the innovations that sewers now enjoy. Computers make it possible to program your own stitch patterns and save your favorite stitch settings on some machines. The list of features is endless, so it's essential to shop carefully for your machine. Ask for hands-on demos, and test-drive the machines you are considering. Buy one with the features that you most need. Then learn how your new machine works; most dealers offer training classes with sewing-machine purchases to jump-start your experience.

A basic machine with a balanced straight stitch and a basic zigzag stitch is essential. Built-in utility stitches are also helpful.

A sewing machine is a major purchase. You may not replace it for many years — or you may decide to upgrade to a pricier model with more "bells and whistles" later. Before you shop, check out sewing publications and *Consumer Reports*. Ask other sewers about their machine experiences and opinions. If you've never sewn, read about how the sewing machine works and what the basic parts are before you go shopping so you can ask the right questions. (*See pages 76–78.*)

Here are a few things to consider:

* **Know your budget.** Don't be persuaded to buy a machine with features you don't need. Hold your ground on this one.

* **Know what types of sewing you plan to do,** so the dealer can help you choose the best machine for your purposes. If you plan to quilt more than sew, you may want a machine with features that quilters love and use a lot.

* **Look at different models and brands** within your price range and test-drive them all. Keep notes.

* **Take along fabrics for test stitching**: a firmly woven one (such as denim) and a lightweight one (like muslin), plus a T-shirt knit and something slippery. Test straight and zigzag stitches, plus the buttonholes. Examine the stitch quality on each one. Do you like what you see?

* **Buy from a local dealer** where help is just a phone call or quick trip away. If you're not comfortable with a dealer during the sales pitch, don't buy from him or her. You want a comfortable, long-term relationship where you can get help, lessons, and repairs from someone you trust.

# Q Which presser feet do I need for my sewing machine?

A Most machines come with a basic set of presser feet, those most used for basic sewing. These include the straight-stitch, zipper, all-purpose zigzag, and the blind-hem feet. Many include a clear or open-toe embroidery/appliqué foot, a special buttonhole foot, and another for sewing buttons on by machine (*see page 388*).

Each presser foot is designed for a specific purpose; the bottoms differ on many of them. The flat sole of the all-purpose foot rides smoothly over straight and utility zigzag stitches without thread buildup. It's the most-used foot on zigzag machines because it's wide enough to hold fabric securely against the feed dogs.

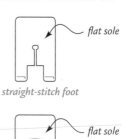

*straight-stitch foot*

*flat sole*

A **straight-stitch** foot has a small needle hole and a smooth sole. It's best used with a straight-stitch needle plate and is appropriate only for straight stitching. For decorative zigzag stitches, use the special **zigzag** foot, which has a small channel on the bottom.

*flat sole*

*zigzag foot*

For satin stitching and other heavy embroidery stitch patterns, use the **open-toe** embroidery/appliqué foot (*see next question*). Its wide channel glides smoothly over embroidery-stitch buildup

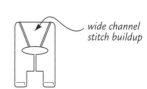

*wide channel stitch buildup*

*open-toe foot*

without snagging or flattening the stitches. A flat-bottomed foot will hang up on them, causing stitch problems. This foot enables you to see edges when satin-stitching over appliqué edges and doing other decorative machine stitching. The **buttonhole** foot has two parallel channels to accommodate the stitched "legs" of the buttonhole. A blind-hem foot has a special built-in guide that runs along the hem fold for accurate stitching (*see pages 312–313*).

---

## Q Will I need any other presser feet for special techniques?

A You can do most sewing with the basic presser feet. Specialty feet make easier work of many sewing techniques. Consider adding the following to your collection as your funds and projects warrant. Your dealer can show you how each foot works for the purpose intended — and often additional "Why didn't I think of that?" uses. Ask about other specialty presser feet and how to use them.

A ¼" **patchwork foot** (even if you don't plan to make quilts) helps you stitch an accurate ¼" seam allowance for home-decor projects as well as for some garment-sewing techniques. It's my most-used presser foot.

A **walking foot** is essential for preventing fabric layers from shifting when stitching thick fabrics and multiple layers. It grips and feeds the top layer of fabric while stitching, just as the feed dogs do the bottom layer. The foot is designed to prevent the machine from pushing the top fabric layer forward, eliminating stretched and puckered seams and uneven layers at the end of a seam. A walking foot is especially useful on denim and corduroy, as well as heavy home-decor fabrics such as upholstery tapestries. It's also essential for machine-quilting through layers of fabric and batting. Some machines have a built-in even-feed mechanism, making a walking foot unnecessary.

Note that the length and shape of the shank on presser feet varies from machine to machine — long, short, and slant-needle are the most common — so you must know the machine brand and model number before purchasing. Bernina feet have a unique clamp-on configuration and many machines now have a universal shank with snap-on presser feet.

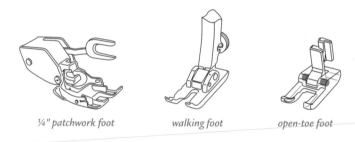

*¼" patchwork foot*                *walking foot*                *open-toe foot*

Q **Why and when would I use a straight-stitch foot and needle plate?**

A Choose them for beautiful straight stitching without puckering on lightweight fabrics. The needle plate has a small, round hole; using it with the narrower straight-stitch foot usually improves the stitch quality and tension. It also helps prevent skipped stitches, because there is no extra room for the needle to push the fabric layers into the hole (called "flagging") like there is in a zigzag plate. It is often used with a spring-loaded embroidery foot for decorative free-motion stitching and quilting; because you move the fabric in many different directions when free-motion stitching, stitch tension can be problematic.

*straight-stitch throat plate*

*zigzag-stitch throat plate*

---

**Q** **Are there general care guidelines for all sewing machines?**

**A** Just like an automobile, your machine needs servicing to keep it in top running order and to eliminate frequent trips to the dealership. The more you sew, the more often your machine will require servicing. For general maintenance:

* Protect your machine(s) with a cover to prevent dust, dirt, pet hairs, and other contaminants from accumulating inside. Buy a cover, make one, or slip a pillowcase over the machine.

* Change needles after eight hours of sewing to avoid skipped stitches, broken thread, and damage to the fabric or your machine.

* Plug your machine into a high-quality surge protector to safeguard against lightning, poor wiring, and power surges. Turn off the machine and turn off the breaker on the surge protector when your machine is not in use.

* Clean and oil the machine after finishing a project or after every 8 to 10 hours of sewing (*see* Cleaning and Oiling Tips *on pages 18–19*).

**Q** Is it okay to use magnetic pin dishes near my computerized sewing machine?

**A** Check your manual or ask your machine dealer. Some machines may be affected, while others are not.

## CLEANING AND OILING TIPS

Some machines require periodic oiling and others don't; read your manual for directions. However, here are some general pointers:

* Use only sewing machine oil — Tri-Flo is often recommended by technicians. Never use 3-in-One oil, because it's too heavy for sewing machines.

* After oiling, use an absorbent cloth or paper towel to remove any oil from the bed of the machine. Then stitch through two layers of scrap cotton several times to absorb any oily film that may remain.

* One of the worst things you can do is put sewing-machine oil in a place it doesn't belong or to mistakenly use the wrong fluid. It's disastrous to use liquid seam sealant instead of sewing-machine oil. (Ask me how I know!) Designate a specific place to keep your sewing-machine oil, so you'll always reach for the right thing.

* If your machine will not be used regularly, take a few minutes every month to stitch at full throttle on fabric scraps to keep it well lubricated.

Q **I bought my machine secondhand and have no manual. What do I do?**

A Visit your local dealer for help. You may be able to locate manuals online in downloadable PDF files. See Resources for website addresses.

In addition to periodic oiling, follow a regular maintenance schedule. For optimal machine function, do the following tasks to clean out lint and other contaminants after each major project or every 8 to 10 hours of sewing.

* Turn off the machine, unthread it, and remove the bobbin and bobbin case first.
* Clean the needle-thread tension disks by running the folded edge of a piece of muslin or similar cotton fabric between them, to dislodge thread bits and fuzz.
* Remove lint and dirt from moving parts and in the bobbin area using a soft brush or a mini-vac. Never use compressed air, as it will drive lint and other contaminants farther into the machine mechanisms, causing problems. Never blow into the machine; the moisture in your breath can cause problems over time.

Try these basic maintenance steps when you encounter stitching problems. If trouble persists, see your dealer. Service may take a few days, longer when parts are needed. Find out what was wrong and what was done to fix it.

**Q** Can I use generic parts and attachments on my machine?

**A** It's best to use replacement parts made specifically for your machine model. Generic parts may invalidate your warranty. Generic presser feet for special sewing applications (sewing on bead strings, for example) are fun to add to your sewing-machine toolbox. Purchase the one that has a shank like the one on your machine.

## What About a Serger?

You can sew just about anything *without* a serger, but many sewers would find it difficult to part with theirs. Sergers can do many basic sewing functions and are wonderful for sewing knits, but if you must choose between machines, invest in a sewing machine first. Once you've stitched a seam with a serger, there's no room for fitting errors. The cutting blade that operates during stitching cuts away excess seam allowance.

**Q** How is a serger different from a sewing machine?

**A** A serger is most commonly used for seams in knits and for seam finishing, as well as for finishing a hem with a neat rolled edge on garments and home-decor items. At its most basic, a serger will make a seam while trimming and overcasting the edge — all in one step. This speeds up the sewing and finishing process. A serger *cannot* backstitch, make buttonholes, embroider, or do traditional topstitching and zipper applications. Like traditional sewing machines, sergers also have special presser feet for special techniques. See Resources for books that cover special serger techniques.

The most basic serger has one or two needles and two loopers, each one requiring its own thread. As the serger runs, a sharp blade moves up and down, making a neatly cut edge on the fabric layer(s), while the upper and lower loopers "knit" their threads over the freshly cut edge. The looper threads are caught into a line of stitches made by the needle thread. The entire process creates a truly ravel-free seam finish. Today, there are sergers with as many as ten threads for special techniques.

---

**Q** **Three or more threads? Doesn't that create a threading and tension nightmare?**

**A** Threading a serger can be intimidating at first, but once you learn how and start using your serger for seam and edge finishing, you'll wonder how you managed without it. After some hands-on threading experience at the dealer, take it home and thread, unthread, and rethread several times until the process is second nature. Keep your manual handy for threading and tension adjustments to create the traditional overlock stitch, as well as the rolled-edge and other seam and edge finishes. Take a beginning class at your dealership. Watch for classes at your local fabric store or community college.

---

SEE ALSO: *Chapter 7, Seams and Seam Finishes, and chapter 8, Hems and Hem-Edge Finishes.*

# Cutting Tools

Buy the very best cutting tools you can afford; they will last a lifetime if you take good care of them. To ensure clean cuts for accurate sewing, every sewer needs a dressmaker's shears, a few pairs of sewing scissors for different cutting tasks, and rotary-cutting equipment.

---

**Q** **What kind of scissors should I buy? Do I really need a rotary cutter?**

**A** **Dressmaker's shears** are essential for cutting out the pieces for any project. These 8" to 10" shears have two long, sharp blades with looped handles to fit your fingers and thumb. The long blades make it easy to make long, smooth cuts. The bent handle allows the bottom blade to glide smoothly along the cutting surface below the fabric; otherwise, you must lift the fabric and pattern from the cutting surface, resulting in inaccurate cuts with choppy edges. Bent-handled shears are also available with microserrated blades for cutting thin, slippery, and slick-surfaced fabrics. If the shears you are considering don't slice easily through four layers of medium-weight fabric, look for a different pair.

*dressmaker's shears*

*embroidery scissors*

*rotary cutter*

*rotary cutter with ergonomic handle*

**Sewing or embroidery scissors** are needed for cutting threads and trimming fabric edges. For all-purpose cutting, invest in 5"- or 6"-long sewing scissors (also called trimmers or tailor's scissors) with a pointed blade and a blunt blade. Embroidery scissors have two fine, sharp points for clipping threads and for cutting single layers or delicate fabrics. They are smaller, usually 3½" to 5" long.

A **rotary cutter, mat, and ruler** make cutting bias strips and rectangular shapes, such as pockets and waistbands, a breeze. You may also use them for other cutting tasks.

A **seam ripper** is essential for "unstitching" mistakes.

- - - - - - - - - - - - - - - - - - - - - - - - - - - - - - - - - - - -

Q **Do I need pinking shears?**

A These special bent-handle shears (also called "pinkers") make zigzag cuts for finishing seam and hem edges, making those edges less prone to raveling. You can also use pinkers to trim and clip enclosed seams (*see pages 282–286*), or for making a decorative edge on firmly woven, nonwoven, or knit fabrics. Similar blades are also available for rotary cutters, along with blades for cutting other fancy decorative edges. To check for quality, make a test cut from the second tooth out to the tip along the edge on scraps of a lightweight and a heavyweight fabric. If the cutting is difficult or uneven, consider a different brand. Look for a deep, rather than shallow, sawtooth cut for the most ravel-resistant finish. This is a major purchase that can wait if you have budget restrictions.

**Q** Are there any guidelines for caring for my sewing scissors and shears?

**A** Keep your cutting tools out of the hands of nonsewers. Find a secure hiding place or mark them in a way that means "for sewing only." For example, tie a pink ribbon to the handle of each pair to indicate "hands off." Other care guidelines include:

* **Use your cutting tools for fabric only.** Keep a pair of general purpose craft scissors handy for cutting paper, cardboard, or plastic for templates.
* **Wipe blades clean after use** to remove lint and thread buildup; lint from tough man-made fibers like polyester and nylon is abrasive and can dull scissor blades. Store scissors and shears in a dry location to prevent rust.
* **Sharpen periodically.** Ask your local fabric store for recommendations.
* **Don't drop your cutting tools.** I tie a long ribbon to my sewing scissors and pin one end to the ironing-board cover. I have a second pair tied to my machine, so they're always handy.
* **Place a tiny drop of sewing-machine oil** on the pivot screw every few months, then open and close the blades. Wipe with a soft cloth to remove excess oil and cut through cotton fabric scraps to absorb any oil you may have missed.
* **To avoid damaging the blades,** never cut over pins or needles.

**Q** **Can I use a rotary cutter in place of dressmaker's shears for cutting?**

**A** Yes, if you feel comfortable using this sharp, pizza-cutter-like tool (*see pages 164–165*). Rotary cutting results in smooth and straight edges for cutting and sewing accuracy. The 45 mm-diameter cutter is the most popular, but smaller and larger sizes are available. You will need a large rotary cutting mat to protect your cutting surface and a 6" × 24" clear acrylic rotary ruler to guide cutting along straight pattern edges.

For cutting along curved edges, choose a small rotary cutter (18 mm). You'll need a very steady hand to cut without a guide, or try using a French curve ruler as a cutting guide. It may be easier to cut curved areas with shears.

Rotary cutting equipment is great for cutting home-decor project pieces, since they are usually large geometric shapes, but this works only if you have a large cutting mat and table. Moving fabric layers can cause slippage and distortion.

---

**CAUTION, CAUTION, CAUTION**

Rotary cutters are razor-sharp! Stay alert and follow basic precautions when using one:

* Keep rotary cutters safely out of the reach of children and pets.
* Always roll the cutter away from your body, never toward it.
* Engage the safety guard every time you put the cutter down, even if you are not finished cutting.

Q **How should I care for my rotary cutter for optimum use and accurate cuts?**

A Using a dull blade can irreparably damage your cutting mat. Also, using too much pressure to force a cut results in inaccuracy. At the first sign of poor cutting action (cuts require more pressure than usual or the blade skips and misses periodically), don't assume the blade is worn. Before you throw it out, try cleaning it:

1. Disassemble the cutting mechanism, placing the pieces on your work surface in the order removed.
2. Use a clean, soft cloth to wipe away any bits of lint on the blade or caught between the nut and blade.
3. Add a tiny drop of sewing-machine oil to the blade in the area that lies under the front sheath.
4. Tighten (but do not overtighten) the nut after reassembly. A too-tight blade will hang up on the fabric layers and cause you to think it's dull or incorrectly assembled.

If, after cleaning, your rotary cutter still won't cut right, replace the blade and discard the used one, wrapped and taped in cardboard (even when too dull for cutting fabric, it's still sharp enough to cut fingers).

## Other Basic Tools

It's easy to assemble a kit of essentials for a modest investment, then add to it as your budget allows and your projects demand more specialized tools.

**Q** Besides good cutting tools, what else do I need in my sewing kit?

**A** Pins, needles, and a thimble are the most basic tools, along with a seam gauge for measuring tasks. See chapter 2 for information on needles. Select a **thimble** that fits your index finger, to protect it while pushing stitches through fabric.

Use **straight pins** to hold fabric layers together for hand sewing and machine stitching:

* **Flat flower-head pins** are my favorites for all-purpose sewing, but for handwork, you may prefer smaller silk pins with tiny round heads or pins with glass heads.
* **Plastic-head pins** are also available. Take care not to touch these with an iron. Pins with fine shafts slip easily through multiple fabric layers.
* **Sequin pins** are shorter and ideal for pinning appliqués.
* You may also like **quilter's straight pins**. These extra-long, fine steel pins with plastic or glass heads are really handy when sewing multiple layers or thick fabrics together.

You'll need a **pincushion** or a magnetic pin dish. Some pincushions fit the wrist; some have an emery cushion attached for cleaning and sharpening pins and needles. The magnetic dish catches pins and is great for sweeping up strays.

A 6" **seam gauge** is a ruler with a sliding marker. Use it to measure and mark hems, for button and buttonhole placement, or for other design details, such as pleats and tucks. You'll also need a **tape measure**, a flexible measuring tape made of fiberglass, to take body measurements, as well as for pattern placement on the fabric grainline (*see page 160*).

# Q Are there other tools that I need for hand- and/or machine-sewing?

A There are numerous sewing tools that make sewing more fun, faster, and easier. I've tried most of them, but the ones I wouldn't be without are listed below. I *can* sew without any of them, but I wouldn't want to! I refer to them in many techniques throughout this book.

* **Bamboo point turner.** Does just what its name implies, without poking a hole in the corner or point (*see page 290*).

* **Basting tape.** Great for temporarily holding zippers in place for stitching (*see page 398*), as well as for matching seams (*see page 220*).

* **Bodkin.** For pulling elastic and drawstring through casings (*see page 346*).

* **Embroidery stabilizers.** Support stitching for a variety of techniques other than machine embroidery, including buttonholes. My stock includes water-soluble, heat-soluble, and nonwoven tearaway and cutaway types. There are many types for specific purposes.

* **Fusible web.** Available in tape (¼" and ½" widths) as well as in 9" × 12" sheets and yardage. Most brands have at least one layer of protective paper to keep the adhesive from sticking to your iron. Fusible web has many uses, including making quick hems (*see page 313*) and repairs.

* **Glue stick.** Holds things in place temporarily. Use it to secure buttons for hand and machine stitching. It will wash out, so don't use it when you need a permanent adhesive.

* **Hot-iron cleaner.** Removes the gunky buildup on the iron soleplate; it's essential if you use fusible interfacings and fusible web.
* **Liquid seam sealant.** Stops raveling and runs in knits, including hosiery.
* **Scotch Magic Tape.** For pattern adjustments (*see pages 148–149*) and to use as a zipper topstitching guideline.
* **Water- and air-soluble marking pens.** For transferring construction marks and details from the pattern tissue, as well as drawing placement lines on fabric.

*SEE ALSO: Marking Tools and Methods, pages 165–174.*

# Sewing Room Ergonomics

Arrange your sewing room for a pleasurable sewing experience to avoid eye strain, fatigue, and neck, back, and shoulder pain. Repetitive stress injuries are not uncommon among those who sew regularly in less-than-ideal sewing setups. Good lighting is an important consideration, along with a comfortable place to cut and mark your sewing projects.

## Q Where do I begin?

A It's ideal to have a separate space devoted to your hobby, but no matter where you sew, setting up the machine, sewing chair, and cutting/ironing space for optimum comfort is essential. Choose a comfortable, adjustable chair, preferably with wheels. Arrange a cutting area at a height that eliminates backbreaking bending. Making do — by cutting on the floor, bending over the kitchen table, or sewing at a table that is too high or too low — can cause great discomfort.

* Choose a chair with an adjustable cushioned seat and cushioned armrests. You should be able to adjust the height of the seat and the back so it comfortably fits the curve of your back. Look for one with good lumbar support and a front edge that curves forward (sometimes called a waterfall-style seat) to avoid strain on the back of your legs and knees.

* Place your machine on the table you will use and adjust the height of your sewing chair so your feet rest comfortably on the floor with your knees at a 90-degree angle and slightly lower than your hips. Sit all the way back, not on the edge of the chair. You may need a footrest so your legs are in the correct position. Adjust the chair or the sewing table so the sewing surface height — where the needle is — is 25" to 29" from the floor (this works for most people). Your hands should be in a straight line with your wrists and forearms, not bent forward. Make sure that you have a direct view of the sewing surface/needle area without bending your neck up or down.

* Place the sewing machine as close to the front edge of the table as possible and bring your chair close to the table so you can reach your work easily without sitting on the edge of the chair.

* Position your cutting surface and ironing board at a comfortable standing height so your elbows are bent and your

hands drop slightly downward. This gives you the perfect view of your work and eliminates backbreaking bending during long cutting and pressing sessions.

---

# Q What do you recommend for lighting my sewing?

A You'll need good light at your sewing machine, pressing area, and cutting table. Ask for color-corrected bulbs to reduce shadows and keep your color selections in perspective. Decorative and utilitarian sewing lamps, in floor and table models, are widely available and are a must for sewing at night and when working with dark colors. Small portable models are a good choice for illuminating your work at your machine and at your easy chair while hand sewing. Bulbs that emit natural, white, or outdoor light are best.

---

# Q When I use the kitchen table for layout and cutting, my back hurts. Is there an alternative?

A To avoid back strain, a counter-height worktable — about 34" from the floor unless you are really short or really tall — is essential for cutting. Try to arrange your cutting surface so you can walk around it, rather than bend over it to reach the other edge, when pinning, marking, and cutting. (Reaching too far also affects accuracy.) The larger the surface, the better. I recommend a surface at least 30" wide (the width of 60" fabric folded in half) and 45" long (an average length for pant legs).

Here are some cutting-surface alternatives:

* A 30" × 45" piece of plywood padded with wool and then covered with cotton canvas or other heavyweight 100% cotton fabric. Place it on top of a dresser or microwave cart.

* A hollow-core door supported by cabinets, microwave carts, or wire basket systems at each end.

* A portable cutting table you can fold and store when not in use, if your space is limited.

* A sturdy ironing board with a slide-on extension that slips around the pointed end.

* A cutting board on top of the washer and dryer or on a kitchen counter (but you won't be able to walk around it, making some cutting and marking a little awkward).

* A large rectangular dining or folding table can be raised temporarily by placing the legs on bed risers or on top of juice cans filled with plaster of Paris.

* As a last resort, pin and cut on the floor. Vacuum first and use a folding cardboard cutting board or large rotary cutting mat, if available.

---

**Q** My shoulders and neck get so tired when I sew. Any other hints for a more comfortable experience?

**A** Take frequent breaks, especially if you are sewing under a deadline. Tilt up the back of the machine a bit so you can better see what you're doing with less neck strain. Purchase a special tabletop apparatus for this or use two rubber doorstops to lift the back of the machine. Or, tuck the thin end of an empty 3-ring 3"-thick notebook binder under the back of the machine and slide it in far enough to tilt the machine. Here are a few other tips to alleviate neck, back, and leg strain:

* **Set a kitchen timer** every 30 minutes to remind you to get up and stretch, roll your shoulders, and get a glass of water!

* **Keep your feet flat on the floor** and don't hunch or slump over your work. Sitting up straight and raising your chest automatically repositions your shoulders and prevents hunching to alleviate neck and shoulder strain. To keep your hips balanced in the chair, it's a good idea to place a small footrest under your left foot.

* **Prevent sliding.** Place a custom-cut piece of nonstick rubber-like mesh (used in refrigerator drawers) underneath the foot pedal and the sewing machine. If your sewing room is carpeted, try a piece of carpet padding (designed to keep a rug in place on top of a carpet) under the foot pedal. A computer mouse pad works, too.

* **Purchase a product like SewSlip** to use when stitching through bulky layers or when maneuvering heavy materials under the needle. The sticky side of the Teflon-like sheet adheres to the machine; it has a hole for the needle. The slippery surface cuts down on resistance so the fabric layers don't drag. Remove the sheet when you're finished, reapply it to its backing paper, roll it up, and store in its tube until you need it the next time.

* **Support your fabric on a second table** (or ironing board) that is cozied up to the sewing table. This prevents strain on you and drag that can break the needle.

# Q Are ergonomic sewing tools available?

A Yes, more and more manufacturers offer these, and they are a good investment in your health. Consider:

* Electric scissors, especially good for those suffering from arthritis
* Scissors with ergonomic handles that fit your hand and pain-free grips to reduce the impact of cutting force; spring-action handles reduce hand fatigue
* Rotary cutters with ergonomic handles to help reduce wrist strain and carpal tunnel syndrome

## Pressing Equipment

"Press as you sew" is one of the most important sewing rules. For a professional finish, you will need quality pressing equipment and a few additional pressing tools. Add to your collection as projects require and your budget allows. A good ironing board and a sturdy steam iron, plus a pressing ham, seam roll, and point presser will make pressing easy and enjoyable. More information on these items to come in this chapter.

# Q What should I look for in an ironing board?

A Height-adjustable, freestanding ironing boards are the most popular. They can be left up, or folded and stored, depending on your space. Locate yours close to your sewing machine, if possible. If it's not close by, keep a small pressing pad on or near the sewing-machine table to eliminate frequent trips to the ironing board. I keep a small craft iron handy for quick pressing jobs that don't require the entire board. The ironing board should have:

* **Vent holes** to allow steam to escape
* **A cover** made of 100% cotton
* **A foam or wool pad** between the cover and the metal board, to prevent vent holes from imprinting on the fabric
* **Adequate space** for an iron to sit (on end) when not in use; some models have an extra storage rack, plus iron rests and cord supports

- - - - - - - - - - - - - - - - - - - - - - - - - - - - - - - - -

Q **Can I use a Teflon-coated ironing board cover instead of cotton?**

A This popular cover, found on many ironing boards, is not recommended for construction sewing. The Teflon reflects heat back into the fabric, which in turn can cause unwanted shine and make fusing difficult. It also interferes with setting the press in synthetics, which must cool to "remember" the pressed shape (*see page 41*).

- - - - - - - - - - - - - - - - - - - - - - - - - - - - - - - - -

Q **I need a new iron. Which features are essential for sewing?**

A You will need a steam iron with a shot-of-steam option. Use it to direct heavier bursts of steam into your work, for shaping and reshaping the fabric. Even if you don't use steam when pressing, you still need it to remove wrinkles prior to lay-out and cutting, and for preshrinking nonwashable fabrics (*see page 190*). A heavier iron is preferable for sewing, as the weight makes pressing easier. Be sure your iron has a wide temperature range so you can adjust it in increments for the fiber content of your project. Helpful features include:

* **A smooth soleplate** and enough weight to make a differ-ence. A too-heavy iron can be wearing, so be sure to test the weight and feel of the iron in your hand.
* **A nonstick surface.** Some say these glide easier than stain-less steel models. Keep pins out of the way of the soleplate since the nonstick coating can peel if you scratch the iron.
* **An automatic shut-off feature** that kicks in periodically if you forget to turn off the iron. This may be a nuisance during a long sewing session; you must wait for the iron to reheat each time you return to the ironing board.
* **A shot-of-steam** and/or a constant-steam feature, like that available with steam-generator irons with high-capacity water tanks. Steam generators hold more water and offer a higher steaming capacity. They're particularly helpful for fusing interfacing and for shaping tailored garments. However, they are more expensive than a basic iron.

- - - - - - - - - - - - - - - - - - - - - - - - - - - - - - -

Q **Is pressing the same as ironing?**

A Ironing involves moving the iron continuously back and forth with downward pressure over fabric to remove wrinkles and creases. You may need to iron your fabric to prepare it for cutting.

Pressing is a more delicate maneuver, used to persuade a seam allowance to lie in a specific direction, or to flatten a finished edge, create a crease or pleat, or train fabric into a new shape. It's an up-and-down motion using the tip or the side of the iron to coax the seams and edges into submission, while taking care not to stretch or distort the shapes.

## Pressing Tools

Begin with a pressing ham and an assortment of press cloths. Add other tools — a seam roll, and a point presser/tailor's clapper combination — as your budget allows, your skills increase, and the projects you tackle grow in complexity.

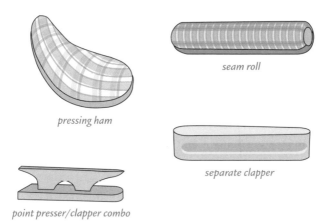

*seam roll*

*pressing ham*

*separate clapper*

*point presser/clapper combo*

## Q What is a seam roll and how do I use it?

A Like the pressing ham, this long, tubular pressing aid is firmly stuffed and covered with wool on one half and heavy cotton on the other. It's rounded at each end and is especially helpful when pressing seams open. Because of its shape, the garment falls away from the seam edges, helping to prevent seam imprints on the right side of your work. It's essential when pressing inside tubular areas such as sleeves and pant legs. You may have a sleeve board, also useful for this purpose; however, pressing a seam open over a sleeve board offers no protection from seam imprinting.

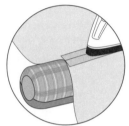

*press seam open over seam roll*

## Q What is the correct procedure for pressing a seam?

A Any seam that will be crossed with another must be pressed first. Even when seam allowances will be pressed to one side or hide inside collars and cuffs, it's usually best to press the seam open first. Exceptions include the seams for set-in sleeves and the curved facing seams around necklines and armholes.

1. Choose the correct temperature setting for the fabric. If there is more than one fiber type, adjust for the most heat-sensitive. Make sure the iron tank has enough water to produce steam.

2. Place the piece you've just stitched flat on the ironing board. Set the stitches by pressing along the line of stitching before you press the seam open or to one side. This helps them sink into the fabric for smoother pressed seams and smoothes out any small puckers that may have occurred during stitching. Allow to cool briefly.

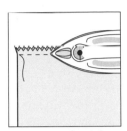

*press to set the stitches*

3. Open up the two pieces of fabric you've sewn together and place the seam over a seam roll. (If you don't have one, see the next question.) Use the point of the iron to direct steam into the fabric while using your fingertips to open the seam. Apply the point of the iron in a lower-and-lift pressing action.

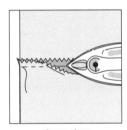

*press open*

After pressing the seam open, then press in the direction necessary for the type of seam you are making. To avoid pressing in any seamline distortion, keep the seam straight and parallel to the ironing board edge.

4. Examine the pressed seam to make sure that the seamline is crisp and flat with no tucks. Flip it over and press lightly from the right side as needed.

---

*SEE ALSO:* Chapter 7, Seams and Seam Finishes.

# Q How do I prevent seam imprints if I don't have a seam roll?

A Substitute a firmly rolled-up terry cloth towel, a rolled-up magazine covered with muslin, or a folded piece of typing paper or a strip of a brown paper bag (with no printing ink) lengthwise. Tuck the folded edge between the seam allowance and the project. You can use adding-machine paper tape or white envelopes, too. Having a seam roll makes it much easier to press seams open inside tubular areas.

---

# Q How do I press seams open that end in points, as in a collar or cuff?

A Enclosed seams like those in a collar are always easier to manipulate into place at the turned edge if you press them open on a point presser. Slip the fabric point over the wooden point of the point presser. This tool is usually attached to a block of wood on the bottom, which is used as clapper or pounding block when pressing seams.

*press enclosed seams open over point presser*

---

# Q Why would I need to pound a seam?

A You won't usually need to pound a seam. Instead, you can use the wooden clapper with firm pressure to help set the steam into the fabric, then cool it in place for a firm press. (*See* Using the Clapper, *below*.) Using a clapper with pressure after using the iron allows you to press longer without damaging the fabric. Enclosed edges on collars and faced edges benefit from this pressing method (*see page 282*).

To use a clapper, first fill the area with steam and heat from the iron. Then replace it with the clapper and hold in place for several seconds to set the press. It's also great for setting the creases in pants legs.

A clapper is also essential for setting seams, creases, and sharp-edged pleats, particularly when working with stubborn synthetic fibers such as polyester, a thermoplastic fiber. You can reshape it while it's warm and set the shape as it cools. Placing the cool block of wood on the warm, pressed polyester and exerting pressure helps it cool faster and "remember" its new pressed shape.

## USING THE CLAPPER

Use a tailor's clapper to "pound" fabric by applying it like a hammer to flatten really bulky areas where seams intersect, or in hemlines. Pounding flat-felled or welt seams in denim or similar heavy fabrics helps flatten layers in a narrow hem allowance, like the ones in blue jeans. Beware: A too-heavy hand with the clapper will break down fibers and weaken the fabric — and may produce unwanted shine.

# Q What is a pressing (tailor's) ham and how do I use it?

A This firmly stuffed item is a little smaller than a football and shaped a bit like a ham (*see page 37*). Its contoured and curved edges assist you when pressing similarly shaped areas in your sewing projects. Darts and shaped seams are stitched to create contours, to make flat fabric fit your body shape. If you press them flat, you will end up with poor fit and appearance. One side of the ham is covered in heavy cotton, the other in wool. Choose the side most like your fabric.

To press a dart, first press it flat — to set the stitches, help them meld into the fabric, and crease the folded edge. Then arrange the fabric over the ham on the curved area that the dart hugs most smoothly. Tuck a strip of clean white paper under the dart and press the dart from wide end to narrow, ending at the point. Use the ham when pressing open curved seams that fit over your hipline. It is also handy when shaping the gathered cap of a set-in sleeve (*see page 364*).

*press stitches to set and to crease fold*

*press dart to one side over pressing ham*

SEE ALSO: *Darts, pages 318–323.*

Q **Are there any other special pressing techniques I should know?**

A Here are some pressing tips for specific pressing situations and special fabrics:

* Don't rush! Careful pressing is the hallmark of finely sewn garments.

* Press in the same direction you stitched (*see pages 104–105*) to avoid stretching and distortion.

* Press straight seams on a flat surface and curved seams over a pressing ham or other padded, curved surface.

* Press toward the flatter layer when the two layers of a seam each have a different amount of fullness. For example, press a gathered skirt waistline seam toward the waistband.

* Aim the point of the iron into any gathers. Keep the soleplate off the gathers to avoid flattening them into unsightly creases.

* Do not press the seam of a set-in sleeve flat (*see page 364* for the correct pressing procedure).

* Clip the concave section of curved seams only where necessary in order to press them open or to one side (*see page 283*).

* Always press darts over a pressing ham to avoid flattening out the fullness beyond the dart point.

*SEE ALSO: Chapter 9, Shaping to Fit.*

Q **Are there any other pressing tools I should consider?**

A It's nice to have a **sleeve board**: a narrow, mini ironing board, for pressing small tubular areas like sleeves. It's also handy for small areas like cuffs and necklines, and on craft projects and clothes for dolls and little ones. A padded **pressing mitt** is handy for steam-pressing a set-in sleeve.

## TIPS FOR PRESSING PERFECTION

1. Fill the iron's water reservoir for steam pressing and adjust the iron to a heat that is safe for the fiber content and the finish on the fabric surface.

2. Test temperature, steam, and pressure on fabric scraps from your project to determine the best pressing technique. Compare a pressed scrap to an unpressed scrap to make sure the iron hasn't changed the surface appearance or color. Look for unwanted shine and texture changes or flattening of the fibers.

3. Use just enough pressure to accomplish the goal. Light to moderate pressure is usually sufficient to avoid scorching, shine, and imprinting seam and dart edges on the outside of the project. Don't overpress; underpressing is the better option. You can always press a little more if needed.

4. Use a lift-and-lower motion, working from section to section, to apply pressure precisely where needed to achieve the desired results.

If you plan to sew on napped or pile fabrics, such as velvet and velveteen, you might want a **needle board** made of stiffened fabric and embedded with point-up steel needles. The napped surface sinks into the needles to protect it from the pressure of the iron when pressing from the wrong side. A terrycloth towel or a piece of napped fabric on your ironing board can substitute.

5. Use your fingers to help coax fabric in the desired direction, but keep them out of the way of hot steam.

6. Press from the wrong side whenever possible to minimize possible damage to the right side of the fabric.

7. Never cross another seam with stitching until it has been pressed in the correct direction. Develop a stitch-and-press attitude to carry through your sewing career.

8. Use a press cloth to protect the surface of delicate and heat- or pressure-sensitive fabrics, particularly when pressing from the right side.

9. Don't press over pins or basting stitches, to avoid imprints on the fabric surface.

10. Allow the pressed piece to cool before moving it from the pressing surface. This helps preserve the newly pressed shape and avoids the problem of heat-set wrinkles in fabrics made of synthetic fibers.

# Q What should I use for a press cloth?

A Using a press cloth between the iron and fabric protects the fabric from excessive heat and shine. You also need a press cloth for applying most fusible interfacings, to protect your iron from picking up and transferring sticky fusible residue to your fabric, iron, and ironing board. Purchase press cloths or use fabrics that you already have. Here are a few options:

* **A clean, white, cotton man's handkerchief** is absorbent and washable.
* **A piece of lightweight muslin** can be used; pink the edges to control raveling.
* **A piece of the actual fashion fabric** works well, particularly if the fabric is wool or has a napped or pile surface (*see page 221*). Keep larger scraps for this.
* **A piece of wool felt** works for pressing wool fabrics.
* **A Teflon pressing sheet** is a good alternative for applying fusible interfacing and for appliqué work. Excess web adheres to the press cloth and is easily scraped away before you use it again.
* **Parchment paper** can be substituted and is available by the roll in the paper-products department at your grocery store.

- - - - - - - - - - - - - - - - - - - - - - - - - - - - - -

# Q How do I remove starch residue and other buildup from the iron soleplate?

A I keep a supply of hot-iron cleaner on hand to clean the soleplate (*see page 29*). Another option is to make a thick paste with two tablespoons of baking soda and a bit of water to rub on the soleplate to loosen and wipe away the gunk. Wipe again with a clean, wet sponge or cloth.

- - - - - - - - - - - - - - - - - - - - - - - - - - -

## Q How do I remove a scorch mark on my fabric?

A Scorching on natural fibers (silk, cotton, linen, wool) and man-made rayon, due to pressing too long or using a too hot iron, leaves a brownish-yellow discoloration. Doing the same on heat-sensitive synthetics causes shine on the surface or melts the fibers, which harden as they cool. You may be able to remove light scorch marks with one of the following methods. *Note:* It's not possible to refresh fabrics that have shiny or melted areas from using high heat on heat-sensitive man-made fibers.

* Lightly brush the fabric surface with a dry sponge, soft-bristle brush, or emery board. You might be able to remove the scorched surface fibers on woolens with this method; a tool for removing pills from fabric surfaces may also work. Proceed with caution.

* For washable fabrics, soak in a solution of 1 quart water and ¼ cup all-fabric (oxygen) bleach. Wash to remove the solution, or plunge the fabric into icy cold water immediately and allow to stand for 24 hours.

* For scorch marks on washable white fabrics (but not on nylon), sponge the area with a diluted solution of hydrogen peroxide and water.

## KEEP A SEWING NOTEBOOK

One of the best things you can do to keep sewing information organized is to create a sewing notebook. A three-ring binder is ideal, because you can add and remove materials easily. Use one with a 2" or 3" spine for room to grow. It can fill up quickly. Use tabbed dividers to organize topics, and add a supply of clear plastic sheet protectors for a place to tuck odds and ends.

Here are a few of the things you will want to keep in the notebook:

* Photos, sketches, and mail-order-catalog clippings of ideas for sewing projects, such as clothing and home-decor items
* Sketches, plans, and ideas for new projects
* Technique directions from classes or clipped from magazines
* Package directions for any tools, notions, and fusible interfacings you've purchased
* Notes on machine and serger tension adjustments
* Photos and records of work in progress
* Photos of completed projects

Your sewing notebook will be an invaluable long-term reference and it can serve as a journal that captures a lifetime of sewing.

# CHAPTER TWO

# Needles and Thread

Whether you sew by hand or machine, stitching requires two important components: the right needle and the perfect thread. To make a perfect stitch in your fabric, choose from a wide assortment of hand-sewing and machine needles and select the right size for the stitching job at hand. Some needle types are designed for success with specific sewing techniques — a jeans or upholstery needle, for example. Then, add the right thread to the equation, choosing from all-purpose sewing thread for basic sewing and special-purpose threads for specific tasks and decorative work.

# Demystifying Machine Needles

You'll need an assortment of sewing-machine needles designed to fit your machine (and serger). Check your manual for needle specifications. Since sewing thread passes up and down and back and forth through the needle many times before it's actually caught into a stitch, the eye of the needle must be smooth and free of burrs and rough spots to avoid thread shredding and stitch problems. It's a good idea to run your fingers over a needle to feel for imperfections before you insert it in your machine. High-quality needles with polished eyes are the best bet.

## SEWING-MACHINE NEEDLE SIZES

| European (mm) | 60 | 65 | 70 | 75 | 80 | 90 | 100 | 110 | 120 |
|---|---|---|---|---|---|---|---|---|---|
| American Size | 8 | 9 | 10 | 11 | 12 | 14 | 16 | 18 | 19 |

**Q** **Why are there so many needle sizes? And what do the numbers and letters on the package mean?**

**A** Sewing-machine needle thickness increases as the size number increases (*see* Sewing-Machine Needle Sizes, *above*). The letters define the needle point type. Both are important in needle selection for your fabric and the thread you are using. As fabric weight and density increases, so should the needle size. American and European manufacturers use different numbering systems, and needles are often referred to in both sizes; for example, 80/12, with the European size coming first.

# Q How do I select the best needle size for my project?

A You need a needle that is strong enough and with the correct point style to pierce the fabric you are sewing without damaging it. You also need one that has an eye and scarf (*see* Parts of a Needle, *page 58*) of the right size and shape to carry and protect the thread diameter as you stitch. Otherwise, the thread will shred and you may damage and weaken the fabric. Lint buildup on a needle can indicate that the needle size is too small. If the needle is too large, holes may be obvious in the fabric, but they may close up during laundering, pressing, or dry cleaning. It's always better to use a needle that is a little too large, rather than one that is too small. Here are a few selection guidelines:

* Size 80/12 is a good all-purpose size for most basic sewing and mid-weight fabrics. For fabrics that have a tight weave, you may have better luck and smoother stitching with a size 70/12. For heavy fabrics, such as denim, duck, and wide-wale corduroy, switch to a larger needle: size 90 and higher.

* Universal needles work on most fabrics, but ballpoint and stretch needles are better for knits.

* A good rule to remember: The finer the thread and the finer the fabric being sewn, the finer the needle should be. The smaller the sewing-machine needle size, the finer the shaft and point. The reverse is true for hand-sewing needles (*see page 62*). For added help with needle selection, *see* Fabric Weight/Needle Compatibility *on page 52*.

## FABRIC WEIGHT/NEEDLE COMPATIBILITY

| Fabric Weight | Fabric Type | Size | Point |
|---|---|---|---|
| **Very sheer/ light** | Wovens: chiffon, organdy, voile, lightweight crepe, lawn, batiste, lamé | 9–10 | sharp |
| | Knits: lightweight tricot | 9–10 | stretch |
| **Medium/light** | Wovens: wool crepe, jersey, cotton gingham, rayon or wool challis, nylon outerwear fabrics, lightweight nonwoven synthetics | 11–12 | sharp |
| | Knits: jersey, single knits | | |
| **Medium** | Wovens: flannel, muslin, gabardine, poplin, broadcloth, percale, velveteen, some denims, nonwoven synthetic suedes and leathers | 12–14 | sharp |
| | Knits: doubleknit, sweater knit, velour, medium-weight stretch corduroy | 12–14 | |
| **Heavy** | Wovens: denim, quilted fabrics, fake fur, heavy woolens, canvas, duck, sailcloth, melton cloth, velvet, corduroy | 14–16 | denim |
| **Leather/ suede** | Kidskin, patent, calf, pigskin, upholstery vinyl | 14–18 | leather |

Q **What's the difference between universal, sharp, and ballpoint needles? Do I need them all?**

A The point of a universal needle is slightly rounded in comparison to a sharp needle. Universal needles are appropriate for stitching on most woven and knit fabrics. A ballpoint needle is even better for knits. Its more rounded point allows the needle to pass between the knit thread loops without piercing and snagging them. Sharp/microtex needles have a sharper point, designed to more easily maneuver between the threads in heavyweight and more firmly woven fabrics, as well as in microfiber and stretch fabrics with special stretch fibers such as lycra.

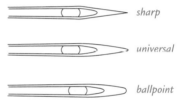

sharp

universal

ballpoint

- - - - - - - - - - - - - - - - - - - - - - - - - - - - - - - -

Q **What do all the letters mean on the needle package?**

A Just as an example, H is the letter used to identify the universal needle. It's the workhorse, the general-purpose needle that is a good choice for most wovens and a variety of medium-weight knits. Keep a stock of these in a wide range of sizes so you have the right one when you need it. A special version of this needle has a slot for self-threading, which is much easier on the eyes! If there is no other letter on the package, the needle is universal. Use the chart on pages 56–57 to identify and choose the right needle (and point) for the sewing task at hand.

**Q** **There's another number on the needle package: 130/705H. Is it important?**

**A** Yes, it identifies the *needle system*. Most home sewing machines require the 130/705H system. The 130 refers to the shank length and 705 means the back of the shank is flat. Always use the correct needle system for the machine you are using. (Sergers and industrial sewing machines require others.)

- - - - - - - - - - - - - - - - - - - - - - - - - - - - - -

**Q** **Is there a special way to insert a sewing-machine needle?**

**A** Machine needles have a shank with a flat side that has a sharp indentation called the scarf, for stitch formation. The other side of the shaft is rounded and has a long groove, where the thread lies as it's carried down into and up out of the fabric (*see* Parts of a Needle *on page 58*). On most machines, the flat side of the needle faces the back of the machine, with the rounded side toward you, and the needle is threaded from front to back. Check your machine manual.

If a needle is not inserted correctly, a stitch won't form. Make sure that the needle shank is firmly seated all the way into the needle opening on the needle bar, and then tighten the screw so the needle won't come loose during stitching. Some older machines require needles with a totally round shank. Industrial machines also require special needles, and sergers usually do, too. Make sure to keep serger, industrial, and sewing-machine needles separate and well labeled to avoid confusion and damage to your sewing machine.

**Q** How often should I change the sewing-machine needle?

**A** Change to a fresh needle when you start a new project or after 8 to 10 hours of sewing. Even cotton will snag and run when hit by a slightly burred or dull needle, and the problem compounds with knits, sheers, and silky-surfaced fabrics. If you hit a pin, change the needle immediately rather than damage the fabric or machine with a bad needle.

---

**Q** Any helpful hints for remembering what type of needle is in my machine?

**A** Place a sticky note on the machine with the needle type and size when you begin a project. Another good thing to do is place a double-thick 2" square of the fabric you've been sewing on under the presser foot. Lower the presser foot and the needle to hold the fabric in place as a reminder of what you were stitching last. This practice also prevents movement of the stitch mechanisms when the machine is not in use, protects the needle point, and prevents the feed dogs from scratching the foot.

### PLAY IT SAFE

If in doubt about the longevity of an already-used needle, throw it out. Needles are the least expensive of all your sewing tools. Don't ruin a project or damage your sewing machine by being stingy with replacement needles.

## NEEDLE LABELS

| Needle Type | Sewing Usage |
| --- | --- |
| DE: Double Eye | Use when you want to stitch with two threads at once to emphasize decorative stitches. |
| DRI: Triple | Three needles, to use for closely spaced rows of topstitching, pintucking, and heirloom stitching techniques. |
| E: Embroidery | Has larger, elongated eye and groove to decrease friction and shredding on more delicate threads such as rayon, silk, and soft cotton thread. |
| J: Jeans/Denim | Very sharp point for penetrating thick and firmly woven fabrics such as denim, canvas, and upholstery fabric; good for topstitching through multiple layers; a substitute for a sharp/microtex needle. |
| L, R, or LL: Leather | Use only on real leather, suede, or vinyls, never on wovens, knits, or nonwoven synthetic suede and leather; has a special wedge-shaped point. |
| M: Sharp/Microtex | For fine or densely woven fabrics, such as microfiber fabrics and synthetic nonwoven suede and leather fabrics; good choice for tightly woven cotton batiks; has a sharp point. |
| MET: Metallic Metafil | For use with metallic and Mylar threads; elongated eye and enlarged groove decreases friction on delicate threads. |
| Metafil | Larger, highly polished eye prevents shredding of rayon and metallic threads. |

| Needle Type | Sewing Usage |
| --- | --- |
| N: Topstitching | Extra sharp for straighter stitches; extra-large rectangular eye and deeper scarf allows room for heavy decorative or multiple threads for more visible topstitching; use smallest size that accommodates thread to avoid large holes. |
| Q: Machine quilting | Slim, sharply tapered point easily pierces quilting cottons, layers at intersecting seams, and multiple fabric layers during quilting process. |
| S: Stretch | Medium ballpoint and special groove help reduce skipped stitches in lightweight knits, stretch wovens, and highly elastic knits (swimwear). |
| Serger | Most sergers require special serger needles (check your manual). |
| SES: Fine ballpoint *and* SUK: Medium ballpoint | For knits and stretch wovens; rounded tip slips between (rather than through) delicate fibers and knit loops; ensures more even stitches; doesn't snag or damage delicate knits or cause them to unravel. |
| Spring | Use for free-motion decorative stitching with dropped feed dogs. |
| WING: Hemstitching | Has a sharp wing on opposite sides of the shaft to create large holes in tightly woven fabric; for heirloom stitching and decorative hemstitching. |
| ZWI: Double or twin | Two needles to use for closely spaced rows of topstitching, pintucking, and heirloom stitching techniques. |

*Note:* H may be used on the package along with the other labels in this chart. It means the needle has a universal point.

## PARTS OF A NEEDLE

FRONT VIEW

SIDE VIEW

*flat side of shank*

*round side of shank*

*shank: inserted and tightened in the needle bar*

*shaft*

*groove*

*groove guides thread in and out of fabric*

*scarf helps form the stitch*

*eyehole for thread*

*point: pierces fabric to draw thread to bobbin for stitch formation*

**Shank.** Heaviest section of the needle; inserted into sewing-machine needle bar.

**Shaft.** Long, narrow section below the shank; diameter of the shaft determines the needle size.

**Groove.** Section that holds and guides the thread down into and out of fabric as stitches are made; larger needles have deeper grooves to protect heavier threads.

**Eye.** Hole for the thread; size increases as shaft size increases; shape differs depending on needle type.

**Point.** In general, use sharps for wovens and ballpoint (rounded) for knits.

**Scarf.** Cutaway section on back of needle above eye; essential to connecting top and bobbin thread for stitch formation.

**Q** What happens if you use the wrong needle for your machine or the fabric?

**A** The wrong needle for your fabric can cause puckering, inferior stitches, or broken or shredding thread or will punch too-large holes in the fabric. It can also throw off the stitch timing and/or damage the bobbin hook. (If either of these last two problems occurs, visit your dealer for repairs.)

--------------------------------------------

**Q** Do I need twin or triple needles?

**A** Several of the basic needle types in the Needle Labels chart (*see pages 56–57*) are also available as twin needles for topstitching two evenly spaced, parallel rows of straight or zigzag stitching. To use one, you must have a zigzag machine with a drop-in or front-loading bobbin. Twin needles are available with needles set different widths apart and are marked with two numbers. The first is the distance between the two needles, and the second designates the needle size (European). For example, a twin needle might be marked 2,0/75. That means the two size-75 needles are spaced 2 mm apart.

It's important to know the needle spacing when using twin or triple needles with zigzag stitches; the overall width of the needle affects how wide a zigzag stitch can be used without breaking the needle on the machine needle plate. Use only a zigzag needle plate (*see page 17*) with these needles and make sure it is large enough to accommodate the needle width and the stitch you plan to use.

Twin needles are ideal for topstitched hems on knits because the bobbin thread zigzags between the two threads, adding a bit of give to the stitch. They are also commonly used with a pintuck presser foot (an add-on accessory) to make decorative tucks, often used for heirloom sewing projects.

------------------------------------------------------------

# Q Why do my needles keep breaking?

A Broken needles result from any of the following situations, all of which are easy to correct:

* **Using a faulty needle;** like everything else, it's possible to get a damaged needle in a fresh package. There is no way to tell until you begin to stitch. Discard.

* **Using the wrong needle system** (*see page 54*) for your machine; check your manual.

* **Incorrect needle insertion;** make sure it's completely and properly seated and the screw is tight in the needle bar.

* **Using a bent needle;** discard.

* **Accumulation of lint** or other debris, including broken needles and pins in the bobbin area; clean your machine (*see* Cleaning and Oiling Tips *on pages 18–19*).

* **Incorrect threading;** unthread the needle and the bobbin completely and start over.

* **Thread hanging up** on the spool edge when it has a slit for storing the thread end; place the spool with the slit end down on a vertical spool holder or at the right-hand end on a horizontal spool holder — always away from the end where the thread feeds from the spool.

## TRUTHS ABOUT MACHINE NEEDLES

* The sewing-machine needle is the least expensive part of any sewing project. Begin each new project with a new needle.

* Needles do get damaged from normal use; they become dull and also may bend or break.

* Some new needles are already defective. If you cannot thread a new needle, the hole for the eye may not be punched out. It happens! If thread breaks after you've inserted a new needle, and you know the machine is threaded correctly, replace the needle and discard the first one. The eye on even a new needle may not be smooth.

* For perfect stitching, use the right needle for the thread: 75/11 or 80/12 with 40-weight thread; 80/12 with 50- or 60-weight thread; 90/14 or 100/16 needle for 30- or 35-weight thread. Use a topstitching needle for heavier threads.

* Sharp needles are designed to easily pierce woven fabrics without damaging them.

* Reserve ballpoint needles for knits; they can cause tears or larger-than-normal holes in woven fabrics, making weak seams.

## BASIC HAND-SEWING NEEDLES

**Sharps:** Medium length with round eye and sharp point; basic needles for a variety of hand-sewing tasks; sizes 1 to 12. Also available as carpet sharps for sewing on heavy, dense fabrics; sizes 16 to 18. Self-threading (calyx-eyed) sharps have a slotted top; thread slides through for easy threading; available in sizes 4 to 8.

**Betweens/Quilting:** Shorter than sharps; have a small, rounded eye; short length makes it easier to stitch fine, short stitches; most often used for hand quilting or very detailed hand sewing; sizes 1 to 12 (the larger the number, the shorter the needle; sizes 8 and 10 are recommended for beginners).

**Crewel/Embroidery:** Sharp needle style with elongated eye to hold several strands of embroidery floss or yarn; sizes 1 to 10.

**Tapestry:** Thicker needle with large eye and blunt tip; available in range of sizes (13 to 28); eye will accommodate several strands of floss, yarn, or decorative threads; blunt tip will not damage fabric; for embroidery and decorative stitching on loosely woven fabrics; can also be used instead of a bodkin (*see page 28*) to thread elastic through casings.

## SPECIALTY NEEDLES

**Beading:** Long, thin needles for sewing beads and sequins onto fabric; sizes 10 to 15.

**Calyx:** Sharp needles with a slot to make it easier to slide the thread down into the needle eye.

**Chenille:** Thick needles with a large, long eye and very sharp point; used for ribbon embroidery or embroidery with heavy threads or yarns; sizes 13 to 26.

**Doll:** Long, fine needles used to soft-sculpture features on handmade fabric dolls; 2½" to 7" long.

**Milliner's:** Longer sharp; used for millinery work but also good for basting and decorative stitching.

**Glover's or Leather:** Has triangular point to make it easy to puncture tough fabrics without tearing them; good for leather, suede, vinyl, or plastic; sizes 3/0 to 10.

**Upholstery:** Heavy needles that may be long or curved, to use when impossible to use a straight needle; use for sewing on thick fabric, as well as for sewing quilt layers together with yarn tufts (tying); straights are 3" to 12" long; curved are 1½" to 6" long.

# Hand Sewing

To choose the appropriate hand-sewing needle, consider the fabric and the technique. Select from those listed in Basic Hand-Sewing Needles on page 62. You'll also need a thimble for easier needle manipulation. Here are some things to consider:

* Choose fine needles for fine fabrics to avoid damaging or stretching the fabric as the needle forces its way through.

* Choose an eye that will accommodate the thread diameter without shredding it.

* Remember, the shorter the needle is, the easier it will be to make short stitches — important when you don't want hand-sewn stitches to show.

- - - - - - - - - - - - - - - - - - - - - - - - - - - - - - - -

**Q** Why do I need a thimble? How do I choose the best one for me?

**A** Even though awkward at first, you'll wonder how you ever sewed without a thimble to help push the needle and thread through the fabric layers. Check out the common thimble types and styles available in the notions department. You may use different types for different sewing tasks. Make sure the thimble fits your index finger snugly but is not too tight. A metal thimble should have small dimples in the flat end to catch, hold, and guide the needle through the fabric. The indentations should be deep enough to hold the needle firmly in place as you guide it through the fabric layers.

* **Metal thimbles** provide the most protection, but your finger may sweat inside during prolonged stitching sessions.

* **Open-ended thimbles** accommodate long fingernails and provide air circulation.
* **Leather thimbles** are soft and comfortable and "grab" the needle better.

- - - - - - - - - - - - - - - - - - - - - - - - - - - - - -

**Q** How do I keep my thimble on? It often slips off while I'm sewing.

**A** First, make sure you are wearing the correct size — not so tight that it cuts off circulation and not so loose that it can slip off easily. To prevent slippage, wear a finger cot (from the drugstore) or cut the fingertips from lightweight surgical gloves to wear underneath your thimble.

## Thread Selection

You'll need different threads for different purposes in your sewing project. Every sewing room needs an assortment of basic colors of all-purpose sewing thread for hand- and machine-sewing. This thread type is easy to sew with, washes and wears well, and lasts over time. Other decorative and functional threads, such as metallic embroidery, topstitching, and heavy-duty carpet threads, are also available for special purposes and sewing techniques.

# Q What should I look for in all-purpose sewing thread?

A Choose either 100 percent polyester or cotton-wrapped polyester-core all-purpose thread. All-poly thread has a bit more "give," so it is often chosen for sewing on knits and stretch-woven fabrics. Cotton-wrapped poly thread is resilient but a bit less heat-sensitive to iron temperatures. Both thread types work well for most fabrics. Sewing thread should be evenly spun, slub-free, and strong. Long-staple polyester thread is the highest quality, a bit more expensive, but worth it for sewing on silk and silkies (silklike fabrics made from synthetics and blends), as well as fine woolens and sheer fabrics.

---

# Q Some threads have numbers, like 50/3, on the label or on the thread display cases. What do they mean?

A Thread diameter is denoted by the first number; the higher the number, the finer the thread. The thread you use should blend into the fabric, not stand on top of the seam-line. A 50- or 60-weight thread (often shortened to "50 wt." or "60 wt.") is the best choice. The second number refers to the number of thread strands that have been twisted together to make a stronger thread. The thread color is also designated by a number, making it easy to purchase additional thread of the same color if necessary.

The typical thread size for most sewing is 50/3 and the tension on most sewing machines is factory-set for this thread weight. For most basic sewing on most fabrics, use the same thread in the bobbin. Embroidery threads, which you might use in the needle for decorative embroidery or special embellishments, are typically 30 wt. and 40 wt. To avoid heavy thread buildup on the back, use special bobbin thread (60 wt.) in the bobbin for machine embroidery or satin stitching appliqués in place.

---

**Q** **What type of thread is best for topstitched details?**

**A** Polyester topstitching thread has replaced silk buttonhole twist (due to expense and availability) as the thread of choice for decorative topstitching. It's thicker, so it requires a needle with a larger eye to avoid shredding (topstitching and denim needles in sizes 16 or 18). If polyester topstitching thread is unavailable in the desired color, substitute long-staple polyester thread and, to make it more pronounced, thread two spools as one through a topstitching needle to accommodate them. Another option is to use the triple straight stitch for highly defined stitches (*see page 108*).

---

**Q** **What's the best way to store my thread? Some of my friends store it in the freezer.**

**A** Don't store thread in the refrigerator or the freezer; cold dries it out. Storing thread in drawers or covered boxes is the best way to prevent dust buildup and prevent fading and damage from sun exposure.

## THREAD FIBER CONTENT

* **Cotton.** Soft, relatively strong for its thickness, easy care, natural fiber; mercerization increases the strength; glazed finishes can rub off and gum up needle and machine; variety of weights and finishes for specific purposes (embroidery, darning, basic sewing, hand quilting, machine quilting); 50-weight for general sewing; matte finish; takes dyes well.
* **Cotton-wrapped Polyester.** Has a little less give than 100 percent polyester all-purpose thread; resilient but a bit less heat-sensitive than polyester to iron temperatures; good for sewing most fabrics.
* **Metallic.** Best have nylon core and outer coating to reduce friction and improve sewing performance and durability; colorfast; some may be heat-sensitive.
* **Nylon.** Synthetic; available as monofilament or tex-turized thread; strong; heat-sensitive; may become brittle with repeated laundering; yellows over time.
* **Polyester.** Durable, strong, colorfast; good shape retention; stretches and recovers (to a point); eco-nomical; 50-weight for general sewing; slight sheen.
* **Rayon.** Soft; high sheen; heat-resistant; not col-orfast; weaker than polyester; less costly than silk; most are 30- and 40-weight; takes dye easily but not colorfast.
* **Silk.** Strong, elastic, high sheen; can be gently washed; damaged by bleach.

**Q Can I use rayon, cotton, or silk thread to sew garments and home-decor items?**

**A Rayon** is soft, not particularly strong, and gets weaker when wet; not a good choice for assembling a project. Its lovely sheen makes it an excellent choice for embellishing and embroidery.

**Silk** thread is often the thread of choice for sewing silks and wools, which are both protein fibers. Although finer than all-purpose thread, it's strong and elastic, making it a good choice for knits (although availability and color range are limited). Silk thread is good for basting (*see* Thread Fiber Content *at left*) because it doesn't leave unwanted holes or stitch imprints in the fabric. It is often used in tailored clothing because it is easily molded when pressing shaped areas.

**Cotton** thread has no elasticity, so stitches can break when stressed, making it a poor choice for knits. You may want to use it in garments made from lightweight woven cotton fabrics, as well as in lightweight silk and silklike fabrics made from synthetics and various fiber blends. Its soft sheen makes it a wonderful choice for machine embroidery, when shine from polyester and rayon threads is undesirable. All-purpose sewing thread is usually the better choice for medium- to heavyweight wovens for garments and home-decor projects.

---

**Q Can I use serger thread on my sewing machine and vice versa?**

**A** Although it's possible to use serger thread on a thread stand for machine sewing, it's generally not recommended; the resulting single-thread seam would be weaker. It's okay to use all-purpose thread on your serger, but the resulting seam will be heavier and firmer, and the stitches may more easily press through so you see their imprint on the right side of the project.

- - - - - - - - - - - - - - - - - - - - - - - - - - - - -

**Q** If my machine is set for 50-weight thread, do I need to make tension adjustments for other weights?

**A** For heavier thread, you will probably need to loosen the top tension to keep the stitch balanced with the top and bobbin threads interlocking in the fabric layers. Use a lower-than-normal needle tension for finer or more fragile threads like metallics; determine this by test-stitching on layers of the same fabrics in your project.

SEE ALSO: *Adjusting Tension, pages 86–87.*

**Q** Are there any other threads to keep on hand for sewing and serging?

**A** There are several specialty threads to consider for specific sewing applications. The list below mentions a few of the most useful to have in your sewing room. There are many other decorative threads, as well as some for special purposes, including assorted quilting types, beading thread, and heavy-duty threads for heavyweight home-decor fabrics and carpet repair.

* **Basting.** Water-soluble thread washes out, but doesn't come out in dry-cleaning solution; use in needle and

bobbin with longer stitch; store in zip-top plastic bag to prevent dissolving in humid conditions

* **Blue-jean thread.** For topstitching; rebalance tension when using; use a (90/14) topstitching needle

* **Bobbin.** Limited colors; use it to draw top thread to bottom for decorative stitching; also for lingerie, fine handwork

* **Fusible.** For positioning appliqués and securing facings and hems; use in bobbin; use press cloth when fusing

* **Gimp.** Strong, fine cordlike thread for corded buttonholes (*see page 377*) and pintucks

* **Monofilament polyester or nylon.** Available in clear and smoke colors; for invisible machine quilting, appliqué, and blindstitching (in needle and bobbin); loosen needle tension when using

* **Serger.** For high-speed serging; sold on cones or tubes; finer, so it may not be strong enough when used alone for machine-stitched seams that are stressed during wear

* **Topstitching.** For highly defined stitching and for hand-sewing buttons in place; use topstitching needle

* **Woolly nylon or polyester.** For lingerie, twin-needle hems and topstitching on knits, serger rolled edges, and attaching elastic; hand-wind on bobbin; stitch at moderate speed; use in loopers for serger rolled hem; use a needle threader (or substitute a dental-floss holder) to thread this soft, fuzzy thread into the needle

**Q** Sometimes I see words such as "core," "monofila-ment," "spun," and "texturized" used to describe thread. What do they mean?

**A** Here's a thread glossary to help you out:

* **Core thread.** Fibers (cotton or polyester) are spun into yarn and then wrapped around a continuous filament of polyester fiber for added strength

* **Monofilament thread.** Polyester or nylon thread made of a single, fine strand of fiber; fine and wiry; transparent; favored for almost-invisible quilting, as well as decorative couching, appliqué, and blindstitching

* **Spun thread.** Fibers are spun into single yarns, which are then twisted together for a smooth, strong thread

* **Texturized thread.** Polyester or nylon filaments that have been texturized and heat-set to make a fuzzy, stretchy thread; most often used in sergers for working on knits

---

**Q** What do I do when I can't find a perfect thread match to my fabric color?

**A** Don't obsess over a perfect match for seaming and gen-eral construction. For the construction seams, find a color that blends into the fabric. Using thread that's a shade darker than the fabric is the best bet, because it will "sew in" a bit lighter and all but disappear along seamlines.

**Q** My thread keeps shredding and breaking while I sew. What's wrong?

**A** It may require some detective work to discover the problem. These are all possibilities:

* **Machine is incorrectly threaded.** This is the primary reason for stitching problems. Rethread carefully; make sure the thread is engaged between the tension discs.

* **Thread is old or of poor quality**, with slubs and weak spots. Discard problematic thread.

* **Needle is the wrong size or type.** A needle that is either too fine for the thread or too fine for the fabric stresses the thread as it is drawn through the machine and fabric. (*See* Fabric Weight/Needle Compatibility *on page 52.*)

* **Needle may be defective.** If thread shreds, replace the needle. If the eye has been roughly punched by the manufacturer, it will damage thread.

* **Needle is incorrectly inserted.** Loosen the needle screw, then make sure the needle is firmly and fully seated in the correct position before tightening.

* **Rough spots on the machine throat plate or thread guides.** Smooth away with a piece of crocus cloth (a fine sandpaper type of cloth available in hardware stores).

* **Top tension is incorrect for the thread.** The discs will flatten and cause shredding of heavier threads if you don't adjust (loosen) the top tension to accommodate thicker threads.

Q **Monofilament thread puddles off the spool, gets hung up, and breaks my needle. Any advice?**

A Wiry monofilament thread has a mind of its own. Place the spool on a separate thread stand (made especially for this purpose) on the table behind the spool pin. The thread goes up through a loop that holds it in place and sends it to your needle with just the right amount of tension.

- - - - - - - - - - - - - - - - - - - - - - - - - - - - - -

Q **I want to use metallic thread for decorative stitching, but it keeps breaking. How do I prevent this?**

A Metallic threads are a bit more fragile than others, requiring care in the machine set-up. Even then, you may get occasional breakage. Keep these tips in mind:

* Use a sewing machine needle designed for metallic threads.

* Make sure all thread guides are smooth and free of any rough spots. Use emery or crocus cloth to smooth away roughness.

* Place spool on a horizontal spool holder so the thread flows off the end of the spool to reduce tension on the thread — or use a thread stand (*see previous question*).

* Reduce the top tension for easier flow and less pressure on the thread. You may need to dial down to a tension setting of 1 or 2 for easy sewing with metallic thread.

* Use polyester-filament bobbin thread to reduce breakage. Cotton thread can grab and break finer threads.

* Stitch more slowly to cut down on friction and heat build-up on the thread.

# CHAPTER THREE

# Stitching Basics

Today, most sewers opt for machine stitching wherever possible. It's faster and easier, and the results are more like what you find in ready-to-wear — only better. Most sewing machines can do much more than you can accomplish by hand. Learning your way around your machine is the first step to successful stitching. Many machines have special stitches built right in; many mimic or can take the place of hand sewing. However, you will still need some basic hand-sewing skills; there are situations when only a hand stitch will do.

# Get Set to Machine-Stitch

Understanding how your sewing machine works is essential to a lifetime of enjoyable sewing experiences. Your sewing-machine manual is an invaluable source of information. Keep it next to your machine until you are comfortable with threading, bobbin winding and insertion, and thread-tension adjustments. Master these first!

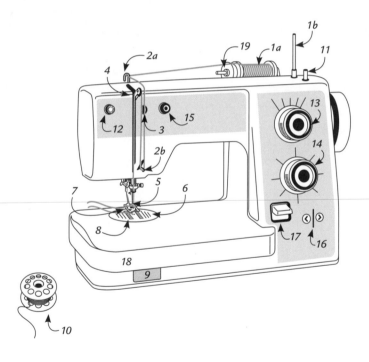

**Q** **What do I need to know about my machine before I start to sew?**

**A** Learn the basic parts and what they do, so you can follow the directions in your machine manual for smooth operation. Machines share common parts that make them work. Study the illustration and read about how each part functions to create stitches. *Note:* On computerized machines, some of the adjustments are made on-screen instead of with knobs.

**1a, 1b** **Spool pin:** horizontal or vertical

**2a, 2b** **Thread guides:** guides thread to 3 and 4

**3** **Tension discs:** control the pressure for even feeding and perfect stitching

**4** **Take-up lever:** raises the needle thread so a stitch can form with the bobbin thread

**5** **Needle:** carries the upper thread to the bobbin under 6

**6** **Throat plate:** has a hole for the needle and fits over the feed dogs (8); usually has engraved seam-width lines

**7** **Presser foot:** puts pressure on the fabric being fed under the needle; lowering the foot engages the needle-thread tension discs for smooth and even fabric feeding

**8** **Feed dogs:** metal teeth below the presser foot move the fabric layer(s) through the machine as each stitch is formed

**9** **Bobbin case or mechanism (separate or built-in):** holds the bobbin

**10** **Bobbin:** holds thread for the stitches that form on the underside of the fabric

**11** **Bobbin-winder tension knob**

12 **Presser-foot pressure knob:** adjusts presser-foot pressure for differing fabric thicknesses

13 **Stitch length knob:** adjusts stitch length

14 **Stitch width knob:** adjusts stitch width

15 **Tension adjustment knob:** adjusts needle-thread tension

16 **Needle position knob:** adjusts needle position several steps to the left or right from normal center for various special stitching applications

17 **Reverse lever or button:** allows you to stitch backward

18 **Free arm:** allows you to "stitch in the round" when working on sleeves, pant legs, and small clothing items

19 **Spool cap:** slips onto horizontal spool pin to keep spool from flying off during stitching

- - - - - - - - - - - - - - - - - - - - - - - - - - - -

**Q** Are there general guidelines for threading the sewing-machine needle?

**A** Most machines follow an "over-down-around-up-down-and-through" threading pattern. Refer to the illustration on page 76 as you read the following sequence:

1. Raise the presser foot (7) to release tension on the tension discs (3) so you can firmly "seat" the thread between them. Forcing thread through unreleased discs damages thread and traps lint in the discs.

2. Place spool on the appropriate spool holder (*see* Vertical or Horizontal Pin *on page 80*).

3. Follow the thread guides (2a) on the top of the machine, leading you from the spool **over** to the tension mechanism.

4. Bring the thread **down** the front of the machine to the tension discs (3). Slip thread between the two discs; make sure it is seated between, not floating in front of the discs.

5. Continue down and then **around** the next thread guide (2b). Continue **up** to the take-up lever (4), which holds the thread as the needle moves up and down. When this lever is up, the needle thread is at its highest point to finish the connection between top and bobbin thread.

6. Follow the remaining thread guides **down** the machine and then insert the thread **through** the needle (5).

7. Give the thread a gentle tug to ensure that you can pull the thread through the machine with ease. Make sure the thread is seated in the discs by lowering the foot and tugging again. If you feel significant resistance, the tension discs are doing their job.

8. Wind and insert the bobbin correctly. See your manual.

9. With the presser foot raised, draw the bobbin thread to the surface by holding the needle thread in your right hand while you lower the needle. Then raise the take-up lever to its highest point to pull a loop of bobbin thread up through the needle hole. Pull threads under the foot to lie behind the presser foot.

## VERTICAL OR HORIZONTAL PIN

If thread is wound on the spool in a parallel fashion (so the threads unwind from the top to the bottom of the spool), use the vertical spool pin for smooth feeding. For cross-wound thread (thread crosses itself as it is wound diagonally from top to bottom), use the horizontal pin for even, stress-free feeding. Add a spool cap (*19 in illustration on page 76*) to keep the spool from flying off the pin while you sew.

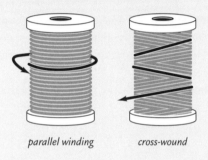

*parallel winding*          *cross-wound*

Serger threads and some specialty threads are cross-wound onto large tubes or cones. To facilitate even feeding, you will need a thread stand with a loop positioned behind your machine at the spool pin. To avoid feeding, stitching, and tension problems, do not put a cone or oversized tube with cross-wound thread on a vertical spool pin. It puts too much drag on the thread and will cause tension and stitch-formation problems, as well as thread and needle breakage.

Q **Is there any way to know if the thread is correctly seated in the tension discs before I begin to sew?**

A Adjust the tension to the correct setting for the thread you are using. Raise the presser foot and thread the machine to, but not past, the last set of thread guides. Pull on the thread as you lower the presser foot. You should feel a change in the tension on the thread. If you feel no change, the thread is not seated in the tension discs. Start over and test again.

Q **Do I need the small felt circles over the spool pin on my machine?**

A Yes. They help stabilize the spool so the thread doesn't unwind incorrectly and get wrapped under the spool, which could cause the thread to snap and the needle to break.

Q **What do I need to know about bobbin winding and insertion for successful sewing?**

A The bottom thread must be smoothly wound and the bobbin correctly inserted into the bobbin mechanism (built-in) or a separate bobbin case. Loosely wound bobbins, or bobbins with threads that crisscross, cause uneven tension and irregular stitching. To ensure smooth stitching, pay attention to these bobbin basics:

∗ Use the bobbin designed for your specific machine so it fits the bobbin case correctly. Bobbins are *not* generic.

* Follow your machine manual for bobbin winding. Wind onto an empty bobbin; don't wind new thread over old.
* Keep the bobbin case and bobbin area lint-free.
* Make sure the thread is engaged in the tension-winding discs for correct winding tension. The thread should wind on smoothly with each strand parallel to the next, not stacked or crossed. Unload and rewind loosely wound bobbins, or those with thread crisscrossing, or where the thread is stacked more thickly on one side of the bobbin. Slow down when winding a bobbin, particularly with polyester thread. Winding too fast will stretch this thread.
* Snip the beginning thread tail close to the bobbin case after winding, so it doesn't get caught and tangled in the stitching when you begin sewing.
* Insert the bobbin with the thread feeding in the correct direction (see your manual). It should move clockwise in the case as you pull the bobbin thread out of the opening (notch) in the tension plate/spring. The direction makes a difference in stitch formation and tension.
* Hand-wind thicker threads for decorative work or with stretchy threads (elastic or woolly nylon, for example). Wind evenly back and forth across the bobbin with uniform tension and no high or low spots.
* Discard cracked or damaged/misshapen bobbins and those that show lots of wear. This prevents bobbins that wobble, which can adversely affect bobbin tension.

*correct*

*incorrect*

Q **How do I eliminate puckers at the beginning of a seam and keep the seam a consistent, accurate width?**
A Grasp both threads when you start to stitch; release threads after the first inch; stitch at a slow to medium steady speed; watch the cut edge glide along the seam guide on the foot as you stitch — don't watch the needle.

- - - - - - - - - - - - - - - - - - - - - - - - - - - - - -

Q **How do I secure the stitches at the beginning and end of a row of sewing?**
A Choose from one of these methods:

* **Backstitch.** Begin stitching the seam at least ¼" below the cut edge, engage your machine's backstitch mechanism, and sew back to the cut edge. Continue forward along the remainder of the seam. Backstitch at the end of the seam for at least ¼". (This is the fastest method.)
* **Tie thread ends.** Leave at least 4"-long thread tails at the beginning and end of the stitching (as when sewing a patch pocket in place). Thread the tails into a needle and bring them to the wrong side before tying with a secure tailor's knot (*see page 121*).
* **Use the lockstitch** feature on your computerized machine. (*Warning:* These tiny stitches are difficult to remove.)
* **Adjust the stitch length** to less than 1 mm and sew several very small stitches at the beginning (and end), before returning to the normal stitch length. (These stitches are also difficult to remove.)
* **Stitch through a thread loop** to knot.

# Tension Tamers

Avoid sewing "tension headaches" by learning how to adjust
the tension and presser-foot pressure for perfectly formed
stitches on your machine, no matter what stitch or thread
you're using.

- - - - - - - - - - - - - - - - - - - - - - - - - - - - - -

**Q** Adjust the tension? How do I do that? I'm afraid to
play with the tension settings.

**A** To make strong seams, it's essential to test and adjust
the thread tension every time you start a new project
on a fabric that's different from the last one you sewed. Thread
tension is also important for making even-length stitches for
visible stitching, such as topstitching and edgestitching (*see
page 111*). Getting the right tension will help you make stitches
that hug the fabric surfaces without lying in loose loops or
digging into the fabric and causing puckers. When handling
multiple or very thick fabric layers, tension adjustments are
also necessary. To test the tension:

1. Set up the machine with the thread type you've chosen for your project, as thread affects tension. Use the
   appropriate needle for your fabric (*see page 52*). Put
   a different color of the same thread in the bobbin to
   make it easy to distinguish between top and bobbin
   threads when checking the stitches. Adjust for a standard sewing stitch length, usually 2.5 to 3.0 mm (or
   10 to 12 spi, or "stitches per inch"). *Note:* Test zigzag
   stitching in the same manner.

84

2. Cut a 2" × 6" rectangle of each of the fabrics that will make up your seam, usually two layers of the same fabric. Stitch through the center of the layers.

3. Examine the stitches. If the bobbin thread is pulled to the top or the top thread is pulled to the back, raise the presser foot and rethread the needle and bobbin to make sure they are correctly threaded. Then stitch another test row and check both sides for one of the results listed in Adjusting Tension on page 86. Make adjustments as needed.

- - - - - - - - - - - - - - - - - - - - - - - - - - - - - -

Q Once I see how the tension is off, is it better to adjust the bobbin or the top tension?

A First, try adjusting the top tension in slight increments, loosening or tightening it as needed. Slight adjustments for varying fabric weights may be required. It's best to adjust the top tension, but you can also adjust bobbin tension by loosening or tightening the tension screw on the bobbin case, no more than ⅛ to ¼ turn at a time. A tiny change can make a big difference. Turn clockwise to tighten and counterclockwise to loosen. Tightening the bobbin thread draws the top thread down farther into the fabric layers.

I have an extra bobbin case (marked with colored nail polish) that I use for special sewing and embellishing techniques with different threads, so I'm not afraid to play with the bobbin tension settings. I don't have to readjust the bobbin tension on the case I use for standard sewing on most fabrics.

## ADJUSTING TENSION

Check your tension test sample (*see question on page 84*).

**Straight stitch.** Balanced stitches look smooth and even on both sides, with the two threads interlocked and buried in the fabric layers, not showing on either surface. If your stitches look like this, you're all set.

If freckles of the bobbin thread show on top, the top tension is too tight. Loosen in small increments by turning the tension dial to a lower number. Test-stitch and adjust again, if needed.

If freckles of the top thread show on the underside, tighten the top tension by turning the knob to a higher number so it will pull the bobbin thread up into the fabric layers. Tighten in small increments and test-stitch until the stitching is perfect on both sides.

**Zigzag.** The top and bobbin thread link at the point of each zig and zag, so look there for thread loops that are pulled to the top or bottom surface. Puckers also indicate tension problems on the side that is puckered. If fabric forms into a ridge underneath the zigs and zags, tension is too tight.

*Note:* If you haven't had your machine serviced and tension problems persist, clean and oil the machine (*see pages 18–19*), and test again. If that doesn't help, it's time for a machine tune-up at your dealer.

|  | Straight Stitch | Zigzag Stitch |
|---|---|---|
| Balanced | | |
| Bobbin-thread freckles (top tension too tight) | | |
| Needle-thread freckles (bottom tension too tight) | | |

# Q I don't have an extra bobbin case. If I change tension, how do I get it back to normal?

A Place a full bobbin in the case and suspend it by the thread tail over your other hand. Jiggle the thread. The bobbin case should gently drop toward your hand in small increments. If it drops fast, tighten the tension screw on the case in increments with a small screwdriver until it's correct.

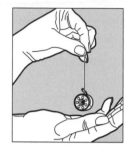

Finally, test the tension by stitching on two layers of quilting fabric. Make additional adjustments, if necessary. Note that this is not possible with built-in bobbin-case mechanisms.

## TENSION TROUBLESHOOTING

| Problem | Possible Cause |
|---|---|
| Top thread shreds and frays | Needle tension too tight (or needle is wrong size for thread diameter; *see page 51*) |
| Top thread breaks | Needle tension too tight |
| Bobbin thread shows on top | Top tension too tight or bobbin tension too loose; lint/dirt in the tension spring: clean the bobbin area and case |
| Nests of thread under the needle plate; jammed stitching | Needle tension too low or threading missed the take-up lever |

**Q** There's a knob on my machine for adjusting the presser-foot pressure. When would I use it?

**A** Different fabric types and weights may require pressure adjustments for smooth feeding and even stitch formation. Too much pressure can cause knit fabrics to stretch, as well as the top layer of a seam in any fabric to scoot forward, resulting in an uneven edge at the end and a pulled or puckered seam.

To test the pressure, raise the needle to its highest point and lower the presser foot on the fabric layers to be stitched. If the fabric slips easily under the foot when you tug on it, there is not enough pressure. If the fabric is so tight that it won't move at all, decrease the pressure a bit. The pressure is correct when:

* Both layers of fabric move under the presser foot at the same rate without bubbles of what appears to be excess fabric forming in the top layer.
* There is no excess fabric on the top or bottom layer at the end of the stitched seam. If there is, don't cut it off! Undo the seam and restitch, after adjusting the pressure.
* The resulting seam is pucker-free.

Some stitching problems result from using the wrong presser foot. For example, the flat-soled zigzag foot has a wider hole to accommodate the utility zigzag stitches. If you try to use this foot for decorative zigzag stitches, it will flatten and/or hang up on the stitches. Instead, use the satin stitch or embroidery foot with a sole designed to accommodate decorative stitch density.

SEE ALSO: *Questions on presser-feet differences, pages 14–16.*

## TWELVE TIPS FOR SMOOTH STITCHING

1. Clean lint from the bobbin area when you finish a project. Oil machine periodically, as outlined in your machine manual.

2. Use the correct needle for the fabric (*see chart on page 52*); make sure it is inserted correctly and securely tightened. Test on fabric scraps.

3. Use high-quality thread. Avoid thread with visible defects, like slubs, bumps, and weak spots.

4. Place the thread on the correct spool pin for smooth feeding (*see* Vertical or Horizontal Pin, *on page 80*).

5. Thread the needle and insert the bobbin correctly. Check your manual.

6. Use the same type of thread in the needle and the bobbin, for a balanced stitch for construction stitching. Rebalance tensions when using different threads together for decorative purposes or special techniques.

7. Test and adjust the tension and stitch length (and width when using other than straight stitches) for your fabric.

8. Do not stitch over pins, to avoid damaging needles and fabric. If you hit a pin, or something happens while sewing that bends or breaks the needle, stop immediately to determine and correct the problem. Discard the needle.

9. Retrieve the broken point of broken needles and pins from the bobbin case before continuing.

10. Stop stitching if your machine starts "talking" with strange or loud sounds, to avoid damaging the stitching mechanism.

11. Use the correct presser foot. A zipper foot makes easier work of maneuvering around zippers. An edgestitching foot ensures accurate stitch placement.

12. Allow the sewing machine to do its job with as little interference or assistance from you as possible. Your job is to guide the fabric under the presser foot smoothly and evenly after setting up the machine for your project. Allow the feed dogs to work correctly. Pulling on fabric to speed the sewing puts undue stress on the needle and can cause it to bend. This can damage fabric and the machine.

Q **Why should I avoid stitching over pins? I've tried it and haven't noticed any problems.**

A Besides the damage it can do to fabric and machine, it's a safety hazard. Broken pins and needles can fly anywhere — into your eyes or into the interior workings of your machine.

* Grazing a pin with the needle may damage the pin; if you don't discard the pin, it may snag on fine fabrics. It may also dull the needle and/or create a burr.
* Hitting a pin directly will bend the pin, rendering it useless. It may not break the needle, but it will damage it.
* Hitting a pin while sewing at high speed (worst of all) will probably break the needle, which can adversely affect the stitch timing on your machine; stitch problems *will* result, and you *will* need to have the machine repaired.

- - - - - - - - - - - - - - - - - - - - - - - - - - - - - -

Q **How do I make sure my straight and curved seams are accurately stitched at the same width?**

A Most sewing machines have a series of lines etched into the throat plate to the right, and sometimes to the left and in front of the needle. If these lines are not marked with the seam widths, use a seam gauge to measure the distances from the needle center position. Select the appropriate guide for the seam width specified on your pattern and sew with the fabric edge aligned with it. To maneuver curved edges, try sewing with a shorter-than-normal stitch length. Depending on the shape of the curve, you may also need to stop and start more often to reposition the edge along the stitching guide.

## AS YE SEW, SO SHALL YE RIP!

For those times when you make a mis-stitch, you'll need a seam ripper (or sharp-pointed scissors) to undo the error. One is often included as a standard tool with your machine presser feet; it's a good idea to have another one in your hand-sewing kit. One of the blades has a sharp point for lifting stitches before cutting them. The other point has a plastic ball to help prevent disastrous slips while you remove stitches. You can also use a seam ripper to carefully slash buttonholes open. Always use with care.

**Q** How do I ensure straight and even stitching when the stitching must be wider than the engraved lines?

**A** My favorite method is an adjustable elastic "bracelet" for the sewing-machine free arm. Use 1"-wide nonroll elastic and overlap the ends, making it tight enough for a snug fit; stitch securely. Slide it on to the free arm and use a sewing gauge to determine where to place it for the desired stitching width. Some sewers use masking tape to mark desired stitching widths on the bed of the machine. That works too! It's a good idea to remove the masking tape when you don't need it any longer. Use rubbing alchohol or a product like Goo Gone or Goof Off to remove any tape residue.

## STITCH LENGTH EQUIVALENTS

| Stitch Type | Stitches/inch | Stitch length in mm |
|---|---|---|
| Regulation (Permanent) | 10–12 | 2–2.5 |
| Basting, Topstitching | 6–8 | 3–4 |
| Ease stitching | 8–10 | 2.5–3 |
| Reinforcement | 18–20 | 1.25–1.5 |
| Stitch in place | 0 | 0 |
| Satin stitching | 100 | 0.25 |

Note: Some machines have even longer basting stitches available. This length makes temporary stitching that holds well but is easy to remove. You may also want this longer stitch length for some topstitching applications.

## Q How do I know which stitch length to use?

A Stitch length is indicated in sewing directions and books as stitches per inch, as in "12 to 15 spi," or in the length of each stitch, expressed in millimeters, as in "2.0 mm to 2.5 mm stitch length." Many computerized machines have built-in sewing advisors that suggest stitch length for particular functions and fabrics. You may need further adjustments after testing the recommendations. (See Stitch Length Equivalents, above.)

- - - - - - - - - - - - - - - - - - - - - - - - - - - - - -

| Purpose |
| --- |
| Standard for most construction sewing |
| Temporary stitching to hold layers for fitting and permanent stitching |
| Easing or gathering layers to fit |
| Use at corners, points, and tight curves, especially where close trimming is required in enclosed seams (*see pages 282 and 283*) |
| Use when bar-tacking buttons in place by machine |
| Securing appliqués and doing other decorative stitching |

## Solving Problems

Q I have "mature eyesight" and threading the machine needle is very difficult. Any hints?

A Many of the newest machines and sergers have automatic needle threaders, and some specialty needles are designed for easier threading. If these are not available, first make sure the area is well lit; a portable sewing lamp is invaluable for this, especially at night. Also try one of these two tricks: (1) Paint the area on the presser-foot shank directly behind the needle with white correction fluid; or (2) Hold a white index card behind the needle while you thread it.

**Q** **What do I do if I can't get the tension balanced on my machine?**

**A** This may indicate that the upper tension spring is worn and should be replaced, or the bobbin tension plate may be bent. Head to your local sewing-machine dealer for these repairs.

- - - - - - - - - - - - - - - - - - - - - - - - - - - - - - - - - - -

**Q** **Sometimes when I start to stitch, the threads disappear into the needle hole and the stitches jam, or the needle comes unthreaded. What's wrong?**

**A** If it happens consistently, it usually indicates the top tension is too loose, causing the needle thread to get pulled into an extra-large loop underneath the needle plate. Because the top tension isn't tight enough to pull that back up, it forms a "bird's nest" on the underside. To prevent the problem:

* Make sure the machine is correctly threaded — top and bottom — so there is enough tension to form a stitch. If the removable bobbin case is not seated correctly, stitches won't form properly and the case will fall out, causing stitch jams.
* Make sure the top tension is correct (*see page 85*).
* Always begin to stitch with the thread take-up (*see pages 76–77*) in the uppermost position. If the lever is down, when it rises to take the first stitch, it will pull the threads up with it, causing the problems you describe.
* Draw at least 5" of top and bobbin thread under and behind the foot to grasp as you begin to stitch.

## LEAD ON!

A stitch leader is a double-layer scrap of fabric that you place under the presser foot to begin your stitching. Center it under the presser foot, lower the foot and needle, and begin stitching, then feed the seam into it. Clip the leader from the seam and save to use again and again. Or, place a piece of tear-away nonwoven stabilizer under the cut edge at the beginning of the seam; begin stitching on it. Tear it away carefully and discard. This is good technique for lightweight, sheer, and silky fabrics, particularly if you are not using a straight-stitch needle plate (*see pages 16–17*).

* Use a stitch leader when you start sewing. (*See* Lead On!, *above.*)
* If the problem continues, visit your sewing-machine dealer to check the stitch timing mechanism and the tension assembly.

Q Why does the upper thread keep breaking while I stitch?

A The most common reasons include:

* Needle is in backward; remove it and reseat it correctly.
* Needle is not the right type for the machine (see your manual).

* Needle hole is not large enough for the thread diameter, causing stress and wear on the thread.
* Needle is slightly bent or may have a blunt point; discard and replace.
* Machine is incorrectly threaded. Unthread and rethread the machine on top and check the bobbin for correct threading. (*See pages 78-79 and/or refer to your manual.*)
* The needle thread tension is too tight; adjust the tension (*see pages 86-87*).
* There is a burr on the presser foot or the hole in the throat plate; use a piece of crocus cloth to gently file away any rough spots you can feel.
* Sewing at a jerky, irregular sewing speed. Slow down and keep your foot steady on the foot pedal.
* Thread is catching on the edge of the spool or the thread slot. Remove the spool and place it with the slotted side down before rethreading the machine.
* Poor quality thread with slubs and bumps is hanging up in the needle hole and breaking off due to the stress of stitching.
* High-speed sewing on synthetic fabrics generates heat, which can heat up the needle and cause thread breakage.

- - - - - - - - - - - - - - - - - - - - - - - - - - - - - -

Q **Why does the bobbin thread keep breaking?**

A The most common reasons are listed on the next page. If correcting any or all of these doesn't solve the problem, it's time for a check up by your dealer.

* Bobbin is incorrectly wound or is not completely and correctly inserted in the bobbin case; remove, check the winding (*see page 82*), and reinsert as directed in your manual.

* Bobbin is too full; remove and discard some of the thread.

* There is a knot in the bobbin thread. Replace low-quality thread if it appears to have lots of slubs or irregular spots or knots along the surface when held up to the light. A knot may just be a fluke.

* Bobbin tension is too tight. Adjust for balanced tension (*see pages 86–87*).

* There is lint in the bobbin case. Clean the case and the bobbin area inside the machine before reinserting the bobbin.

* The spring on the bobbin case may be worn; ask your dealer to check it out.

- - - - - - - - - - - - - - - - - - - - - - - - - - - - - -

Q **What causes skipped stitches and how can I prevent them?**

A Consider and correct the following as they apply to your sewing situation:

* **Incorrect needle selection and insertion.** Make sure you are using the correct needle type (point style) for the fabric (*see page 52*). A ballpoint needle doesn't pierce woven fabrics like a universal or sharp needle, which may cause poor stitch quality if used on the wrong fabric. Make sure the needle is correctly seated and secure. If it's skewed, not in far enough, or loose, the stitches won't form correctly.

* **Sewing with a damaged needle.** Burrs make it difficult to pierce the fabric layers for correct stitch formation. Bent needles may form stitches sporadically.
* **Incorrect threading.** Completely unthread and rethread the top and the bobbin.
* **Stitching with the zigzag plate** on the machine when sewing on lightweight knits and wovens. The fabric "flags" (gets caught in the wide hole), interrupting stitch formation. Change to a straight-stitch throat — unless you need the wider plate for seam finishing or decorative stitching. Use taut sewing (*see next page*) to prevent flagging.
* **Adhesive on the needle,** from stitching through fusible interfacings, fusible web, or fabrics basted with temporary spray adhesive. This may cause drag on the needle. Remove adhesive buildup on the needle with rubbing alcohol.
* **Lint accumulation.** Check for and remove lint in the tension discs, in the bobbin case and/or around the bobbin case housing inside the machine (*see pages 18–19*).
* **Excessive fabric finishes.** Prewash washable fabrics to remove sizing that can cause the needle to stick and skip rather than forming a stitch.

If none of these appear to be the problem, clean and oil moving parts, following the directions in your owner's manual, rethread, and test-stitch on scraps. If the skipping continues, try adding a line of liquid thread conditioner, such as All-Purpose Sewer's Aid, to the spool of thread to soften and condition the thread for smoother stitching.

Also, faulty timing or a damaged hook in the bobbin mechanism may be the culprit. These are mechanical problems to be addressed by a trained mechanic. Once-a-year servicing, or more often if you sew a lot, is essential for the health of your machine.

---

**Q** **What causes puckered stitching and how can I prevent it?**

**A** This results from using the wrong thread, needle, stitch, or tension — or any combination of these. On lightweight and sheer fabrics, sewing with a layer of tissue paper or tear-away embroidery stabilizer underneath helps alleviate the problem. Also, winding a bobbin too fast with polyester thread stretches the thread and can contribute to puckered seams.

You may need to use "taut sewing" to assist the machine when sewing on some fabrics. It's an easy way to prevent puckered stitching as you join seam layers on fabrics that are prone to the problem. Simply grasp both layers of the fabric in front of and behind the presser foot and tug *gently* to eliminate any slack in the fabric layers. Take care not to pull too hard; that will adversely affect the feed dogs and bend the needle, causing it to hit the machine throat plate and snap. Light, even pressure keeps the feed dogs and fabric moving smoothly for smooth

tug gently and evenly

TAUT SEWING

101

seams. It also works when topstitching (*see page 107*), and it's an integral part of stitching wavy lettuce edges on knit fabrics or bias edges. (Pulling the stretchy fabric taut while stitching, and then releasing the stretch, creates the "wave.")

- - - - - - - - - - - - - - - - - - - - - - - - - - - - - - - - -

**Q** Is there a quick and easy way to rip out inaccurate machine stitches?

**A** There are several ways to "unstitch a seam," but I find this method the fastest, easiest, and safest. On the bobbin-thread side of the seam, use a sharp seam ripper (or small, sharp scissors) to lift and snip every fifth or sixth stitch. Flip the piece over and pull the thread. It should lift away easily in one piece, leaving only small thread tufts on the reverse to remove. Run a piece of masking tape over the seamline to pick them up or use a lint roller, a small foam paintbrush, or a pink pencil eraser to whisk them away.

- - - - - - - - - - - - - - - - - - - - - - - - - - - - - - - - -

**Q** My sewing machine needle makes a popping noise and the stitches aren't always perfect. What's wrong?

**A** The needle is probably dull and worn; change it. When making a project with extensive machine stitching, you may need to stop midway and change to a fresh needle. Tough synthetic fibers, such as polyester and nylon, dull machine needles faster, so changing the needle more often is essential.

# Machine-Stitching Know-How

You will need to master several different types of machine stitching to create quality garments and home-decor projects. You will use a straight stitch, a simple zigzag, or one of several basic zigzag variations for most construction and seam finishing. Master the basics of straight and simple zigzagging and you are on your way to perfect seams and finishes and beautiful topstitching. Then add basting, staystitching, blindstitching, and "stitching in the ditch" to your sewing repertoire to tame edges and hold layers securely in place.

**Q Are there guidelines for achieving perfect straight and zigzag stitching?**

**A** Test the tension (*see pages 84–85*) and adjust the stitch length (and width for zigzagging) on scraps of the same number of fabric layers you will be sewing on. Make note of favorite settings for different types of fabric/stitch combinations on your machine and keep them in your sewing notebook (*see page 48*) for future reference.

**Q How do I machine-baste?**

**A** Set the machine for a longer-than-normal straight stitch — at least 3 mm to 4 mm (6 to 8 spi, or stitches per inch). Loosen the top tension a setting or two and then stitch, guiding the cut edges along the desired seam width. Do not backstitch, and leave long thread tails.

If the basting will not remain in the work, use a different thread on the bobbin for easy identification. When it's time to remove it, clip the bobbin stitches every inch or so, then pull on the top thread. It should pull out with ease (unless it's caught in a stitch), leaving only bits of bobbin thread to remove on the other side of the seam.

- - - - - - - - - - - - - - - - - - - - - - - - - - - - - - -

Q **What is staystitching? How and when should I do it?**

A Staystitching prevents shaped and angled edges of garment pieces from stretching out of shape during construction and fitting. It keeps cut edges on the grain. Staystitch curved and angled V-neckline edges, as well as armholes, shoulder edges, waistlines, and the curved side seams in fitted skirts and pants. Straight-grain or nearly straight-grain seams usually don't require it. It's a good idea to staystitch all seams in garments cut from loosely woven or very stretchy fabrics, to ensure that pieces retain their shape. Some staystitching guidelines:

1. Staystitch immediately after removing the pattern piece, stitching ⅛" inside the seamline and using a standard stitch length. For standard commercial patterns with ⅝"-wide seam allowances, staystitch ½" from the cut edge. *Do not backstitch.*
2. Attach the underlining (*see page 249*) in an underlined garment and then staystitch; otherwise staystitching is done on a single fabric layer.
3. Don't pivot when you reach a corner. Stop, clip the threads, and stitch the next edge in the same manner.

4. Stitch directionally to prevent stretching the edge while you staystitch — usually this means stitching from the widest to the narrowest point of the piece (as shown by the arrows in the illustration). To maneuver smoothly around curved edges without stretching them, stop often and adjust the piece to align with the stitching guide on the machine.

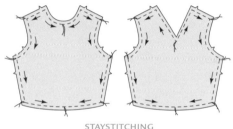

STAYSTITCHING

5. Do not remove staystitching. It remains in the garment.
6. Never staystitch long bias edges. They will stretch out of shape.
7. On pile fabrics, such as velvet, velveteen, and corduroy, it's best to staystitch with the direction of the pile (the smoothest direction), to avoid roughing up and damaging the surface.

- - - - - - - - - - - - - - - - - - - - - - - - - - - - - - - - - -

Q How do I determine which direction is *with* the fabric grain and which is *against* it on a cut edge?

A Think about what happens when stroking a cat. When you rub the edge of the fabric and it stays smooth, *that's with the grain.* If it roughs up when you stroke the edge, like a cat's fur does when you pet it the "wrong" way, that's against the grain.

---

Q How can I be sure that I don't stretch the piece while I'm staystitching?

A Stretching or otherwise changing the shape of the curve as you stitch causes uneven, roughly shaped edges on outward curves, as well as armholes and necklines that gape or flare around inside curves.

When you stitch around a curve, think of the fabric as a piece of poster board, which you can't stretch or reshape. Use your hands to keep your fabric in the shape it was cut, as you stitch around the curve. On concave curves, like armholes and necklines, hold your hands around the area you're stitching in a hooplike shape, holding the edges in place so they don't stretch or distort. *Don't stretch the curved edge as you sew* — that will actually shorten the curve. When the fabric relaxes after stitching, it will no longer match the curve on the pattern piece. On a convex curve, place the left hand to the left of the needle and the right hand perpendicular to it, to hold the edge in shape as you "drive" smoothly around it.

After staystitching, replace the pattern piece to make sure the fabric piece is still the correct size and shape. If the piece has stretched a bit and doesn't match the pattern, carefully pick up stitches with a pin to draw up the staystitching every 2" or so to coax the piece to match the pattern shape (*see illustration on page 199*.) Sometimes it's necessary to clip a stitch every six stitches or so to release tight stitching. Fabric pieces that pulled in a bit during staystitching can then relax into shape to match the pattern piece.

*SEE ALSO: Convex or Concave?, page 277.*

# Q When and why do topstitching?

A Topstitching is essential when making flat-fell seams (*see page 271*) or when machine-stitching a hem (*see pages 302–303*). Use it to stabilize the edge and hold fabric layers together along collars, lapels, and front edges of faced garments. It draws attention to design details, and it is often done for decorative purposes in single or multiple rows to emphasize an edge or a seamline. Use the same sewing thread you used to construct the item, or a heavier thread, such as topstitching thread or buttonhole thread, to match or contrast as desired. It's essential to topstitch accurately, at a slow, even speed.

**For construction purposes,** as in flat-fell seams: Use the same stitch length as used for other stitching (2 mm to 2.5 mm, or 10 to 12 spi).

**For decorative purposes:** Lengthen the stitch (2.5 mm to 3 mm, or 8 to 10 spi is standard) for more obvious stitching. Use the thread-appropriate needle (*see page 52*) with all-purpose sewing thread in the bobbin, and rebalance the tension (*see page 84*). If the item is reversible, use the same thread in the bobbin and needle.

> ## TRIPLE-STITCH IT!
>
> If your machine has this capacity, use the triple straight stitch for topstitching, lengthening it to make it more obvious (8 to 10 stitches per inch). This technique layers three stitches on top of each other for a more visible stitch. Stitch slowly and carefully. It's not fun or easy to "unstitch" this one! For decorative topstitching that looks a little like rickrack, try the triple zigzag stitch, if available on your machine.

**Q** **My topstitching thread keeps shredding and break-ing. What's wrong?**

**A** If you are using a topstitching or denim needle, it's possible the needle has a burr. Try a new needle. In addition, some machines are a bit persnickety about thread combinations. Try the following options to find the best combination for the fabric:

* Use topstitching thread on top, and polyester all-purpose thread on the bobbin.
* Use topstitching thread on the bobbin, and polyester all-purpose thread in the needle. Turn the fabric over, so the side where stitching will show is on the bottom while you stitch.
* Use topstitching thread in the needle and on the bobbin.
* If none of these combinations work, try using two threads (all-purpose) threaded through the needle as one, with the project thread on the bobbin. Have the side where the

topstitching will show facing you while you stitch. Using two threads will result in more pronounced topstitching.

- - - - - - - - - - - - - - - - - - - - - - - -

## Q How do I keep rows of topstitching an even distance apart without marking them on the fabric?

A Use the edge of one of the presser feet as a guide for evenly spaced rows. The ¼" patchwork presser foot is great, unless, of course, you want wider spacing between the rows. The edge of an all-purpose presser foot is slightly wider, but you can also adjust the spacing by adjusting the needle position to the right or left. Here are some options:

* Attach an adjustable quilting/stitching guide to the presser foot. (*See page 110.*)

* Use narrow masking tape. It adheres to and is easily removed from most fabrics (but not on napped surfaces). It's great for marking straight rows of stitching; apply carefully, using an acrylic ruler to guide its placement. Stitch along both edges to create parallel rows ¼" apart.

* Use a twin needle (two needles attached to a single shank) to quickly double the topstitching or other decorative stitches. It's particularly effective on knit hems (*see page 207*) and around knit necklines, because the bobbin thread zigzags between the two needle threads, adding flexibility and preventing threads from breaking under strain.

SEE ALSO: *Demystifying Sewing-Machine Needles, pages 50–63.*

# Q How do I use a quilting/stitching guide?

A Make sure your presser foot has a screw on the back with a hole for the guide. Loosen the screw and slip the bar through the hole. Here's how to use it:

1. Mark and do the first row of topstitching. Use a guide on the machine or the edge of the presser foot for the first placement if possible.

2. Adjust the guide to the desired distance from the needle and tighten the screw. Place the work under the foot and guide.

3. Lower the foot and adjust the "toe" of the guide so it just grazes the fabric surface along the first line of stitching. Tighten the screw to hold this position.

4. Lower the foot and stitch slowly, with the guide following the first marked row to keep stitching lines straight. Complete all rows. Maintain a slow, steady speed and stop often to ensure evenly spaced rows.

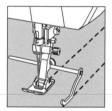

# Q How do I neatly end topstitching?

A Never backstitch; instead, leave long thread tails where you begin and end. Thread them into a large-eye needle and draw between the fabric layers, bringing out on the under-side several inches from where you started. Clip close to the fabric surface so they will slip back between the layers.

# Q How does edgestitching differ from topstitching?

A It's really a form of topstitching, but it is done close to an edge to control the fabric layers. It may also be used as a decorative touch.

---

# Q How do I keep edgestitching straight? Mine is often crooked and wobbly.

A The edgestitching foot has a "blade" between the toes (much like that on some blindstitch presser feet, *page 312*) against which to guide the fabric edge. Select the desired distance from the edge by adjusting the needle position. Some sewers use the inner edge of a ¼" patchwork foot as a guide. Or, try using the inner edge of the toe on an open-toe presser foot and adjusting the needle position to place it close to the edge. With any of these options, take your time and stitch slowly to ensure edgestitching that makes the grade.

---

# Q How do you turn a corner when edgestitching and topstitching? I always miss a stitch when I pivot and continue stitching.

A That's because there's not much for the feed dogs to grab onto at the edge. Here's a neat little trick that works every time:

1. Use a hand-sewing needle with doubled thread to take a stitch through the corner before you begin and leave long tails to hold onto.

2. Edgestitch to the corner, stop with the needle in the fabric, and pivot the work. After lowering the presser foot, hold onto the thread tails to gently tug the corner and get it moving between the foot and the feed dogs. Remove the thread.

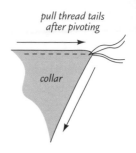

*pull thread tails after pivoting*

*collar*

SEE ALSO: *Chapter 8, Hem and Hem-Edge Finishes.*

# Q What does "stitch in the ditch" mean?

A Used to hold layers in place, this almost invisible stitching is done in the well or ditch of the seam. It's easier to do when the seam allowances are pressed to one side, creating a high-low surface along which to stitch. Always stitch in the low side of the seam. Use stitching in the ditch to secure facings so they stay put (*see page 292*) and to hold elastic in place inside casings (*see page 349*).

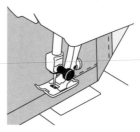

*stitching in the ditch*

# Q Are there guidelines for using patterned stitches?

A Many mechanical machines and all computerized machines have built-in patterned and utility stitches. You can use some of the utility stitches for decorative work, as well as the open, tri-motion, and closed (satin-stitch-based) patterns that are intended for decorative work. Test-stitch on your fabric layers to determine stitch-pattern suitability.

* **Lightweight fabrics.** Choose simple, less dense stitch patterns. These patterns are more open. Heavily satin-stitched details are not appropriate for lightweight fabrics.
* **Medium-weight fabrics.** Designs can be a bit more complex, with some satin-stitched details.
* **Heavyweight fabrics.** More intricate stitches with lots of satin stitching are a good choice. These are considered "closed" stitches.

| OPEN STITCHES | CLOSED STITCHES |
|---|---|

*honeycomb stitch*

*scallop stitch*

*feather stitch*

*arrowhead stitch*

> **SAMPLE THEM!**
>
> Use a firmly woven fabric to make a sampler of all the utility and decorative stitches available on your machine, and keep it in your sewing notebook (*see page 48*). *Hint:* Striped ticking is a great fabric choice, because it gives you rows to follow.
>
> Stitch length and width affects each of the stitches and often creates some interesting results. I recommend trying each stitch at the factory setting first, and then gradually changing the stitch length and widths. Use an indelible pen to write down the settings you like, on the fabric right next to the stitches.

Q My decorative stitches are often unattractive — sometimes I can see the bobbin thread on the surface. Any guidelines?

A Adjusting the tension correctly yields smooth stitching without puckers or bunching under the stitches, and with the bobbin thread pulled to the underside, rather than showing on the top. For best results:

* Test and perfect the stitch tension on samples of the actual fabric and layers used for your project.

* Attach the satin-stitch (also called embroidery) presser foot (not the free-motion embroidery foot) to your machine. The wide channel on the bottom will ride smoothly over the thread buildup typical of embroidery

stitches. The bar between the toes helps keep fabric flat. The open-toe presser foot is also useful for machine embroidery.

* Use the same thread color in the needle and bobbin.
* Use bobbin-weight thread to help draw the stitches to the back of the work.
* Check the needle tension. Decrease it to prevent the fabric from bunching up under the stitches. Too-tight needle-thread tension can also draw the bobbin thread to the surface.
* Place an embroidery stabilizer on the wrong side of the fabric for better stitch formation. Use an additional water-soluble stabilizer on the surface, particularly on pile fabrics (fleece, velvet, velveteen, terry cloth). Gently tear the stabilizer away from the stitches, rather than wash it out. Test first.
* Feed the fabric through without pulling or pushing it.

- - - - - - - - - - - - - - - - - - - - - - - - - - - - - - -

Q **My project calls for satin stitching. How do I do that?**

A Attach the satin-stitch (or embroidery) foot. Adjust the machine for a closely spaced (short) zigzag stitch of the desired width (*see* Stitch Length Equivalents *on pages 94–95*). The stitch length will vary, depending on the fabric and the desired look; you should use a size of 1 mm or less. Loosen the top thread tension a bit, so the bobbin thread will pull it to the underside of the work. Use bobbin-weight thread on the bobbin to facilitate this.

# Special Stitching Challenges

Stitching curves, points, and inset corners, as well as stitching over thick intersections, all offer their own special challenges. Matching seams at intersections where they meet is another important skill to master.

---

Q My project has a piece that must be set into a corner. How do I do that without creating ugly puckers or a hole at the corner of the finished seam?

A Master inset corners in a flash with these easy steps:

1. Reinforce the corner by stitching just shy of the seamline. (Use a fine-point removable marker to mark the seamline first, then stitch to the right of the line.) Adjust the stitch to a shorter-than-normal stitch length and begin and end the reinforcement stitching 1" from the inside corner. Clip to the stitching as shown.

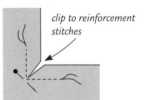

clip to reinforcement stitches

*Step 1*

2. Carefully mark the seam intersection on the outside corner using a fine-point removable marking pen.

3. Pin the clipped section to the outside corner, allowing it to spread and making sure the inside corner is aligned

pivot at clipped-and-spread corner

*Step 3*

with the seamlines on the outward corner. Stitch with the clipped side up, pivoting carefully at the corner and making sure to stitch just inside the reinforcement stitches so they won't show on the outside of the finished seam.

---

**Q** When stitching multiple layers, the machine either skips stitches or the needle breaks. What's the solution?

**A** You'll often encounter bumps where seams cross each other or when sewing through several seam layers — in a hem, for example. Your machine may need extra help at these spots to stitch smoothly without stalling, skipping stitches, or breaking the needle.

To master the bumps with ease, keep the presser foot parallel with the feed dogs; the heel shouldn't angle down in back. You can purchase a special leveler or shim (a Jean-a-ma-jig or Seam Buster) to place beneath the back of the presser foot. Or, make one with a scrap of fabric folded into enough layers to lift the heel of the presser foot so the entire foot is parallel to the feed dogs as you sail across the bump. When the toe drops, move the shim to the front under the toes, again to keep the foot parallel. Keep the shim under the foot (but don't catch it in the stitching) until the heel drops back into position when it leaves the bump. When sewing on hook-and-loop tape, you may need a leveler along the edge so the foot isn't lopsided.

Q How do I smoothly change directions when stitching around corners and points?

A Use a fine-point marking pencil or dressmaker's chalk wheel to draw the seam intersections on the side you will be stitching. For a perfect pivot, use the hand wheel on your sewing machine for the last few stitches, to be sure your needle will land precisely in the intersection. If the last stitch looks like it will overshoot the mark, *gently* tug the fabric toward you so the needle will hit correctly, or shorten the stitch length. Then return to the normal stitch length. *Always stop with the needle down in the fabric when you are ready to pivot.* Lift the presser foot and rotate the fabric into the new position. Lower the foot and continue stitching.

---

Q Intersecting and crossing seams never match up when I'm setting in sleeves. Any advice?

A This can also be a problem when sewing on facings and matching seams on two pieces being joined. Pin carefully, and then machine-baste across the challenging areas where things must match. Check the match, remove basting, and restitch if necessary. When sure of a match, stitch permanently. When seams are pressed to one side instead of open, press in opposing directions so it's easy to nest the seams into each other. This balances the bulk of the two seam allowances and avoids lumps.

# Hand-Sewing Essentials

Threading your needle and sewing by hand can be a soothing process. Some hand stitches are temporary and others remain in the completed project.

**Q** Is there anything special I need to know about threading a needle?

**A** To prevent thread twisting and knotting, cut an 18" length from the spool (A), making the cut at an angle to make it easier to thread (twice that length if you are planning to sew with the thread doubled as for button sewing (*see pages 386–387*). Insert the fresh-cut end into the needle (B). Draw the thread through the needle and make a tailor's knot at that end (C).

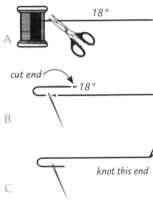

A

*cut end* → 18"

B

*knot this end*

C

*Note:* If you are left-handed, reverse this direction, threading the cut end from the spooled thread into the needle and then drawing it through and knotting.

**Q** Should I hand-sew with a single thread or doubled thread? Why does thread length matter?

**A** Hand sewing is done with a single thread for finer, neater, less noticeable stitches. I've found that doubled

119

threads tend to kink and knot more often, so I prefer the single-thread method for most hand sewing, even though doubling threads can make some tasks, such as button sewing, faster. If you must use two threads, cut two lengths and thread them through the needle, just-cut end first. Knot the two threads together at each end, rather than knotting all four together.

Drawing thread through fabric weakens it somewhat. Longer threads often get caught on pins, or curl, kink, or knot. Stopping to thread a needle periodically is often easier than trying to remove knots in your thread. It's also easier to draw a shorter length of thread through the fabric. The time saved using shorter lengths is worth the time it takes to stop and thread a fresh needle.

## THREADING AND KNOTTING TIPS

* **Cut thread at an angle** with sharp scissors to make a neat end for inserting into the eye.
* **Wet the eye of the needle** with a little saliva, which will attract the thread end to it. Don't wet the thread.
* **Use a needle threader,** a fine wire loop that inserts easily into small needle eyes. Insert the loop through the eye and then insert the thread through the loop. Draw the loop (and thread) through the eye. Place the needle eye in front of something white to make it easier to see and thread it.

# Q How do I make a neat knot for hand sewing?

A Make a tailor's knot (or quilter's knot): After threading the needle and drawing it through, place the cut end that went through the eye perpendicular to the needle and extending about ½" above it. Make three thread wraps around the needle and use your fingernail to hold them firmly as you slide the wraps down the length of the needle, over the eye, and down the length of the thread, ending the "slide" within ½" of the end. The result is a small, secure knot. For a heavier knot, make a second knot over the first one or make more thread wraps around the needle before completing the knot as described above.

*place needle across thread end*

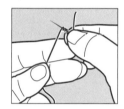

*make 3 wraps and then slide wraps down needle to end of thread*

# Q How do I secure the stitches when I'm finished sewing?

A Usually a few hidden backstitches in place will suffice. Clip the thread close to the fabric.

Q **What are the basic hand stitches I will need and how do I make them?**

A Mastering the basic straight stitches shown at right and hemming stitches shown on pages 302–305 is essential. Although most of these can also be done on today's sewing machines, sometimes it's easier to manipulate fabric by hand rather than working within the constraints of the machine. The running stitch is the most basic stitch, used for hand-basting, as well as for traditional hand-quilting and for hand-sewing trims in place.

- - - - - - - - - - - - - - - - - - - - - - - - - - - - - - - - - -

Q **What is hand-basting? Should I use a special thread for it?**

A For most hand-basting, choose **all-purpose thread** in a slightly contrasting color, so it's easy to remove. **Silk thread** is a good choice for delicate fabrics, or when it may be necessary to press over basting stitches. It's strong but fine, so it is less likely to leave indentations in the fabric. **Darning cotton** is another good choice; it is softer than high-twist sewing thread, but not as strong as silk. Use what seems best for the fabric and project. (*See* Basic Hand Stitches *starting at right.*)

- - - - - - - - - - - - - - - - - - - - - - - - - - - - - - - - - -

Q **How do I keep my thread from kinking and knotting while I hand sew?**

A Cut a short length and then thread it as directed on page 119. To strengthen thread for hand sewing and help prevent kinking and knotting, see Wax It! on page 389.

## BASIC HAND STITCHES

Here are the most often-used hand stitches, as well as a few other commonly used ones. You'll find hand-hemming stitches on pages 302–305. The illustrations that follow are for a right-handed sewer. If you are left-handed, turning the page upside down should help you.

### Straight Stitches

**Running/basting.** Temporarily holds fabric layers together for checking fit or doing permanent stitching. Often used for better control when matching plaids and checks, sewing slippery fabric layers together, or positioning trims for machine

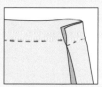

*running/basting stitch*

stitching. Make short, even-length (¼" or shorter) stitches. Use this stitch to gather a length of fabric by drawing up the thread to create the gathers before knotting or ending the stitching. You may also use it for topstitching by hand and for mending tasks.

**Backstitch.** Use for a strong permanent stitch to hold a seam or a trim in place. Looks like machine stitching on the top, with overlapping stitches on the under-side. Good for repairing split seams for hand mending.

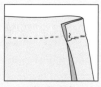

*backstitch*

**Prickstitch.** Use this backstitch variation for almost invisible topstitching when inserting a zipper (*see page 402*) in fine fabrics. Tiny, evenly spaced stitches on the surface look like dots or "pricks" and all but disappear when made with matching silk thread.

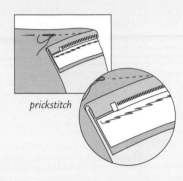

*prickstitch*

Pickstitching (no "r") is similar but is for decorative topstitching. Stitches do not catch the lowest layer of the fabric and are not pulled taut, so they lie on the fabric surface like tiny beads.

## Other Useful Hand Stitches

**Blanket stitch.** Decorative stitch worked from left to right over an edge. Also for making neat thread loops (*see page 394*), and French tacks (*see page 256*). It can be done on most zigzag sewing machines; often used to finish raw-edge

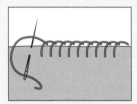

*blanket/buttonhole stitch*

appliqués. Called buttonhole stitch when making hand-worked buttonholes and to repair buttonholes by hand. Used to securely and neatly sew on snaps and hooks and eyes. (*See pages 392–393.*)

**Overcasting.** Used to hand-finish raw edges. Stitches should be evenly spaced and of uniform

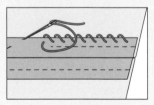

*overcasting*

depth (*see page 263*). Machine stitch the edge first as a guide for even stitch placement. Machine-stitched versions of this time-consuming hand stitch are available on most zigzag sewing machines.

**Serging.** Another similar seam-finishing method that is faster than hand overcasting and provides a sturdier, longer-wearing finish (*see page 262*).

**Slip basting.** Use this slipstitch variation (*see page 314*) to make sure that plaids, stripes, print motifs, and curved seam sections are securely matched for perma-nent machine or hand stitching. Fold under one edge, position at the seamline; slip the needle

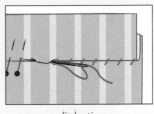

*slip basting*

through the fold and then through the single fabric layer close to the folded edge. On the inside, you'll find a row of short basting stitches to follow for permanent stitching.

**Whipstitch.** A slanted overhand stitch to hold two finished edges together.

SEE ALSO: *Chapter 8, Hems and Hem-Edge Finishes, and chapter 11, Fasteners and Closures.*

**Q** I pricked myself while I was sewing and bled on the fabric. How do I get the blood out?

**A** If it's still wet, use a bit of your own saliva to dissolve it and then dab it with a little cold water. Or, dip a cotton ball or cotton swab in hydrogen peroxide and dab it on the stain, then follow with a little cold water. If any blood is left and you plan to wash the item, treat it with a stain remover before you wash it.

# CHAPTER FOUR

# Working with Patterns

Several commercial companies offer broad selections of clothing patterns for all figure types and sizes, as well as patterns for home-decor items, costumes, and accessories. Independent designers also market their own pattern lines of basic and not-so-basic designs. These are available in quilt shops, fabric stores, and from Internet websites. A few pattern-software companies offer patterns customized to your figure. Knowing how to "read" a pattern envelope, guide sheet, and the pattern pieces is essential to successful fabric selection and fitting adjustments, as well as to pattern layout, cutting, marking, and sewing for any project.

# Reading the Pattern Envelope

Since you cannot return sewing patterns for a refund, take time to study the pattern envelope before you purchase to understand the complexity, fit, and drape of the design. Examine the guide sheet for a better understanding of how the pattern goes together to avoid getting in over your head. Use the envelope to guide your size selection and fabric choice.

- - - - - - - - - - - - - - - - - - - - - - - - - - - - - - - - -

**Q** **How do I read the pattern envelope to ensure choosing a design and fabric that will work together?**

**A** Examine the front illustration of the designs and views included, making note of how the garment fits and drapes on the figure, and which fabrics are shown. Trying on similar styles in ready-to-wear will give you a good idea of how it will look on you. The back of the envelope is information-rich; it is your guide to size selection and fabric purchase. Look for the following:

* **Garment description.** Contains info and descriptions on silhouette and details not visible on the front.

* **Back views.** Study carefully to better understand style, fit, and details of the view you're planning to sew. Look for fitting cues. For example, simple styles with few seams are often more difficult to fit to a curvy body than those with multiple seams.

* **Body measurements.** Use these to choose the pattern size that matches or comes close to your accurate body measurements. Wearing ease and style ease are added to these in the actual pattern tissue to create the fit and silhouette

illustrated on the pattern front (*see* Understanding Silhouette *on page 135*).

* **Recommended fabrics.** For the best result, select only those listed or others that are similar in weight, drape, and stretch; make note of fabrics that are not suitable.

* **Yardage requirements.** Buy fabric, interfacing, and lining yardages for your size. Increase the amount if you are tall, need to make lots of fitting adjustments, or have chosen a fabric with a nap, a one-way design, or one that requires matching fabric. You may also want extra fabric to allow for loss from preshrinking. Choose the correct yardage for "with nap" or "without nap" layouts, indicated by one (*) and two (**) asterisks, respectively. When written as */**, yardage is appropriate for either type of layout.

* **Widths at lower edge.** Look for the hemline circumference of skirts, dresses, pants, coats, jackets, shirts, and blouses to use as a helpful fitting clue. A 42" hem circumference reflects a far more fitted garment than one with a 60" circumference.

* **Finished back lengths.** This information may be helpful when determining necessary lengthening or shortening adjustments.

* **Notions.** Thread and the other extras you need to finish the garment: zippers, trims, and elastic, for example.

* **Stretch gauge.** Available on "knits only" patterns to help you determine if the knit you've chosen has the correct amount of stretch for the design.

SEE ALSO: *Knit Know-How, starting on page 193.*

# Following the Pattern Guide Sheet

The guide sheet is your sewing road map. Study it before you begin. With experience, you may find ways to shortcut and improve on the illustrated sewing process. For example, you can group tasks: sew all darts in one sitting; or construct the lining while you're sewing the garment, rather than waiting until the garment is completely ready for the lining.

- - - - - - - - - - - - - - - - - - - - - - - - - - - - - - - -

**Q** What should I find in a pattern guide sheet?

**A** The first page includes the information you need to follow for cutting the pieces:

* Front- and back-view illustrations of each garment, project, or view in the pattern

* Numbered illustrations and a list of each pattern piece with grainlines marked

* Cutting layouts for each view and fabric width and for special fabrics when appropriate (with and without nap layouts); circle the appropriate one for the project you are making

* Fabric key to identify right and wrong side of fabric and pattern, for pattern-tissue placement

* Other helpful cutting information

* Body measurements/sizing chart (optional)

* The pattern identification number and an illustration key, along with basic sewing information

The remaining pages include:

* Step-by-step assembly directions for each garment or view in the pattern
* Helpful highlighted tips to improve, speed, or ease your sewing experience

---

## Reading the Pattern Pieces

Pattern pieces are like an architect's blueprint, containing all the information you need to sew the designed project. However, patterns can be adjusted to create a perfect fit. In addition to pattern name, brand, and style number, the pattern pieces may also include a view number or letter; the size or sizes; multiple cutting lines on multisize patterns; the name of the pattern piece and its number (usually indicating sewing order as directed in the guide sheet); cutting information; and information on lining and interfacing.

- - - - - - - - - - - - - - - - - - - - - - - - - - - - - - - - -

**Q** **There is other information on my pattern pieces, like arrows, symbols, and notches. What do they mean?**

**A** Pattern tissues have fitting-adjustment lines, layout guidelines, and construction symbols, usually explained within the pattern instructions. These are intended to help you join the right pieces together, fold facings in place, position details, such as pockets, and sew buttonholes in the finished garment. They are there to ensure accuracy and help achieve a good fit.

# Selecting Pattern Size

Check out the pattern sizing charts in the back of commercial pattern books to determine your best (closest) pattern size. Patterns are sized by body type, as well as by body measurements; use the size chart with measurements closest to yours. (For patterns from independent designers, you must rely on the sizing chart printed on the pattern itself.) Accurate body measurements and a basic understanding of wearing and pattern ease will guide you to the right pattern for your size and shape.

- - - - - - - - - - - - - - - - - - - - - - - - - - - - - - - -

## Q How do I ensure accurate body measurements?

## A Enlist the help of a sewing buddy and follow these steps:

* Wear the undergarments you plan to wear with the finished garment. Make sure your bra fits well and the straps are correctly adjusted.
* Tie a piece of narrow elastic around your waist — the crease where you bend at the side — and make sure it's settled there; some measurements are based on waistline location.
* Use a nonstretchy tape measure. Keep the tape measure straight and parallel to floor when taking the horizontal measurements shown in the illustration. Pull the tape snug but not tight.

Refer to the illustration for the location of each measurement in the list. You will need additional measurements (*see pages 144–145*) for making pattern adjustments to fit the adult female figure. For other body types, refer to the pattern catalog sizing charts. Record your measurements and the date taken in your sewing notebook for future reference (*see page 48*). Update periodically — a six-month check/comparison is a good idea.

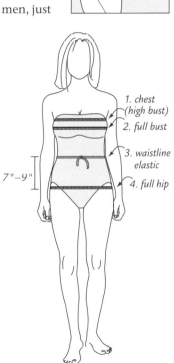

1. **Chest.** For women, under the arms and above the full bust; for men, just under the arms and over the shoulder blades.

2. **Full bust.** Over the fullest part, with tape straight across the back.

3. **Waist.** At the point where you bend at the side (measure over the elastic).

4. **Full hip.** For women, 7" (Misses Petite) to 9" (Misses and Women's) below waistline, or at full thigh if wider than hip; for men, the full hip is 8" to 10" below the natural waistline.

1. chest (high bust)
2. full bust
3. waistline elastic
4. full hip

7"–9"

133

# Q What is wearing ease? What about design ease?

A **Wearing ease** is the extra room added to most garments to give you room to move, bend, reach, and sit comfortably. Most designs include minimum amounts of wearing ease in key locations. (Swimwear and some activewear patterns have 0 or even –1" or –2" of wearing ease when designed for knits with stretchy spandex fiber.) Knits and stretch-woven fabrics (with a bit of Lycra for give) require less design ease than woven fabrics. The basic amounts of wearing ease are included in the chart on pages 146–147.

**Design ease** is any extra fullness beyond the minimum wearing-ease standards, added to create the desired shape or silhouette. A straight skirt cut from a woven fabric requires a minimum of 2" wearing ease at the full hipline on the Misses figure type (*see* Minimum Wearing-Ease Standards *on pages 146–147*). If you are making a gathered style, there will be much more ease at the hip.

*Note:* You can often "borrow" some design ease for fitting ease when sewing a full style; just know that the overall finished look on your figure may not be exactly as the designer intended. However, if you are happy with it, it works!

- - - - - - - - - - - - - - - - - - - - - - - - - - - - - - - - - - -

# Q How do I know how much ease a pattern has included in its design?

A Examine the photo or drawing on the envelope and read the description on the back for clues. Look for the fitting terms in Understanding Silhouette (*see next page*) for an idea of the intended fit. To help determine required pattern adjustments, examine the printed pattern pieces. Commercial pattern companies include the actual pattern measurements for bust, waist, and hip on the tissue. These printed measurements include the measurement for the size *plus* any wearing and design ease.

## UNDERSTANDING SILHOUETTE

The words used to describe a garment on the back of the pattern can give you an idea of how much room is built into the design (design ease). This chart will help you understand design ease for various silhouettes.

| Fit Description (Pattern Envelope) | Dress, Shirt, Vest at Full Bust | Skirt, Slacks, Shirts, Shorts, Culottes at Hip | Jacket at Full Bust/ Chest | Coat |
|---|---|---|---|---|
| Close-fitting | 0"–3" | 0"–2" | N/A | N/A |
| Fitted | 3"–4" | 2"–3" | 3¾"–4¼" | 5¼"–6¾" |
| Semi-fitted | 4"–5" | 3"–4" | 4⅜"–5¾" | 7"–8" |
| Loose-fitting | 5"–8" | 4"–6" | 5⅞"–10" | 8"–12" |
| Very loose-fitting | over 8" | over 6" | over 10" | over 12" |

## MISSES VS. WOMEN'S

What's the difference? In women's patterns, the amount of design ease differs depending on the body type. Larger, fuller bodies (Women's) usually need a bit more wearing ease than slimmer types (Misses) as shown in the chart below.

| Body Type | Misses | Women's |
|-----------|--------|---------|
| Bust | 2½" | 3½" |
| Waist | 1" | 1" |
| Hip | 2" | 2¾" |

# Q What is a back waist length, and why is it important?

A Back waist length is the measurement from the bone at the base of the neck to the waistline in back. This measurement, plus height, helps you determine your proportion and necessary pattern shortening or lengthening. If you are under 5'5" and your back waist length is at least 1" shorter than the one that matches your bust size, you probably need a Misses Petite pattern. Choices are limited in this size range, but you can use a Misses size if you shorten it on lines provided on the pattern to match your length. If you are taller than 5'6" or your back waist length is longer than average, you may need to lengthen the upper body pattern and shorten or lengthen the lower body pattern, depending on your proportions.

**Q** How do I use my body measurements to choose a pattern?

**A** Follow the guidelines below to choose your best pattern size from the pattern sizing chart on the back of the pattern or in the pattern catalog.

* **For men,** use the chest measurement.

* **For women:** Compare your bust and chest (high bust) measurements. If the difference is more than 2", use the chest (high bust) measurement for the bust measurement on the pattern sizing chart. Why? Patterns are made for a standard B-cup bra size (*see* Bust Cup Measurements *below*). If your cup size is larger and you use the full bust measurement to purchase the pattern, it *might* fit your bust, but the neck, shoulder, and armhole areas will be too large. It's easier to adjust for a full-bust cup size than to try to change the fit at the other three areas.

* **If your measurements fall between two sizes,** choose the smaller one if you are small-boned. The wearing ease in the pattern will make up some of the room, and you can let out the vertical seams to gain a bit more room. For differences of ⅛" or ¼", or if you are large-boned, use the larger size. I measure 33¼" in the bustline but use a size 10 (32½" bust), which gives a perfect fit in the neck and armhole. I make a full-bust

| BUST CUP MEASUREMENTS | |
|---|---|
| Cup Size | Difference between chest & full bust |
| A | 1" or less |
| B | 1¼" to 2" |
| C | 2¼" to 3" |
| D | 3¼" to 4" |
| Larger | 4¼" or more |

137

adjustment for a perfect fit there. The other option is to
purchase patterns that are multisized, so you can use the
appropriate cutting lines for each half of your body.

* **For most pants and skirts,** use your full hip measurement
  to select the size. It's easier to adjust the waistline, and
  buying by the hip size ensures plenty of room to fit around
  you. Adjusting at the side seams is always an option for a
  more snug fit.

* **For very full styles** (skirts and pants) with lots of design
  ease, purchase by your waistline measurement.

---

SEE ALSO: *Make Mine Multisize, pages 140–142.*

---

Q **When I sew with a size that matches ready-to-wear
sizing, the results are mixed. How do I use the measurements to choose the right pattern size for a good fit?**

A Forget ready-to-wear sizing when you purchase a pattern! It's less standardized than pattern sizing. One
designer's size 2 is another's size 6. If you are a size 12 in ready-
to-wear, do all size 12s fit you? Probably not.

Pattern sizing is based on a set of standard measurements, if
you are using a pattern from one of the major commercial pattern companies. (Independent companies may not follow these
same standards.) The chances that one pattern size matches
all of your measurements precisely is very slim, unless you try

ordering patterns that are available from computerized services that print custom-sized patterns (and even these may require fitting adjustments).

*Important:* If a flattering and comfortable fit is important to you, it's essential to approach pattern adjustments with a positive attitude. The pattern tissue, in the size that best accommodates your body type and size, is only a guide.

- - - - - - - - - - - - - - - - - - - - - - - - - - - - - - - - -

**Q What size do I buy when the pattern has coordinating top and bottom pieces?**

**A** Buy to fit your top and alter to fit the bottom. It's a lot easier to make the bottom smaller or larger where needed than to adjust the top to fit.

- - - - - - - - - - - - - - - - - - - - - - - - - - - - - - - - -

**Q How do I know if I'm a Small, Medium, or Large in patterns that are sized that way?**

**A** These patterns are drafted to fit the largest size in the range given. For example, a Medium, sized for a 12/14 range should fit a size 14 body but may be too large for the 12. They are usually loose-fitting styles that give several sizes an acceptable, average fit. In unisex patterns, the man's chest measurement determines the size range. If you are female, use your bust measurement to determine pattern size.

# Make Mine Multisize

Today, most patterns are sold with multiple sizes in one envelope — sometimes as many as six sizes. Some have cutting lines for all sizes for the figure type. Most have at least three: 8/10/12, for example. These patterns offer convenience, economy, and their own special challenges: following the cutting lines for your size or using the multiple lines to your advantage to fit a body that doesn't match the standard pattern measurements.

---

**Q** **When I'm using a multisize pattern, can I just cut out my pattern pieces along the tissue lines, or must I trace them onto tissue paper or cloth?**

**A** Multisize patterns have multiple cutting lines and construction marks, but usually no marked seam allowances (stitching lines). The cutting lines for different sizes are often identified by different graphic patterns of lines, dashes, and dots. Determine the graphic pattern for cutting lines in your size, then trace along them with a colored permanent marking pen. Highlight the notches and construction matching dots for that size.

*Note:* Seamline dots and other construction marks are ⅝" from the cutting line *into* the pattern tissue, not at the cutting line; those belong to the next size up. On some pattern pieces, a cutting line may be shared by all sizes (most typically the straight-grain center front or center back seam) with multiple cutting lines at other locations. Neckline, armholes, and side seams usually vary, since these affect fit. Small pieces (such as facings) may be given as separate pattern pieces, rather than drawn with multisize lines; be sure to cut out or trace the correct one for your size.

After marking your cutting lines, you can trim the pattern pieces along the marked lines or trace the pattern pieces onto pattern-tracing cloth or tissue to make a new pattern. Transfer grainline arrows, fold lines, detail placement lines, and any other construction marks within the boundaries of your cutting lines. Write *all* label information (pattern number, view, piece number, and so forth) on each piece.

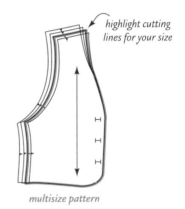

*highlight cutting lines for your size*

Cut out the tissue pieces on the cutting lines you've marked, unless you want to preserve the original pattern as a master to cut other sizes. I always cut them out, as I rarely use a pattern again unless it's something really basic, such as a chef's apron or a classic straight skirt.

*multisize pattern*

---

Q **I'm a different size on top (10) than on the bottom (14). How do I make multisize patterns fit me?**

A When making a one-piece dress, a jacket, a coat, or a shirt or blouse, taper the sizing between the lines, creating a pattern shape that more accurately reflects your body shape. Remember, a body is a series of interconnected lines and curves. Increases in size flow gradually from bust to waist to hip. If both sizes you need (to fit the bust and to fit the hip) are available in the purchased size range, simply blend from the cutting line for the top size at the underarm to the size line for the full hip at the location of your full hip (which may not be where the full hip is marked on the pattern itself).

1. Purchase the pattern with the size grouping that best matches your measurements, making sure that one of the sizes in the range is the best fit for the upper half of your body. For example, if you are a size 12 on top and 16 on the bottom, a 12/14/16 range is ideal.

2. Draw between the lines to create a pattern that fits your full hip. Make sure you have accurate body measurements (*see pages 132–133*), so you can select the right size pieces for the top and bottom half of your body. In curved areas, use a French curve ruler to blend and smooth out the new cutting lines. Trace or cut out the customized pattern and test the fit (*see pages 149–151*) before cutting from your fabric.

*Note:* If your bottom size is not included in the range, add a strip of tissue at the side seam, measure out the required amount for the hip adjustment (including wearing ease and any additional desired fullness), and then blend from the underarm to the full hip, continuing to the bottom edge. As with any other pattern, expect to fine-tune the adjusted multisize pattern fit before cutting and also during the sewing process. If the garment has a waistline seam, you will need to adjust the top and bottom pieces so they meet in the middle.

# Fitting Adjustments

Learning to fit your body is a lifelong commitment. Body changes due to weight fluctuation, aging, shape-altering accidents, and illness affect how a garment fits. Most people cannot simply cut out the pieces for a garment, sew them together, and expect a perfect fit.

Because the fitting process is complex, I've addressed a few basic pattern adjustment questions to get you started. If you are serious about achieving a flattering fit, now and as your body changes over your lifetime, invest in a comprehensive book on fitting. Several favorites are listed in Resources.

---

**Q** **None of my measurements are a perfect match for the ones given in the sizing charts in the pattern books. How do I know what size to choose so the pattern will fit?**

**A** In most cases, you will need to adjust the pattern before you cut, test the adjustments, and fit as you sew to ensure the best fit in the fabric you've chosen (different fabrics fit differently).

* Make sure the pattern pieces are the correct length: sleeves aren't too long or too short, the waistline is in the right place on fitted garments, and the overall length is right for you.

* Also ensure the pattern is large enough around to accommodate your body with the right amount of wearing ease, plus any added design ease (*see pages 146–147*).

Q **How do I compare pattern and body measurements to determine necessary adjustments before cutting?**

A I'll use the female figure as an example. The same basic steps apply for other figure types. First, take the body measurements shown in the illustration on the next page.

1. Measure the pattern pieces at the bust (chest for men), waist, and full hip (these are the key fitting locations), not including seam allowances and any dart, tuck, or pleat take-up, to determine how large the garment will be when sewn. If you are using a multisize pattern, don't forget to deduct the seam allowances — *they are not marked on the tissue*. Measure the pattern piece from cutting line to cutting line and then subtract the necessary seam allowances. Some patterns include finished garment measurements at those key locations to make this process easier.

2. To determine if there will be enough room in the finished garment, add the minimum wearing ease to your body measurement (*see the chart on pages 146–147*) and compare it to the flat-pattern measurement.

3. If there isn't enough pattern to "cover the subject," you can increase the seam allowance width. I always make any necessary fitting adjustments first and then cut 1"-wide seam allowances on all vertical seams and at the shoulders, so there will be extra fabric in key locations, in case I need it. I can always cut away any excess during the fit-as-you-sew process, but if I cut too small at the start, it's usually impossible to rescue the fit.

**BODY MEASUREMENTS FOR
PATTERN ADJUSTMENTS**

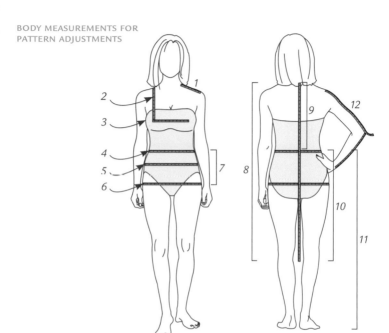

1 Shoulder width

2 Length from shoulder center
to bust apex

3 Bust apex to apex
(point to point)

4 Waistline

5 High hip/tummy circumference
(about 3" below waist or across
full tummy)

6 Full hip

7 Waist to full hip length (7" to
9" below waist or to full thigh
if wider than full hip)

8 Dress length: neck bone to hem

9 Back waist length from neck
bone to waistline

10 Skirt length: waist to hem at
side seam

11 Pant length: waist to hem at
side seam

12 Sleeve length from shoulder
pivot bone (over elbow for long
sleeves) to mid-wrist bone

## MINIMUM WEARING-EASE STANDARDS

| Garment | Bust | Waist | Full Hip | |
|---------|------|-------|----------|---|
| Blouse/shirt | 2½"–3" | NA | 2" | |
| Fitted dress | 2½"–3" | 1" | 2"–2½" | |
| Unlined jacket | 3"–4" | NA | 3"–4" | |
| Lined jacket | 3"–4½" | NA | 4"–5" | |
| Coat | 4"–5" | NA | 4"–5" | |
| Fitted skirt | NA | 1" | 2"–2½" | |
| Fitted pants | NA | 1" | 2"–2½" | |
| Trousers | NA | 1" | 3"–5" | |

**Q** Where do I begin? How do I decide which adjustments need to be made?

**A** Remove only the pattern pieces required for the garment or view you are making. Use one of the two methods below to determine and make the adjustments that will ensure ample fabric to fit around your body and enough length for hems at unfinished edges. Personally, I do both, making obviously needed width and length adjustments based on Method 1 and testing my adjustments with Method 2, particularly for fitted and semifitted styles.

| | Thigh | Back Waist Length | Back Width* | Full Upper Arm | Shoulder Center over Bust to Waist |
|---|---|---|---|---|---|
| | NA | NA | ¼" | 1"–1½" | NA |
| | NA | ¼" | ¼" | 1½"–2" | ¼" |
| | NA | NA | ¼"–½" | 3"–4" | NA |
| | NA | NA | ¼"–½" | 3"–4½" | NA |
| | NA | NA | ½" or more | 4"–5½" | NA |
| | NA | NA | NA | NA | NA |
| | 2" | NA | NA | NA | NA |
| | 3" | NA | NA | NA | NA |

*\* Armhole to armhole, 4" to 6" below base of neck, for reaching room*

**Method 1**. Take flat pattern measurements at key locations and compare them to your own, taking into account wearing and design ease (*see chart above*). Make the necessary adjustments and proceed to layout and cutting, *or* first test your adjustments as described in Method 2.

**Method 2**. Pin the tissue pattern together with pins parallel to and along the seam lines, and try on the "garment" to determine the necessary changes (this is called "tissue fitting").

# Q What supplies do I need for pattern adjustments?

A Use a ruler, a pencil or permanent-ink pen, and light-weight paper, plus a scissors or paper shears for cutting out the pattern and tape. Scotch Magic Tape works best, or try 3M Micropore Paper Tape (available at the drugstore). I use pattern-tracing paper; it's marked with an accurate 1" grid and ⅛" increments within the inches. It provides straight lines to follow when copying a pattern — for grainline arrows and pattern straight edges — and accurate measuring when lengthening or widening patterns. Other possibilities are colored tissue paper, pattern-tracing cloth (nonwoven interfacing with a printed 1" grid), and Swedish tracing paper; the last two are sewable, if you want to test-sew and fit before cutting the actual garment pieces. In a pinch, you could use a roll of gift-wrap paper, which sometimes has a grid printed on the back.

- - - - - - - - - - - - - - - - - - - - - - - - - - - - - - - - -

# Q How do I use the lengthen/shorten lines on the pattern?

A **To lengthen.** Cut between the two lines and spread the two pieces the necessary amount. Place a piece of tissue paper (cut 1" wider than the amount you need to spread the tissue) under the cut edges. Tape in place.

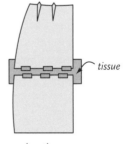

*tissue*

*lengthen*

**To shorten.** Draw a line (b) on the pattern below the lengthen/shorten lines (a) and equal to the total amount

148

you need to remove. Fold between the two lines and bring the fold to the drawn line. Pin or tape in place. (The fold is half the depth of the desired change because there are two layers of tissue in the fold). Connect and smooth the outer edges of the pattern to taper it into the original cutting line above the tuck.

*Note:* Make sure to lengthen or shorten (by the same amount) any corresponding pattern pieces, such as facings, linings, and interfacings.

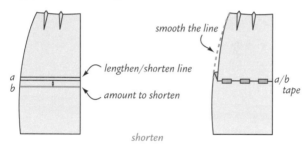

smooth the line

lengthen/shorten line

*a*
*b*

amount to shorten

*a/b*
tape

shorten

---

**Q** How do I test the pattern and the fitting adjustments I've made *before* I cut?

**A** Try on the pattern, either the tissue pattern itself or one cut from pattern-tracing cloth, as described below. For specific pattern adjustments for your figure, invest in a good book on fitting (see Resources).

1. Accurately cut out every tissue pattern piece that you need, following the outside edge of the printed cutting line. Press pattern pieces with a dry iron to remove all wrinkles.

2. If you are using a multisize pattern, draw accurate seam stitching lines. Multisize patterns have cutting lines only;

you will need stitching lines to check the pattern fit (*see page 140*). Use a fine-point permanent pen to avoid ink running onto your fabric when cutting later.

3. To try on the tissue, you must reinforce curved seams with short pieces of ½"-wide transparent tape. Place them with *one edge right at the stitching line and within the seam allowance.* Overlap the short pieces as needed to reinforce the entire curved section. Clip the tissue to within ⅛" of the seamline in *the curved areas only* on each pattern piece.

clip curves to seamline

overlap short pieces of tape around curved seamlines

Step 3

4. Fold out construction details, such as darts, pleats and tucks. Pin in place with pins placed along stitching lines on the *outside* of the pattern, so you can reach the pins if adjustments are needed when you try on the tissue garment.

5. Pin the major pattern pieces together with wrong sides facing, seamlines matching, and pins pointing to the floor and away from the body at the neckline and underarm.

6. Tie a length of ¼"-wide elastic around your waist.

7. Try on the tissue garment you've constructed, and gently adjust it into the correct position on your body. If the pattern is for a skirt or a bodice, anchor the piece under the elastic tied at your waist. If the center fronts and center

back lines don't reach the correct place, move pins as needed to adjust the fit at the side seams. Make sure there's enough wearing ease (*see pages 146–147*).

8. Evaluate the tissue fit. Make sure it's large enough to fit around your curves, adding tissue and making any required adjustments so the pattern fits. Follow the fitting sequence in Fitting Order on page 152.

9. Fine-tune the pins on the vertical seams for a smooth fit, adding tracing paper or cloth if necessary to allow enough room around.

10. Remove the tissue and mark the final positions of all the seams and construction points with a red pen (permanent ink is best). Remove the pins and trim or add tissue as needed, so all seam allowances are at least ⅝" wide. It's better to make all vertical seam allowances 1" wide, to give you extra insurance for fitting while you sew.

11. Use the adjusted pattern pieces to cut out the garment pieces.

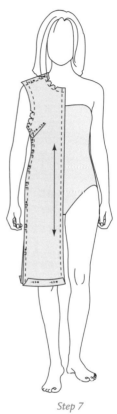

*Step 7*

## FITTING ORDER

Check the following fitting points in the order below (as they apply to the garment you are making). Every adjustment you make affects the others, so adjust each area in the order listed before checking the next area in the list. For example, adding to the tissue for more upper back width makes the pattern bigger around — which might make the front fit better over the bust.

* Back width
* Bustline fullness (if you are larger than a B-cup, you will need to adjust this area in most styles; refer to a fitting reference for how-tos)
* High round back (area between neck and shoulder blades)
* Midriff and waistline
* Back-waist and front-waist length
* Shoulder seam position — make sure it lies in a straight line from the base of your neck to the shoulder bone; many need a forward-shoulder adjustment due to posture changes (too much computer and sewing-machine time)
* Sleeve length and ease in upper arm of a fitted sleeve (pin the sleeve underarm seam and slip on so the underarm seam edge is next to your underarm; a full upper arm adjustment may be necessary)
* Fullness across waistline, tummy, derriere, hip (check if there is enough room around for comfort)
* Length

**Q** So, if I do a good job of tissue fitting, I should be able to sew the garment together for a perfect fit?

**A** Maybe. It's best to pin-fit the garment the same way you tested the tissue because every fabric is unique and will fit a little differently. Thin fabrics may actually cut smaller, and thick fabrics may cut larger than the pattern pieces. Knit and stretch-woven fabrics may need the fit tweaked a bit because of their inherent give. To pin-fit the garment:

1. Staystitch the waistline and any other seam allowances that require it (*see pages 104–105*).

2. Machine-baste the garment pieces together *with wrong sides facing,* including darts, tucks, and other construction details. (Don't baste the sleeves in, though; you can test that fit when you're ready to set them in.) Be sure to use the appropriate seam width; if you cut the seam allowances 1" wide, baste those seams at 1".

3. If shoulder pads are required, pin them in place. Tie elastic around your waist if you are fitting pants or skirt styles.

4. Try the basted garment on over the same type of undergarments you plan to wear, as they can affect fit. Make any adjustments required. In knits, you may need to reposition bustline darts that are too low due to the "give" in the fabric, even though they were correct in your tissue fitting. Follow the same order given for pin-fitting the tissue (*see previous page*).

5. When you are happy with the adjusted fit, remove the garment, spread open the seams, and use a piece of

chalk or other fabric-marking tool to mark the lines along the pins. Mark stitching positions on other adjusted areas, such as darts and tucks. (*See* Marking Tools and Methods *on pages 165–174.*)

6. Machine-baste the garment together with right sides facing and check the fit again before final stitching. Don't be surprised if it still needs a bit of fine-tuning. If the garment has sleeves, prepare them and baste them into the armholes to check the fit before stitching permanently.

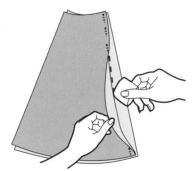

*mark pin locations with chalk or fabric-marking pen*

- - - - - - - - - - - - - - - - - - - - - - - - - - -

Q How do you recommend preserving and storing a tissue-paper pattern that you will use over and over? I can't ever get them back into the original envelope.

A Press the pieces to eliminate creases and wrinkles, then prepare and pack them in the following manner:

1. Place each piece right side up on the fusible-resin side of a piece of lightweight nonwoven fusible interfacing. Position the iron in the center for a few seconds to "fuse-baste" the piece to the interfacing. Using a lift-and-press motion, continue to fuse-baste out to within ½" of the cut edges.

2. Cut out each piece and then permanently fuse the entire piece to the interfacing.

3. Store the pattern in a large zip-top bag with the pattern envelope in front of it. Or, roll the pattern pieces on a cardboard tube labeled at one end with the pattern name and number, and file the pattern envelope in a file cabinet or box for easy retrieval.

# Pattern Layout

After you've prepared your fabric for cutting (*see pages 186–193*), and you've made necessary fitting adjustments to your pattern, you're ready to cut out the pieces. Now's the fun part: turning pieces of fabric into a new garment or decorative accessory. To begin, locate the appropriate cutting layout on the guide sheet for the design view and fabric width you've chosen, and circle or highlight it with a colored pen, pencil, or marker to avoid visual confusion while you work at the cutting board.

**Q** How do I prepare fabric on the cutting surface when I'm ready to arrange the pattern pieces for cutting?

**A** Do a quick trial layout of the pieces with only a few pins to make sure you have enough fabric. If the entire piece of fabric won't fit on the cutting surface, do this layout on the floor, your bed, or a large dining-room table. Fold the fabric as shown for the layout you've chosen and circled on your guide sheet. See the next page for some general suggestions.

155

**A** In the majority of patterns, the fabric is folded in half lengthwise with selvages even.

**B** Others may show folding with selvages meeting in the center, giving two fold lines along the lengthwise edges.

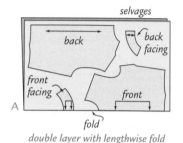

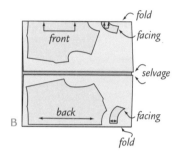

*double layer with lengthwise fold*

**C** In some cases, you will need a crosswise fold with cut edges even and selvages aligned at each edge. Some layouts show single-layer cutting or a combination of single- and double-layer cutting.

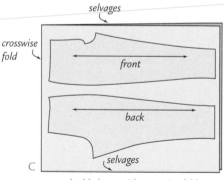

*double layer with crosswise fold*

**D** In single-layer layouts, some pattern pieces may need to be flipped, so you cut left and right pieces.

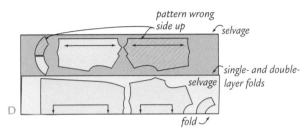

Q **What's the difference between a "with nap" and "without nap" layout?**

A When following a layout *without* nap, the hem or lower edges of the pattern pieces may point to opposite ends of the fabric. For a layout *with* nap, all lower edges point to the same end of the fabric. This type of layout is essential for napped and pile fabrics (velvet, for example), as well as for one-way designs in prints, plaids, and stripes.

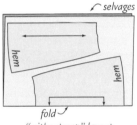

*"without nap" layout*

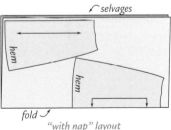

*"with nap" layout*

SEE ALSO: *Plaids, Stripes, and One-Way Designs, pages 213–220.*

**Q** My yardage won't all fit on the cutting surface. What do I do with the excess?

**A** Don't ever allow the excess to hang over the edge of the cutting board. The drag of the added weight will pull one or both layers, causing unwanted stretching and grainline distortion. It will also affect cutting accuracy and fit. Instead, accordion-fold the excess at one end and place it on the cutting table. Pin and cut only those pieces that will fit on the cutting surface.

---

**Q** How do I determine the fabric right and wrong side when there is no obvious difference? Also, should I fold fabric with right sides together or right sides out?

**A** Cotton and linen fabrics are usually folded right side out on the fabric bolt. Wool and silks are folded wrong side out. The right side of tube-rolled fabrics usually faces the tube. If you can't determine an obvious right and wrong side, use the side that is most appealing visually and to the touch. Once you've chosen the side you prefer to show, even if it's really the wrong side, be consistent. Mark it with short pieces of masking tape spaced along the selvage as a reminder — or use spaced chalk marks along the selvage.

In most cases, it doesn't really matter if you fold with right sides facing or right sides out for cutting. Just be consistent. Sometimes the marking method you plan to use will dictate whether to fold with right and wrong sides facing *(see pages 165–174)*.

**Q** Do I need to do anything special to the fabric and pattern before I do the layout?

**A** Press the tissue pieces with a warm dry iron to remove any wrinkles, tucks, or creases. All of these affect the accuracy of the pattern shape. If you have used tape to secure pattern adjustments, press on the side without the tape, to avoid melting it and causing the tissue to shrink up. If necessary, press fabric to remove all creases or wrinkles. If there is a crease where the fabric was folded on the bolt, press it out, if possible. If the fabric is discolored along the fold, you may need to plan a new layout so you can fold the fabric to avoid the discoloration showing up in any of the cut pieces.

- - - - - - - - - - - - - - - - - - - - - - - - - - - - - - - - - - - - - - - - -

**Q** Any tips for layout accuracy?

**A** Locate the fabric key on the guide sheet to familiarize yourself with the shading and marks used to identify the fabric and pattern right and wrong sides for placement purposes. Also determine what shading is used to indicate interfacing if it's not on the pattern/fabric layout key. Incorrect pattern placement will result in duplicate or missing pieces for the project. Pattern shading guides you to flip pattern pieces, so that all the pieces are cut correctly.

* Fold the fabric as shown in the layout you are following and loosely arrange the pattern pieces on the fabric following the layout.

* Pin each one in place for grainline accuracy (*see page 179*).
  For the most accurate results, extend the grainlines to the
  outer edges on all but the small pieces (neckline facings,
  pocket flaps, and the like), using a ruler and a pencil or
  permanent ink pen. Use a tape measure or ruler to measure
  and match the distance of the line at each end and in the
  center from the selvage or fabric fold. Pin in place. When a
  pattern piece is placed on a fold, the pattern fold line *is* the
  grainline, so folding the fabric accurately and on the grain
  is an essential first step.

* Always pin with the pins crossing the stitching line (or
  the fold line) — perpendicular to the cutting line, never
  parallel (*see the illustration*). Insert the pins ¼" from the cut
  edge of the pattern piece and space every 3" to 4" for the
  most control.

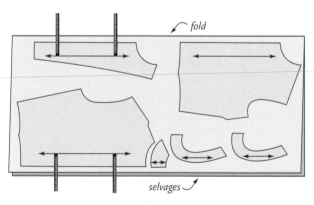

*place pieces on straight of grain*

For delicate fabrics that are easily marred by pins, place them within the seam allowance only or use pattern weights. After cutting and marking, use a few pins in the seam allowances to keep the tissue attached until you are ready to sew.

- - - - - - - - - - - - - - - - - - - - - - - - - - - -

**Q** **Is it okay to change the pattern layout?**

**A** Yes, as long as you can cut all the required pieces with the grainline and fold-line arrows positioned correctly on the fabric (*see previous question*). Sometimes a new layout is necessary due to fabric flaws or pattern-fitting adjustments.

*Note:* With woven fabrics, it's *not* a good idea to align arrows on the crosswise grain, *unless* you can position all pieces that way. Using the crossgrain along the length of the pattern pieces could result in a garment that sags during wear because the stretchier filling yarns won't hang as straight as the warp yarns. Crosswise layouts are not appropriate for knits: you'll lose the "give" that's inherent to the crosswise direction.

═══════════════════════════════════════

# Cutting the Pieces

Allow time during the cutting session to transfer all construction marks to the cut pieces (*see pages 165–174*). Why is this important?

* Trying to smooth the pattern tissue back into place after the pieces have been removed from the cutting surface and then trying to mark accurately is all but impossible,

especially on slippery and soft lightweight fabrics, and on bias-cut pieces.

* Poorly transferred marks can cause sewing problems, as well as fitting problems.

* Marking as you cut or just before you remove the pieces from the cutting board ensures accurate marks for accurate sewing.

* When you're finished cutting, you're ready to remove the pattern tissue, pin the fabric pieces together, and sit down to sew — the fun part!

---

**Q** How can I ensure cutting accuracy? Sometimes my cut edges are really choppy.

**A** Here are my rules for cutting accuracy:

1. Always place your noncutting hand on the pattern and cut to the right-hand edge of the pattern piece if right-handed (reverse for left-handed). This gives you full view of the edge — your cutting hand isn't obscuring it — and the weight of the noncutting hand helps prevent patterns from shifting out of place. Keep the fabric as flat on the table as possible while you cut.

2. Use bent-handled dressmaker's shears to make long, steady slashes, using the entire blade of the shears when cutting long lines and around large curves. Shorter curves and intricate shapes require shorter cutting strokes.

3. Cut past the notches if you haven't already trimmed them from the pattern tissue (not out and around them). Use a sharp-pointed sewing scissors to snip-mark the notches. Cutting out and around notches is inaccurate and only recommended if fabric ravels badly or you have very narrow seam allowances.

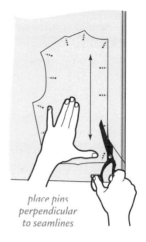

*place pins perpendicular to seamlines*

---

**Q** Can I use pinking shears instead of dressmaker's shears?

**A** Here are two good reasons *not* to do this:

1. It wears out your pinking shears faster and sharpening them usually means sending them out.
2. Pinked edges are inaccurately cut, and matching the pinked edges leaves additional room for error. Cut out pieces with clean, straight edges and finish the seam edges later, using the best seam finish for the fabric and the garment (*see pages 261–263*).

**Q** Any tips for using a rotary cutter instead of a shears?

**A** Rotary cutters work well when you have a large cutting surface and a rotary-cutting mat to protect that surface from the blade. If you've never used rotary-cutting tools, practice on fabric scraps first. Here are few tips for handling them when cutting garment pieces:

* Use large blades for straight lines and large pieces. Use a cutter with a small blade for easier maneuvering around curves — or use your dressmaker's shears to cut more intricate pieces.

* Use flat-head flower pins to pin pattern pieces in place and use a rotary-cutting acrylic ruler as a cutting edge along all straight lines whenever possible. It will lie flat on top of the flat-head flower pins.

* Use your noncutting hand to hold the rotary ruler securely in place and cut away from your body, rolling firmly against the ruler edge. Walk your fingers along the ruler as you cut to reach the end. Reposition the ruler carefully as needed when it doesn't reach along the entire length of the piece.

* Forsake the pattern piece if it is a true square or rectangle; instead, measure the tissue and

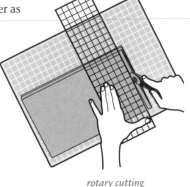

*rotary cutting*

cut the required pieces. Then pin the tissue piece to the
cut fabric piece for easy identification. This method is
faster and far more accurate than pinning and cutting
around a pattern piece.

* Purchase a French-curve ruler for an edge to follow when
cutting curves. It's also very handy for making pattern
adjustments in curved areas.

*SEE ALSO: Guidelines and cautions, pages 24–26.*

## Marking Tools and Methods

Choose the best marking method and tool for the job; the one
that is easiest, fastest, and most accurate, as well as best for the
fabric. You will probably use more than one marking method
in most garments.

Q **What tools do I need to have on hand for marking?**

A The marking tool depends on the fabric/fiber content
and the mark that must be transferred from pattern to
fabric. In addition to your sewing scissors for snip marking
and a see-through ruler, you should have a marking kit that
includes the following, so you'll always have the right tools
for your project:

* **Nonpermanent marking pens.** Water-soluble and
vanishing-ink pens are available. Choose fine-point pens
for accurate marking. Don't use a vanishing-ink pen unless

you are prepared to sit down and sew *immediately* after cutting and marking. These inks usually disappear within a day, sooner in humid climates. *Caution:* Test on scraps first to make sure the marks can be removed, and never press over them, as heat may make them permanent.

* **Chalk.** Available in small square cakes, in pencil form, or as a powder to fill the container of a special chalk wheel. Don't use waxy chalk on synthetic fibers; it's difficult to remove. Keep a small brush handy to dust away marks that don't disappear on their own during the sewing process.

* **Tracing wheel and dressmaker's carbon paper.** Choose a wheel with a smooth edge for delicate fabrics; otherwise the serrated-edge type works for most fabrics. Tracing paper is available in a variety of colors and may be waxy (difficult to remove, so use only on the wrong side of your fabric) or water-soluble (easy to remove with a damp cloth).

* **Soap slivers.** Save slivers of *white* bar soap to mark fabric for projects that will be laundered. Avoid soap with oil content. Periodically sharpen the edge with a knife so you'll have a sharp-edged marking tool.

### DON'T BREAK THIS MARKING RULE

Don't cut unless you have time to mark as you go. To ensure accurate marks for accurate sewing, transfer construction marks *immediately* after cutting the piece and *before moving* it from the cutting board.

**Q** Are the chemicals in the water- and air-soluble marking pens really safe on my fabrics?

**A** Be forewarned, these chemicals *might not* come out, due to fabric and dye interactions — a result that could ruin your project. As with any marking product, test first to make sure the marks disappear. Some new pens claim the marks can be removed with water or heat, but it's still best to test first on the project fabric to make sure.

---

**Q** How do I remove the temporary-ink marks after stitching, if I don't want to launder the garment?

**A** Remove the marks before you press because heat may set the inks. Usually, a damp washcloth will do the trick. I keep a sponge-tipped envelope moistener at my ironing board. I give it a gentle squeeze along the marks and use a paper towel to blot up any excess moisture. You may be able to find a special refillable pen for this purpose at your fabric store.

---

**Q** What should I mark?

**A** Mark the things that matter, most especially the things that will help you match the appropriate sections, position add-on details (such as pockets), and create dart folds, tucks, and pleats. Mark these things as you cut:

* Snip mark upper and lower ends of fold lines, the center front and center back of pieces cut on the fold, and both ends of marked hemlines that are drawn on the pattern piece

* All notches, dots, squares, and triangles on the pattern tissue (for matching and detail positioning)
* Stitching lines for darts, pleats, or tucks
* Beginning and end points for easing or gathering sections
* Placement lines for pockets, flaps, and other add-on details
* Positioning lines for trim, decorative stitching, embroidery, or appliqués

---

**Q** Should I mark stitching lines for seams? What about buttonholes and buttons?

**A** Generally, it's not necessary to mark seamlines. I prefer to mark buttonhole positions when I'm ready to make them. This allows me to precisely position the buttonholes where I want them, which may not be where the pattern recommends. I never mark button positions, as those can shift due to both intentional changes and/or placement inaccuracies. It's best to mark their positions as described on page 386.

---

**Q** How do I transfer the construction symbols and marks efficiently and accurately?

**A** The method depends on the fabric type and the location of the symbol. Do as much snip marking as possible while you cut; after that, choose one of the following methods that works best for your project: pin marking, making tailor tacks, thread basting, or transferring lines and marks with dressmaker's carbon and a tracing wheel. (These marking methods are all described in the questions that follow.)

# Q How and where should I snip mark?

A Snip marking is accurate, easy, and the fastest way to mark. Study the pattern pieces shown to see where you can snip-mark. Use sharp scissors to make ⅛"-long snips at construction lines that intersect the cut edge of the pattern piece: hemlines, fold lines, and dart lines, for example. If your fabric ravels easily, choose one of the other marking methods. You cannot snip interior marks, so you will need to choose a second marking method for those.

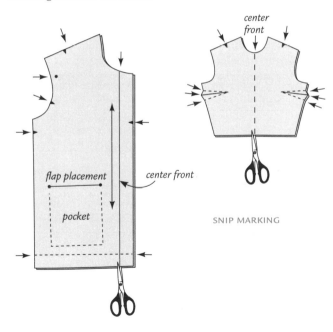

flap placement

center front

pocket

center front

SNIP MARKING

# Q Which method is best for transferring interior marks?

A Study these methods and select the one(s) that will work best for marking on your specific fabric. Using carbon and a tracing wheel could damage fine fabrics or pile surfaces, such as velvet. Tailor tacks and thread basting are time-consuming but often the best choice for these. Pin marking is quick and accurate but may show through on sheer fabrics if not done with a removable marker.

**Pin marking.** This is my second-favorite method — it's fast and accurate. Fold fabric for cutting with wrong sides facing. Use a sharp pencil, marking pencil, chalk, or a fine-point nonpermanent marking pen. Carefully insert a pin through the center of the mark, and lift the tissue and the upper fabric layer so that you can mark the precise exit point on both layers of fabric with chalk, marking pen, or a pencil. Work from the cut edge in to the

PIN MARKING

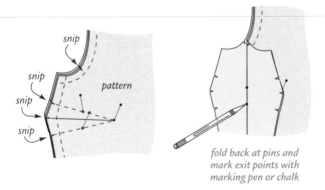

fold back at pins and
mark exit points with
marking pen or chalk

interior. You can also mark straight lines with a series of dots to connect after you've removed the pattern tissue.

**Dressmaker's carbon.** Use a sawtooth or smooth-edge tracing wheel (for delicate or easily damaged fabrics). It's best to cut with the wrong sides of your fabric facing for this method. Place the area to be marked on top of a rotary-cutting mat or firm cardboard to protect your work surface and make it easier to mark crisp lines. Fold the tracing carbon paper in half or place two sheets back to back. Remove pins only in the area where you will be marking and slip the paper in between the two fabric layers. When marking straight lines, use a ruler to guide smooth marking. Otherwise, take care as you run the wheel along the marks so they are accurate. Make X marks through dots or squares to precisely mark the spot.

*Note:* This method works best on flat, smooth-surfaced (not soft) fabrics. It's especially easy to rip the pattern tissue with the wheel on napped and thick fabrics. For those kinds of fabrics, choose a thread-marking method from those that follow instead.

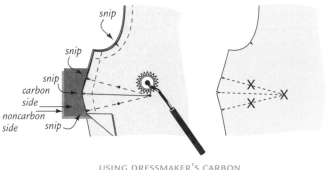

USING DRESSMAKER'S CARBON

**Tailor tacks.** Use a hand-sewing needle threaded with a double strand of sewing thread, cotton darning thread, or embroidery floss. To make a tailor tack, take a small stitch at the point to be marked, through the pattern and both fabric layers. Leave a thread tail at least 1" long. Take a second stitch, leaving a large loop above the tissue. Move to the next point, leaving a loose thread to connect the loops. After completing all marking on the piece, clip the loops and *carefully* remove the pattern tissue. Separate the fabric layers and clip the threads halfway between them, leaving small tufts of thread on both layers.

TAILOR TACKS

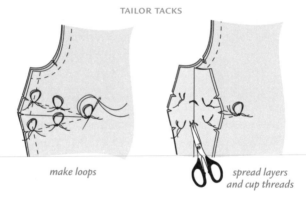

*make loops*

*spread layers
and cup threads*

**Thread basting/tracing.** Use this to transfer marks made with other methods to the fabric right side: it's good for marking flap placement lines, for example. Use a contrasting thread and hand- or machine-baste along the marked lines. To protect napped and pile fabrics and lightweight or delicate fabrics from stitch imprints, use silk sewing thread or basting thread (*see pages 70–71*).

172

**Q** **How do I keep slippery, wiggly, and lightweight fabrics like chiffon in place on the cutting board?**

**A** For best results, use a single-layer thickness for the layout. Here are two options to help control shifting:

1. If not already covered with muslin or canvas, prevent slippage by covering work-table surface with one of these fabrics (pulled tautly and stapled to the underside).

2. For double-layer layouts, fold the fabric and pin to a layer of tissue paper before pinning patterns in place. Pin all the way through the fabric, the pattern pieces, and the tissue paper. Leave pieces attached to the tissue paper until you are ready to sew, to prevent stretching.

- - - - - - - - - - - - - - - - - - - - - - - - - - - - - -

**Q** **Help! I've cut several pieces for my garment, but now there's not enough fabric left for the remaining ones that didn't fit on the cutting board.**

**A** To prevent this situation, always do a trial layout to make sure there's enough fabric. You can lay everything out on the floor if the cutting table isn't large enough to hold the entire piece. If there isn't enough fabric, you have time to rethink the project or make some creative design changes so the pieces will fit. Ask yourself:

* Can you face a hem, requiring only a ⅝" seam allowance instead of a 2" hem allowance to make up for a shortage?

* Can you cut facings from a different fabric or cut collars and cuffs from a contrasting fabric?

* Can you eliminate some of the fullness in a flared skirt to gain the required room?

173

* Use your "noodle" to discover design solutions that will help you find ways to make the fabric work. If you can't find a creative solution, you may have to abandon the project and use the remaining fabric and the cut pieces for an entirely different project.

- - - - - - - - - - - - - - - - - - - - - - - - - - - - - - -

**Q** **If I transfer placement lines to the wrong side, how do I transfer them to the right side?**

**A** Machine-baste carefully and precisely along the marked lines with a contrasting color thread on the bobbin. It's not necessary to remove the placement lines. They're on the inside and will not show or will disappear if you used chalk or a marking pen.

# CHAPTER FIVE

# All About Fabrics

Today's fabric offerings are broad and enticing, ranging from simple broadcloth to gorgeous special-occasion fabrics, some of them costing $500 per yard and up. For sewing success, refer to the back of the pattern envelope for a list of the suggested fabrics for your project. Choose fabric you love; it's not fun to sew on fabric that you're not crazy about! Allow adequate time to prepare your fabric for cutting and sewing to ensure satisfactory results. Some popular fabrics require special handling; techniques are included in this chapter for knits, plaids and stripes, and pile/napped fabrics.

# Fabric Selection

Once you've selected your pattern, it's time to wander the aisles of your favorite store to find the perfect fabric.

- - - - - - - - - - - - - - - - - - - - - - - - - - - - - - - - -

**Q** **Are there any guidelines for choosing the best fabric for the project?**

**A** Fabric selection is a matter of personal preference combined with selectively narrowing the available choices.

* Study the pattern envelope photo or illustration for ideas and read the list of recommended fabrics on the back to narrow your search.

* Watch for a list of unsuitable fabrics for the design, as well as warnings, such as "for knits only."

* Decide on color, fiber content, and fabric type (knit, woven, or other). Make sure you like the fabric "hand" (the way it feels against your skin).

* Decide if the fabric drapes or hangs correctly for the silhouette of your garment, and check how it flows (or doesn't) over body curves. Unroll a length of it in front of a full-length mirror and allow it to hang from your waistline. Then move one leg forward to see how it falls over curves. Softer fabrics require fewer seams and are best in styles with a looser fit, to avoid straining the fabric at stressed seamlines.

* Purchase and prepare your pattern pieces, including any fitting adjustments, before purchasing expensive fabric. Do a trial layout to determine what you need.

* Purchase the yardage specified on the pattern for your size, based on the fabric width. Buy extra if you are taller

than average or need lots of fitting adjustments. You will also need extra fabric for matching prints, plaids, and stripes (*see pages 215–218*) or if you must follow a "with nap" layout (*see pages 222–223*).

- - - - - - - - - - - - - - - - - - - - - - - - - - - - - - -

**Q** Is there any way to change the drape of a fabric?

**A** Launder a washable fabric so excess finishing agents and dyes disappear; the fabric may feel softer and a bit more drapeable. Laundering can turn crisp linen into a softer fabric, appropriate for a less tailored jacket, for example. However, it may also turn the fabric into a mass of difficult-to-remove wrinkles, as well as shrink it considerably.

Applying a lightweight interfacing to a fabric changes its drape and hand. This is a good technique to firm up a fabric that may not be quite heavy enough for the intended project. (*See* Interfacing *on pages 230–234*.)

Cutting a garment on the bias also affects the drape, making it mold to the shape underneath and reveal body contours. Sewing on bias-cut garment pieces is challenging, however, because every seamline is prone to stretching while you sew — not something for a beginner, to be sure.

- - - - - - - - - - - - - - - - - - - - - - - - - - - - - - -

**Q** Once I've chosen the fabric, how do I make sure I have the right amount?

**A** Check the bolt end for the fabric width and check the pattern yardage chart for the fabric width. Most fabrics are available in 44/45", 54", or 60" widths, but other narrower and wider selections are available. Buy extra fabric to allow for preshrinking, extensive fitting adjustments, matching large plaids and patterns (*see pages 216–218*), or "with nap" layouts (*see pages 222–223*).

Also, jot down the fiber content and any special care techniques required and attach the note to the fabric for reference. Purchase all other "ingredients" for your project — interfacing, lining, buttons, zipper, and other notions listed on the pattern envelope — so you can go right home and sew!

## FAVORITE FABRIC BUYING TIPS

* **Avoid forbidden fabrics;** if the pattern envelope says the design is not suitable for knits, napped fabrics, plaids, diagonal weaves, or a one-way design, avoid them for that design.
* **Buy fabric you love** that fits your lifestyle and enhances your personal coloring and body type. It's more satisfying to work on fabric that you can't resist — and to wear the finished garment.
* **Buy the best you can afford;** quality makes a difference in the sewing process and in the finished project.
* **If you haven't tried using a special fabric before,** make a small project from it first to learn how to handle it.

# Fabric Facts

Before you cut the pieces for your project, it's important to understand how fabric is made and to know about fiber content. Both will affect how you will prepare the fabric for cutting and sewing, as well as which sewing techniques you will use.

- - - - - - - - - - - - - - - - - - - - - - - - - - - - - - - - -

**Q** **What do I need to know about fabric before I begin to cut out the pieces for my project?**

**A** Before you start a project, it's important to know the difference between knit, woven, and nonwoven fabrics, as well as the basic terms used to describe them. Woven fabrics are created on a loom and have two sets of threads (also called yarns). The **lengthwise** set (warp yarns) are held taut across the loom; the **crosswise** yarns (the filling, weft, or woof yarns) are woven in and out of the warp yarns in a specific pattern to create the desired surface texture and design.

Because of this structure, the cut edges of woven fabrics are prone to raveling, making seam finishes necessary to curtail it. Woven fabrics have two finished edges, made by packing lengthwise threads closely together to create firm edges that won't ravel on the bolt. These are the **selvages**.

**True bias** grain lies at a 45-degree angle to the selvages. It can have a significant amount of give and is used to create softly draped and flowing garments, as well as for making

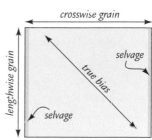

binding. It is a challenge to sew with bias-cut pieces because of the inherent stretch.

- - - - - - - - - - - - - - - - - - - - - - - - - - -

## Q Why does grainline matter?

A For most garment pieces and for draperies, it's essential to place the length of the piece along the lengthwise grain so the finished project hangs straight. The lengthwise threads are the strongest and have little give, so they resist bagging and stretching in the direction that gravity most affects. Crosswise yarns have more give, so they can take the strain placed on garments when you sit or when you reach, but they can also bag out from strain. Sometimes, pattern pieces are placed with the lengthwise grainline around the body, usually for taking advantage of border prints or other design details that run along the selvage. Small pieces, such as cuffs, may be cut on the crossgrain, but interfacing can support and stabilize them if need be.

Bias-cut pieces have lots of give. Take advantage of the drape that results when the fabric threads run diagonally, rather than vertically and horizontally, across the body.

*straight of grain*

*straight cut*          *bias cut*

## KNIT GLOSSARY

**Wale.** Vertical row of knit stitches (loops).

**Course.** Horizontal row of knit stitches.

**Warp knit.** Made with multiple vertical yarns that are interconnected; vertical rows of loops are visible on both sides of the fabric, as in a *doubleknit* fabric. *Tricot* is also a warp-knit fabric. These knits are run-resistant and don't unravel. They have almost no give in the vertical direction, with varying degrees of horizontal give. They are generally more stable than other knits and have a smooth, flat surface.

**Weft knit.** Made with a single yarn of interconnected loops, with the rows formed horizontally (as in hand knitting) back and forth across the fabric. These knits can unravel but only from the yarn end at the end of the knit. Breaking a yarn in these knits causes vertical runs. *Jersey* knit is a weft-knit fabric; it has vertical loops visible on the right (smoother) side, with visible stitches forming horizontal rows on the reverse. These usually have moderate to large amounts of crosswise give. Edges curl on most of these knits.

**Rib knit.** Composed of alternating rows of knit and purl stitches to create visible vertical rows; fabric has lots of horizontal give with good stretch recovery; most commonly used for neckline, wrist, and ankle finishing, sometimes referred to as ribbing.

## ESSENTIAL DIFFERENCES

Look at the front and back of the fabric, compare it to the illustrations, and check the chart below for visible characteristics.

| Woven | Knit |
|---|---|
|  | |
| Two sets of threads that interlace at right angles. Long edges have finished selvages. | Loops on one or both surfaces (front and back); no selvages; some have dots of glue or heavy starch along lengthwise edges to prevent natural edge-curling. |
| Fabric has little or no stretch lengthwise and limited stretch crosswise. | Substantial crosswise stretch; some have stretch in both directions; tiny runs also form at the cut edge of some knits. |
| Individual threads easily come undone (they might fray or ravel) along the cut edges from selvage to selvage. | Edges don't fray or ravel. Unraveling the stitching of a hand knit results in one continuous thread. It's difficult to unravel most commercially made knit fabrics. |
| Most wovens crush and retain wrinkles when balled up and released. | Knits spring back to shape when balled up and released. |

Q What's the difference between woven and knit fabrics?

A Knits are made with needles that loop yarns together to create a fabric with built-in stretch (elasticity), making them comfortable to wear. Knits don't ravel, making seam and hem finishing easier or unnecessary. Technically, knits don't have a grainline, but they are directional and most have more stretch or give in the crosswise direction. Knits don't have a bias grain, but they do have give when pulled on an angle across the ribs and courses. The rows of lengthwise loops are called ribs or wales, similar to the lengthwise grain in wovens. The rows of crosswise loops are called courses. Lacy-looking raschel knits have no stretch, and knits for activewear and swimwear have a lot of stretch in both directions for a body-hugging fit. Check out the Knit Glossary (*page 181*) and Essential Differences (*previous page*) to identify different kinds of knits. Ask for help in the store if you're not sure.

---

Q Can I use the selvage edges in my garment?

A Because they are firm and sometimes stiff, selvages are not generally used. However, you can use selvages when applying a waistband (*see pages 340–344*) or cuffs on sleeves (*see pages 367–370*). Sometimes selvages are so tightly woven that they look a bit pulled or drawn along the edge. They should not be used if this is the case! They will not lie flat unless you clip them, negating the reason for using their clean-finished edge.

## FIBER FACTS

When choosing fabric, fiber content plays an important role. Study the characteristics of some of the most commonly used fibers for fashion and home-decor fabrics.

### Natural Fibers

Cotton. Relatively inexpensive; absorbent and comfortable for year-round wear and in hot and humid climates; wrinkles; shrinks; generally easy to sew and easy to clean.

Linen. Crisp, strong, breathable, very absorbent; comfortable but wrinkles easily; available in light- to heavyweight versions; often blended with rayon or polyester to lessen cost and decrease wrinkling; easy to sew and press; ravels.

Rayon. Man-made from wood fibers; cool and comfortable to wear; dyes beautifully; washability depends on the rayon type and fabric weave; soft and drapeable; weak when wet; not very resilient; wrinkles unless treated.

Silk. Strong, somewhat wrinkle-resistant; takes dyes beautifully; most require dry cleaning; often blended with synthetics to lower the cost; sometimes blended with wool or other animal fibers; weakened by sunlight and perspiration; absorbent but dries quickly; shrinks.

Wool. Warm in winter but cool in summer; absorbent and water-repellent; flame-resistant; dyes well; resists wrinkling; may lose its shape during wear; relaxes back to its original shape; not washable unless pretreated; available in very sheer to very heavy fabrications; absorbent, so can be comfortable in warm weather; attracts moths.

## Synthetic Fibers

**Acetate.** Silklike luster, good drape, weak when wet; has static cling; low resistance to abrasion; fabrics used for lining and formalwear.

**Acrylic.** Dries quickly, washable, but weak when wet so must be handled carefully during laundering; may pill and is heat-sensitive; often used in blends with wool and cotton to cut down on cost; used to make the pile for many faux-fur fabrics; resists mildew and moths; has static cling.

**Nylon.** Lightweight; heat-sensitive, strong; often used in swimwear and outerwear; resists moths and mildew.

**Polyester.** Strong; warm, wrinkle-resistant; pills, has static cling; attracts oily stains; used in blends and many different fabrications, from light- to heavyweight.

## Why Does Fiber Content Matter?

You need to know how to prepare the fabric for cutting (preshrinking), as well as the correct iron temperature for construction pressing. It's important to know if the fabric can be laundered or whether it must be dry-cleaned due to the fiber content. Fiber content may also affect sewing and pressing methods. Wool shrinks when steam is applied, for example; this can be helpful when shaping a sleeve head before setting it into an armhole. Some synthetics are difficult to press flat, requiring special pressing equipment to ensure a sharp press and a press cloth to avoid surface damage.

# Q Why are fibers blended in fabrics?

A Blends are done to offset manufacturing costs or to create fabrics that perform better or differently. Adding Lycra to wool gabardine or cotton broadcloth builds in a little stretch for wearing comfort, creating a fabric type called stretch-woven. Mixing a little silk with cotton adds a little luxury. Mixing fine, soft, and expensive cashmere with wool adds softness and creates a different hand. Combining acrylic with wool cuts down on expense. Blending fibers lends some of the best and worst features of both fibers; launder or dry-clean as directed on the fabric label. Choose an iron temperature for the most heat-sensitive fiber in the blend.

# Prepare for Cutting

Get ready to cut the pieces for your project by straightening the fabric grain and cut ends prior to preshrinking. Choose the appropriate preshrinking method for your fabric to prevent shrinkage during construction pressing and/or during laundering or dry cleaning.

# Q How do I straighten the grain on a woven fabric? Why is this necessary?

A Straightening ensures that the pieces you cut are correctly positioned so the finished project hangs straight and true, or with the desired drape when working with bias-cut pieces. If the threads in your woven fabric are not perpendicular to each other before you cut out the pieces, the fabric is "off grain" and the finished project will twist or hang crooked. To straighten woven fabrics, you will need to "square off" the cut ends by making a more precise cut that is truly perpendicular to the selvages. Work as close to the cut edge as possible, but before you start, be sure you have room to make a new cut that goes all the way from selvage to selvage. Here's how:

1. *If you can see the crosswise-grain threads clearly,* simply follow one of these threads as you cut away the uneven end. This works for coarsely woven fabrics, as well as on crosswise woven stripes, and woven plaids and checks.

2. *If it's difficult to see the crosswise threads,* make a cut into the fabric past the inner edge of the selvage. Pull one or two threads away from the cut edge, grasp the fabric a few inches from the selvage, and gently pull the threads. Use the other hand to gently slide the fabric along the pulled thread(s). When the thread breaks (it usually does), stop and cut carefully along the line that you can see. Repeat the process until you have trimmed the entire edge.

*pull a thread and cut along the pull*

3. After you've straightened both cut ends of a woven fabric, check the fabric for grain alignment; fold in half with selvages aligned and no ripples or wrinkles along the fold. You may find that the cut edges still don't match up even though you carefully straightened them. (*See page 188.*)

Q Can't I just tear the fabric across the cut end instead of pulling a thread?

A While that works on some firmly woven fabrics, the force of the tear causes stretched edges, snags, tiny pulls, and wispy ends of thread along the torn edge on most woven fabrics. Test for tearing, but if your first effort meets with resistance or damages the fabric, revert to other methods.

---

Q What do I do if the cut edges don't match?

A Depending on how the fabric was made, finished, and rolled on the bolt, you may not be able to correct this. If the grainline is distorted, try these alternatives for straightening or "squaring" it. They might also work for realigning a knit with stretched cut ends.

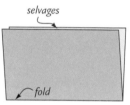

*selvages*

*fold*

*straightened ends lie off-grain*

For natural-fiber woven fabrics or natural-fiber blends (not for synthetics or permanent-press fabrics):

1. Fold lengthwise with selvages even.
2. Hand-baste the straightened cut edges together, using silk or soft cotton thread.
3. Pin-baste the selvages together.
4. Lay out on a padded surface and steam-press lightly to dampen the fabric; smooth the fabric into place, with no wrinkles along the fold.
5. Allow the fabric to cool completely before cutting.

**For synthetics and any fabric that is really off-grain** (the folded fabric looks like a parallelogram):

1. Tug the fabric gently on the bias in the direction opposite the distortion, to readjust the lengthwise and crosswise threads orientation.

2. Repeat as needed along the length of the fabric before refolding and checking the ends. This may help a little or a lot — or it may have no effect at all. If the fabric is still off-grain, decide whether the fabric is worthy of your work.

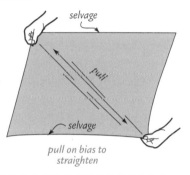

*pull on bias to straighten*

- - - - - - - - - - - - - - - - - - - - - - - - - - - - - - - - - - -

**Q** **Since knit fabrics don't have a true grainline, do they require straightening?**

**A** Technically, no, but you must prepare them for cutting. On some textured knits, it's easy to follow a row of horizontal loops or courses to straighten the cut ends. To "straighten" a cut knit end, fold the fabric carefully along the centermost row of vertical loops (*see page 182*), making sure there are no wrinkles along the fold. Then use a rotary ruler placed with a horizontal line along the fold and cut off the uneven cut ends, using the ruler edge as your guide. If your knit is tubular, fold so there are no wrinkles at either folded edge and then cut the ends and along one fold (*see pages 196–197*).

# Q How do I preshrink fabric?

A The method you choose depends on the fiber content, fabric type, and the intended end use:

* If the fabric is washable and you plan to launder the finished garment, launder the fabric in the same manner.
* Wash dark colors alone and check for colorfastness by laundering with a scrap of white fabric (an old nylon tricot undergarment will attract stray dyes). If the dye bleeds, you many want to wash the fabric a second time.
* Launder cotton denim and cotton knits two or three times to eliminate the residual shrinkage common with these fabrics; buy extra yardage to allow for this.
* For dry-clean-only fabrics or those you plan to dry-clean because they have trim or inner components that cannot be laundered, ask your dry cleaner to steam-shrink only. They usually charge by the yard or the piece. As an alternative, you can steam-shrink it at home.
* Steam-press home-decor fabrics; do not launder those that have stain-repellent finishes unless you are prepared to reapply them.

- - - - - - - - - - - - - - - - - - - - - - - - - - - - - - -

# Q I'm not sure I have enough fabric to allow for shrinkage. How can I tell how much a fabric will shrink before I actually wash it?

A Cut a 4" square of fabric from one corner of the yardage. Mark the lengthwise grain with a permanent marking pen. Wet the square (don't just get it damp) and press it dry.

Draw a 4" square on white paper or graph paper and place the pressed square on top. If it fills the square, the fabric didn't shrink. Fabrics usually shrink more in the length than the width. If the degree of lengthwise shrinkage is ¼", then the fabric will shrink 2¼" in length per yard. That's probably too much to gamble on if you didn't purchase extra yardage to allow for preshrinking.

- - - - - - - - - - - - - - - - - - - - - - - - - - - - - - - -

## Q Are there any laundering guidelines to follow?

A Yes, here are a few to heed to minimize wrinkling and fabric wear:

* Use the same water temperature as when you will be laundering the garment: warm for synthetics, warm or hot for natural fibers (cotton and linen).
* Avoid crowding the washer, to avoid excessive wrinkling or abrasion that causes pilling.
* Use detergent to help eliminate excessive finishes and soften fabric for maximum shrinkage.
* Use a cool rinse and short spin cycle; remove from the washer immediately to minimize wrinkles.
* Use a wash-and-wear or permanent-press dryer setting to avoid heat-set wrinkles.
* Dry to a barely damp stage to eliminate static electricity and undue wear; air-dry or press to remove residual dampness.
* To prevent woven fabric from raveling in the wash, serge the edges or zigzag with a wide, medium-length stitch.

# Q Can I launder silk fabrics to preshrink them?

A Some lightweight silks, such as flat, firmly woven silks for shirts and blouses, can be hand-laundered even if the label says "dry-clean only." This saves on dry-cleaning costs. Do the laundering test described earlier. Silks usually shrink in length. Check for too much shrinkage or any unwanted change in appearance or hand. If you will be preshrinking, buy ⅛ yard extra per yard required for the project.

However, *never wash silk suitings*; they lose their body and color. It's best not to launder silk brocade, dupioni, chiffon, crepe, and satin-surfaced fabrics. Many silk fabrics tend to water-spot, so have your dry cleaner steam shrink them if you feel it's necessary, or do it yourself *(see next question)*.

---

# Q How do I steam-shrink fabric yardage at home?

A You'll need a large, flat, padded pressing surface and an iron that produces steady steam. Fill the reservoir with water before you begin and allow the iron time to reach the desired temperature to heat the water. Spread the fabric on the padded surface and hold your steam iron an inch or so above it. Work section by section and steam the fabric until damp — *without* pressing the iron to the fabric. Leave in place to dry completely before moving it, folding it, or laying it out to cut the pattern pieces.

**Q** What about linings, interfacings, zippers, hem tapes, twill tape, and trims. Should I preshrink those too?

**A** It's best to preshrink all components, so choose them with laundering in mind. Preshrink zippers, tapes, elastics, and trims in a zip-top mesh laundry bag in the washing machine, or in a sink with hot water. Allow the water to cool before machine- or air-drying to the barely damp stage, then press. To preshrink fusible interfacings, see pages 235–236.

# Knit Know-How

You can use many of the same techniques for sewing knits as you use for woven fabrics, but it's good to know a few special handling techniques. There are also some special considerations for knit pattern selection, cutting and layout, and seams and hems.

**Q** How do patterns for knits differ from those for wovens?

**A** Most, but not all, knits have built-in ease because of the stretch factor. A "knits only" pattern has less wearing ease (*see pages 146–147*) than one for wovens. "Knits only" patterns are designed for specific types of knits with specific degrees of stretch. Swimwear patterns are sized for 0 ease or minus (negative) ease; the spandex stretch fiber in the two-way stretch fabrics designed for swimsuits has enough give to stretch and hug the body for the snug fit required. Heavier double knits and fleece knits require more pattern wearing ease because they fit the body more like woven fabrics. If figuring out which knit is right for your project seems complicated, carefully read the pattern envelope for the recommended fabrics and you'll get it right.

- - - - - - - - - - - - - - - - - - - - - - - - - - - - - -

**Q** **How do I test the amount of knit stretch on a pattern stretch gauge?**

**A** Most "knits only" patterns include a numbered stretch gauge on the back, so you can check your fabric's stretch suitability. Test the stretch by making a fold at least 3" below the crosswise cut edge (don't test the cut edge). With hands positioned about 4" apart (or the number indicated on the pattern), stretch the folded fabric toward the right-hand end of the gauge. If it doesn't reach without overstretching and distorting the knit, it's not stretchy enough for the pattern you've chosen. (*See* Knit Stretch Guidelines *on the next page*).

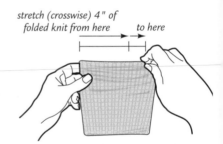

*stretch (crosswise) 4" of folded knit from here* *to here*

## KNIT STRETCH GUIDELINES

| Knit Type | Stretch Factor | Stretch Percentage |
|---|---|---|
| Stable | ½" for every 4" of fabric | less than 15% |
| Moderately stretchy | 1"–1½" for every 4" of fabric | 25%–30% |
| Very stretchy | 2" or more for every 4" of fabric | 50% or more |

*Note: Some exceptionally stretchy knits, such as rib knits and spandex knits, have stretch that exceeds 100%*

Q **Can I use a pattern meant for knits with woven fabrics instead, and vice versa?**

A No, you can't use knit patterns for wovens. They don't have the necessary wearing ease (*see pages 146–147*) for woven fabrics. But yes, it's sometimes possible to use a woven pattern with some types of knits. Here are a few guidelines:

* Use a stable knit fabric for a pattern designed for wovens; these have the least amount of stretch and fit more like woven fabrics. You will need some fitting adjustments.

* Select designs with simple lines and minimal seamlines for the most success when using a woven pattern for knits. Avoid designs with sharp edges and details, as knits don't hold sharp creases.

* Expect to make fitting adjustments while you sew to achieve the desired fit and silhouette.

* *Never* substitute a pattern for wovens when sewing with two-way stretch knits.
* If possible, eliminate zippers, substitute bindings for facings around armholes and necklines (*see pages 292–294*), and consider using ribbing for necklines and sleeve-edge finishing if appropriate to the style.
* Check out the appropriate seam and hem finishes for knits (*see pages 201–206*). Hem allowances on patterns for woven fabrics are often wider than those for knits.

---

**Q** Do knits require special preparation? Should I preshrink? And how do I straighten the cut ends?

**A** To eliminate residual shrinkage, preshrink washable knits by laundering them in the same way you plan to launder the finished garments. They usually shrink more in the length. Cotton and rayon knits may shrink more in the next washes; launder them two or three times to minimize shrinkage. Laundering also removes excess dye and finishing agents, which will make for easier sewing. Some sewers don't preshrink polyester and nylon knits because shrinkage is minimal, and the finishing agents actually make them easier to pin, cut, and handle while sewing.

Steam (without pressing) wool and silk knits and sweater knits on the wrong side prior to cutting. Allow the fabric to lie flat and dry thoroughly (for 24 hours) before doing the pattern layout and cutting. If you prefer, you can have knits steam-shrunk at your local dry cleaner (*see page 192*).

If you must press knit fabrics before pattern layout, press lightly in the lengthwise direction and take care not to stretch the fabric out of shape. *Don't press a crease* at the lengthwise fold. There should be no wrinkles along the fold, which means the long edges of the knit may not align precisely. As for straightening a knit, there's no thread to pull or follow as you do when straightening woven fabrics. Instead, follow along a crosswise row of loops if you can see them.

---

Q **Are there any special considerations when doing pattern layout, cutting, and marking on knits?**

A Cutting and layout is the same for any fabric, but here are a few things to remember for knits:

* Lengthwise folds should follow a lengthwise rib of the knit, even if the two outer edges don't quite match up (they may not be straight due to manufacturing processes). Fold with right or wrong sides facing, depending on which side the ribs are most visible and easy to follow.

* Fold napped or textured knits with wrong sides facing; follow a "with nap" layout (*see page 157*).

* To avoid snags, use pattern weights, fine straight pins, or ballpoint pins confined to the outer edges or close to seam and hem allowances. Because all but the thinnest knit fabrics tend to be spongy, it's best to pin through the pattern tissue and only the upper fabric layer, to avoid ripping the pattern tissue. Trying to pin through bulky layers also distorts the pattern, affecting cutting accuracy.

* Make sure all of the fabric is on your cutting surface. Don't allow excess to hang off one end of the cutting surface; the give in the knit, plus the weight of the fabric, will cause the fabric on the table to stretch; the pieces you cut from a stressed knit will not be accurate.
* Don't pull on the fabric when cutting; it will stretch the knit. When you let go after cutting, the piece will be smaller than the pattern, adversely affecting fit.
* Use a single-layer layout when cutting the pieces from slippery or bulky knits. When you need a mirror-image piece, cut and mark the first piece with the pattern piece right side up. Transfer any marks, remove the pattern piece, and flip it wrong side up on the fabric. *Never use the cut piece as your pattern!* This could lead to disastrous stretching and inaccurate cutting; your pieces might not be the same size.

- - - - - - - - - - - - - - - - - - - - - - - - - - - - -

**Q** Do I need to do anything special to prepare my sewing machine for knits?

**A** Here are a few things to remember:

* Always start a knit project with a new sewing-machine needle. Even a tiny burr on a needle that's been lightly used on other fabrics could cause snagging.
* On all but the sheerest and bulkiest knits, a size 80 ball-point or stretch needle is a good choice, but test it first on two layers of the knit.

* Use a high-quality long-staple polyester thread. This thread type has a bit of built-in give. Polyester-wrapped cotton all-purpose sewing thread is a second option.

* Change to a straight-stitch presser foot and needle plate for straight stitching on lightweight knits, to prevent the needle from dragging the fabric down into the wider hole of the zigzag plate, which can cause skipped stitches.

* Use a stitch length of 5 to 6 mm (12 to 15 stitches per inch) for straight stitching. A shorter length puts a little more give into a straight-stitched seam.

* Attach a walking foot (*see page 16*) if available, particularly when sewing on medium- to heavyweight and highly textured knits.

- - - - - - - - - - - - - - - - - - - - - - - - - - - - -

Q **Do I need to staystitch knits?**

A Yes, follow the same guidelines for woven fabrics, and then place the tissue on top of the staystitched piece to make sure the shape still matches. If not, use a needle or pin to lift and draw up the staystitching, as needed, so the cut edges match the pattern edges. (*See pages 104–105.*)

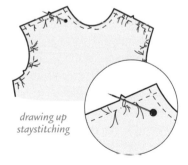

*drawing up staystitching*

## Q Do I need to interface knits the same way I do woven fabrics?

A Styles that must stretch over your head — T-shirts, for example — don't require interfacing. Other necklines and front-faced edges usually need it for stability. Use light-weight fusible tricot knit interfacings or weft-insertion inter-facings (*see page 231*). They have crosswise give, just like knits. Apply fusible interfacings to the wrong side of the facing, not to the garment side, to avoid shadow-through and puckering. If the neckline is bound or has ribbing, interfacing is not neces-sary; in fact, it's not advisable.

---

## Q Can I serge seams in knits?

A Yes, in fact, most ready-to-wear garments are sewn together with overlocked seams on a 3- or 4-thread serger. If you don't have a serger, there are many machine-stitched options using built-in stretch stitches or a combina-tion of straight stitching and zigzag stitching.

If you choose serged seams for knit garments, check the fit *before* serging. This all-in-one seaming-and-finishing method cuts away any excess seam allowance, leaving no room for adjusting the fit after stitching. Use a ⅝"-wide seam allowance and trim away the excess seam allowance as you serge, unless your pattern for knits has narrower seam allowances. Check the tissue and the pattern guide sheet.

**Q** **Which sewing-machine seams and seam finishes are most appropriate for knit fabrics?**

**A** Looking at seams in knit ready-to-wear in your closet or in the store provides guidance for seam and seam finishing choices. Plain seams with straight stitching are always appropriate for knits, but your sewing machine may also have an assortment of built-in stretch zigzag stitches for knits (*see illustrations on page 203*). Do a test sample on two layers of your fabric for appropriate stitch selection and tension adjustments. (*See* Troubleshooting Stitch Problems on Knits, *on page 206.*)

* **Add a little give to straight-stitched knit seams** by stretching the layers very gently as they pass under the presser foot. (If you pull too hard, the resulting seam will ripple, not lie flat.) Press the seam open. This seaming option is particularly appropriate for stable medium- to heavyweight double knits.

* **Serge-finish the seam allowance edges of plain seams** together for a neater look, particularly on textured and bulky knits. If knit seams won't stay pressed open (which is not uncommon), then serge the edges together, trimming away excess seam allowance, and press to one side. The 4-thread stitch has two rows of needle stitching, so it is more stable and secure, which is the best choice for stable knits in styles that fit the body more closely. A 3-thread stitch is a little lighter and more fluid and works fine on most knit garments.

* **Use a simple zigzag stitch for seaming** (*see* A Crooked Little Stitch *below*), but do not stretch the seam as you sew. (Some sewing machines have a special crooked zigzag stitch for seaming knits.) If the fabric doesn't feed smoothly and the top fabric layer wants to bubble and scoot ahead, loosen the pressure on the presser foot or use your thumb to push down lightly on the back of the presser foot while you stitch to lift the toes at the front of the foot.

* **For a narrow seam, stitch twice:** once at the seamline and a second time ⅛" from the first row in the seam allowance. Choose a very narrow zigzag, blindstitch, 3-step zigzag, or a special knit stitch. Trim the seam allowance close to the second stitch and press the seam allowance to one side. Use the straight stitch, a very narrow zigzag, or a special knit stitch on your machine. You can also do the first

### A CROOKED LITTLE STITCH

To build in a little stretch when seaming knits, adjust for a "crooked straight stitch." To the naked eye, the stitching looks almost straight, but the bit of zigzagging improves seam stretchability and helps prevent popped stitches from straining the completed seams. Use a very narrow (0.5 mm) medium-length (2.5 mm) zigzag. You can actually press this type of zigzagged seam open if you wish — a good idea for wool and cotton knits.

row with a straight stitch along the seamline and when you are sure of the fit, stitch the second row on the serger, trimming away the excess seam allowance.

* **Consider a French seam** (*see pages 269–270*) for a neat finish on sheer, see-through knits. Very narrow serged seams are also appropriate.

* **If you plan to use a walking foot** to stitch knit seams, you'll need a ½"- or ⅝"-wide seam allowance so there is adequate fabric to ride under and make contact with the presser foot and the feed dogs.

DOUBLE STITCH-AND-TRIM OPTIONS

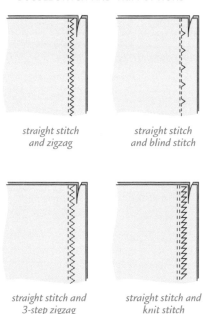

*straight stitch and zigzag*

*straight stitch and blind stitch*

*straight stitch and 3-step zigzag*

*straight stitch and knit stitch*

**Q** My sewing machine has overlock and stretch-over-lock stitches. How do I use these on knits?

**A** These are good substitutes for serger overlocking. Use for stitching and finishing in one step, but first trim the seam allowances to ¼" if the pattern has standard-width ⅝" seam allowances. Use a special overlock or overedge foot (often standard with the machine) for best results and smooth finished edge. (*See* Common Serger Seams *on page 273* for illustrations of these stitches.)

## WHICH STRETCH STITCH?

| Stitch | Best for |
|--------|----------|
| Overlock * | lightweight jersey, tricot, and interlock knits |
| Double overlock | firm knits and those with a coarser hand |
| Stretch overlock ** | swimwear and activewear knits; lightweight or loosely knit ones |

*\* You can stitch knit seams with a straight stitch first, trim to ¼" and finish with the overlock stitch.*

*\*\* For more control on bulky knits and loosely knit ones, use the stretch overlock stitch and standard presser foot to stitch along the ⅝" seamline and then trim close to the stitching; do not trim seam allowances first.*

Q How do I prevent knit seams from stretching during wear?

A Lengthwise seams probably won't stretch, but it's good to stabilize shoulder seams in particular, as well as V-necklines or wrap-front bodices. Choose one of the following methods, which work on straight-stitched as well as serged seams:

* Cut a strip of ⅝"-wide nylon tricot seam binding and center it over the stitching line on the wrong side of one of the two pieces. Catch in the stitching.
* Cut a strip of fusible knit tricot interfacing along the lengthwise (nonstretchy) direction, ¼" wider than the seam allowance. With raw edges even, fuse to the wrong side of one of the two pieces, with the excess width extending into the garment past the seamline. Stitch the seam using the desired stitch and seam finish.

- - - - - - - - - - - - - - - - - - - - - - - - - - - - - - - -

Q How do I make the flat seam with visible loops of stitching on both sides of the seam that I see in ready-made knit activewear?

A Use a serger to make a flatlocked seam, which has loops on one side and ladder-like stitches across the seam on the other (*see illustration on page 273*). Flatlocked seams eliminate bulk in fleece, velour, sweatshirt, and terry knits. *Caution:* Once stitched, there is no way to let out these seams.

# Q Which hem finishes are best for knit fabrics?

A Simply turn, press, and topstitch with a single or a twin needle. No edge finish is necessary. Using a twin needle puts a little more give in the finished hem (*see page 311*). Try a 4 mm twin needle and 10 stitches per inch.

## TROUBLESHOOTING STITCH PROBLEMS ON KNITS

For the perfect machine setting for your knit fabric, look for these problems in your test seams and make the necessary adjustments before testing again. Save a sample of the perfect stitch in your sewing notebook (*see page 48*), making note of the settings used. (Save the setting in your computerized machine if it has a "favorites" stitch storage option.)

* Seam is wavy or rippled: The stitch is too short.
* Seam looks puckered and the stitches break when you tug on the seam: The stitch is too long.
* Fabric forms into creases or tunnels under the zigzag stitch: The stitch is too wide.
* Seam edges roll: This happens on jerseys. If you are not serging the seams, choose one of the other twice-stitched seams recommended for knits (*see pages 202–203*). Trim the excess seam allowance close to the stitching.

**Q** When I machine-stitch a stretchy knit hem, the fabric tunnels and ripples. Why is that?

**A** Most knits stretch the most along the crosswise edges. To control this, turn up the hem allowance and trim to ½". Cut ½"-wide strips of soft, fusible knit interfacing long enough to reach from seamline to seamline in the garment. Place them on the wrong side of the hem allowance *with the fusible resin facing you.* Tuck the cut ends of the interfacing strips underneath the seam allowances. Serge or zigzag the interfacing to the hem cut edge. Turn up the hem and fuse in place. Then use a twin needle to topstitch, or you can do two rows of closely spaced topstitching.

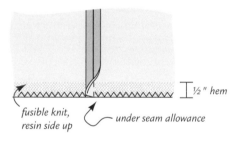

fusible knit, resin side up — under seam allowance — ½" hem

**Q** Are there any guidelines for hem-allowance widths on knits?

**A** When in doubt, remember that on knits that have a tendency to curl (jersey, tricot, and single knits), hems should be 1" or 1½" wide. If the bottom edge of the knit garment flares, stick with a narrow hem finish, ¼" to ½" wide.

Q **Are there other hem finishes I can use in place of the topstitched hem if I don't want visible stitches?**

A Try a machine-blindstitched hem (*see page 312*), or a hand-catchstitched hem (*see page 314*). On stretchy lightweight knits, you can add a flirty flare at the hem by doing a rolled edge on the serger, stretching the fabric edge as you stitch to create a rippled edge (also called a lettuce edge). Test on scraps first to determine how much to stretch the fabric to create the desired look. A variety of specialty hems are possible on sergers; check your manual and serger sewing references for more options.

- - - - - - - - - - - - - - - - - - - - - - - - - -

Q **Are there any special handling tips for sweater knits?**

A The bulk of these fabrics require a few special handling techniques:

* **Use pattern weights to hold tissue in place** on thick knits for accurate cutting.
* **Baste with long quilter's pins** or flat-head flower pins, and use as few as possible. It's easy to "lose" them in the knit, causing needle damage.
* **Use a serger to sew the seams** or use one of the twice-stitched knit seams shown on page 203.
* **Always stabilize shoulder seams** (as shown for pockets on page 357).
* **Sew sleeves into open armholes** with the sleeve on the bottom, so the feed dogs ease the sleeve to the armhole. Then stitch the underarm/side seam in one step.

* **Use vertical buttonholes only** and prevent stretching by placing a strip of water-soluble stabilizer on the top and underneath. If you don't have stabilizer, substitute strips of fusible web. Pin in place *but don't fuse!* Make the fusible web disappear under the completed buttonholes by holding a steam iron above each one until the web "melts" into the fabric and disappears under the stitches.

* **Use light pressure for construction pressing,** or hold the steam iron just above the fabric to avoid flattening the texture.

- - - - - - - - - - - - - - - - - - - - - - - - - - - - - -

**Q** I don't want ribbing or binding around the neckline of my knit garment. Is there any other way to finish the neckline quickly and easily?

**A** On most knits (with the exception of very stable ones with little or no stretch), turn and press the neckline seam allowance to the wrong side *after* stitching the shoulder seams. To make this easy, first machine-baste along the seamline to create a turning guide. Pin the turned edge in place with pins perpendicular to the turned edge. Topstitch (*see page 107*) from the right side using a twin needle (*see page 311*) or a medium zigzag (2 mm wide; 2 mm long). Stitch no more than ¼" from the turned edge. Trim the excess seam allowance close to the stitching on the inside. You can do this finish around armholes of sleeveless knit tops, too.

# Solving Problems

**Q** My knit fabric is a tube. Do I need to do anything special before cutting the pieces for my garment?

**A** Cut along one fold and steam or press gently to remove the remaining fold line. If it won't press out, you'll need to take care to avoid it when laying out pattern pieces. Never use it as the center front or center back fold line; it will show in the finished garment.

- - - - - - - - - - - - - - - - - - - - - - - - - - - - - - - -

**Q** There are runs at one end of my knit yardage. Is it bad fabric? What can I do to stop them?

**A** You have an interlock knit, which runs in one direction only — an inherent quality of this knit type. (When you don't see any runs, determine if it is an interlock by stretching both cut edges. Only one cut edge will develop little runs.) To avoid runs that develop from the neckline, shoulder, or waistline down into the garment, position pattern pieces following a "with nap" layout (*see page 157*), placing the bottom edges of all pattern pieces toward the end of the knit with the runs. To further prevent runs from forming while you sew the garment, machine-stitch ¼" from the lower cut edges of bodices, hem edges, and sleeves.

**Q** How do I prevent the presser-foot toes from hanging up in the loops of my textured sweater knits?

**A** Wrap a piece of masking tape over the ends of the presser foot to create a "mono" toe that will be less likely to catch in the loops. Another option is to place a strip of tissue paper or tearaway stabilizer on the top and bottom fabric layers, to prevent the toe from catching on top and the feed dogs from catching on the bottom layer. Stitch and then *carefully* tear away the strips along the stitching.

- - - - - - - - - - - - - - - - - - - - - - - - - - - - - -

**Q** The test buttonholes I made in my knit fabric scraps are stretched out of shape and the stitching is lumpy. What can I do to correct this problem?

**A** Corded buttonholes (*see page 377*) are a great choice for knit fabrics. On spongy and bulky knits, lengthen the buttonhole stitch a bit to help the fabric feed through the machine more smoothly without stitch buildup. Place a strip of water-soluble or tear-away stabilizer between the knit fabric and the feed dogs on the underside of the garment to make it easier for the fabric to feed while stitching the buttonhole. Add a layer of water-soluble stabilizer on the top layer. (In other words, you're using two layers of stabilizer, and the fabric is sandwiched between them.) Carefully tear away the stabilizer after stitching; use needle-nose tweezers to remove stubborn bits of paper or tearaway stabilizer caught under stitches. Dab away visible bits of water-soluble stabilizer with a damp cloth, unless you cannot use water on the fabric.

Here's another way to stabilize a buttonhole in knits: Cut a piece of ½"-wide transparent elastic 1" longer than the desired buttonhole length. Center and baste it in place over the buttonhole position. Make the buttonhole and then carefully trim the excess elastic close to the stitching.

---

**Q** Both sides of my knit fabric look the same. How do I tell right and wrong side?

**A** Interlock and doubleknits usually look the same on both sides. Choose the side you like the best — the one that may look slightly more "finished." Fold for pattern layout with the right sides facing. As you remove pattern pieces, attach a small piece of masking tape to the wrong side of all of your pieces to keep them easily identified for sewing.

---

**Q** How do I prevent curling on the seam allowance edges of plain seams in knits?

**A** Lightweight single knits, such as jersey, have a tendency to curl. (When you stretch the crosswise cut edge, it curls to the right side.) Keeping cut edges aligned for accurate stitching can be a problem. Tame cut edges by applying a bit of spray starch to the seam allowances. Cover your ironing board with parchment paper or a piece of muslin to prevent starch buildup first. Press after starching. For those fabrics that curl, a narrow, double-layer seam allowance/finish, like those described on pages 201–203, is the best bet.

**Q** Why does the zipper in my knit garment buckle and how can I prevent this from happening?

**A** It's possible that you stretched the fabric as you were inserting the zipper. To prevent this in knits, cut 1"-wide strips of lightweight woven or weft-insertion interfacing (along the direction with the least stretch). Center one over each seamline of the opening and fuse in place before basting the seam and setting the zipper.

SEE ALSO: *Chapter 6, Interfacings and Linings.*

# Plaids, Stripes, and One-Way Designs

Plaids, stripes, and checks, plus fabrics with one-way woven or printed motifs or patterns, require careful attention in layout and cutting. Most require using a "with nap" layout. They usually require additional yardage to allow for pattern matching. Large plaids and pattern-repeats require more additional yardage than small ones.

**Q** What are the best pattern styles for plaids and stripes?

**A** Because of their geometric nature, stripes and plaids are at their best in designs that are also more linear: with points, rather than curves; square corners, rather than rounded ones; simple, straight seaming, rather than lots of fussy details.

* If the design is shown in a plaid or stripe in the illustration or photo on the pattern envelope, that's a clear go-ahead.

If these fabric types are not suitable, that will be stated in
the fabric suggestions on the envelope back. If it says don't
use a plaid or a stripe, don't!

* Choose simple designs with minimal add-on details and
  fewer seams. Every vertical seam in a plaid requires careful
  matching during layout and cutting.
* Stay away from designs with circular detailing, curved
  seams (such as princess seams) that come from the armhole (very difficult to match), rounded corner collars, and
  darts that slant up from the waistline.

- - - - - - - - - - - - - - - - - - - - - - - - - - - - - - - - - -

Q **What do I need to know about plaids so they match
up in the finished project?**

A Identify the plaid type first. An *even* or *balanced* plaid
has mirror-image patterns on each side of the main bar
of color in the vertical *and* the horizontal direction. An *uneven*
plaid has a one-way pattern in the vertical and/or the horizontal direction. The easiest way to determine which you have is to
fold the fabric in half lengthwise and then flip back one corner
on a 45-degree angle. If it's an even plaid, the sequence of the
lines, spaces, and colors will match up in the vertical *and* horizontal directions. If they don't match, the plaid is uneven or
unbalanced in one or both directions.

*Note:* Some unbalanced plaids are difficult to identify. If in
doubt, cut a narrow strip that includes at least two of the pattern repeats and pin it to a piece of paper. Choose a bar in the
center of each edge and label as number 1. Then number the
bars on either side of it, using a new number for each bar that

is different before you reach the bar that matches number 1. Do this in both directions. A number pattern that is the same on each side of the center 1, as in 543212345 is balanced. If the pattern repeat is 1234512345, it is unbalanced: *not* a mirror image to either side of the bar or space numbered 5. Check the plaid along the crosswise and lengthwise edges.

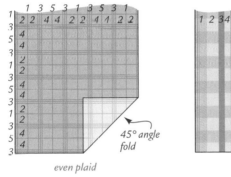

*even plaid*

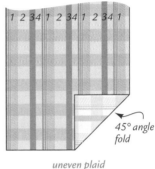

*uneven plaid*

---

# Q How does the plaid type affect pattern layout?

A For even plaids, you can fold the fabric through the exact center of a dominant "stripe" in the plaid, pin the layers together in several locations, and do a double-layer layout. Follow a "with nap" layout, even though the plaid is balanced. For uneven plaids, it's usually best to do a single-layer "with nap" layout, so the plaid sequence is unbroken going around the body. Make duplicate pattern pieces for those that are cut double, or remember to flip the pattern piece to cut the second piece (or half of a piece that must be placed on the fold; center front, for example).

------------------------------------------------

**Q** **Are there guidelines to follow for plaid placement in the pattern layout?**

**A** Follow these pointers carefully to ensure success:

* Don't cut until you have adjusted the pattern pieces to the desired finished length, plus hem allowance. The finished hem edge on pants, skirts, dresses, coats, jackets, and sleeves should fall at the lower edge of a dominant horizontal bar of color to visually weight the bottom edge. You must determine the desired finished length *before* you cut and adjust the pattern pieces accordingly.

* Plaids should match at the side seams and other vertical seams. They should flow around the body without a break at the side seams and up and down as much as possible. If a bodice has vertical darts from the waistline to the bust, the plaid can only match between the darts. Use the notches at the pattern edges when cutting to ensure a match (A).

* Place the dominant vertical section of a plaid at center front and center back for a balanced look (B).

* Cut add-on details, such as pockets, so the plaids match horizontally and vertically as much as possible. Cut major garment pieces first, then position the pattern piece for the detail on the garment piece. Draw the plaid lines on the tissue to guide your placement for cutting (C).

If the area is interrupted with a vertical dart, start the vertical match toward the center front; once past the dart, the pocket won't match.

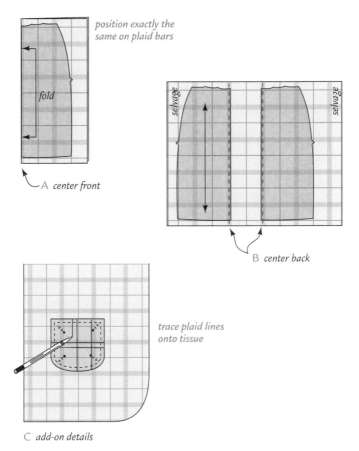

*position exactly the same on plaid bars*

*fold*

A *center front*

B *center back*

*trace plaid lines onto tissue*

C *add-on details*

* For set-in sleeves, match the front armhole notches on the sleeve to the plaid lines that intersect the notches on garment front armhole edges (D).

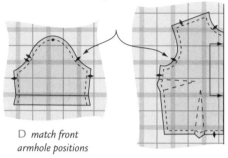

D *match front armhole positions*

* Double-check pattern positioning on the fabric before cutting. Make sure every pattern piece that must match is securely and accurately pinned in place.

---

## Q What do I need to know about working with striped fabrics?

A Like plaids, they can be even (balanced) or uneven (unbalanced), but they are a bit easier to handle because the matching is in only one direction. With horizontal stripes, follow the above guidelines for plaids to match the pieces at the side seams and front armhole and to position hemlines. It may be impossible to match vertical stripes at the shoulder seams. Pockets and other add-on details should be cut to match the stripe within the placement area.

**Q** Now that the plaid pieces are cut, how do I make sure the plaid lines match during the actual sewing?

**A** Line up and pin the plaid lines together with pins perpendicular to the seamline. For a precise match, insert the pins at the seamline from the top layer to the underlayer and check before reinserting the pin along the line and bringing it to the top layer. Machine-baste and check the match before permanently stitching. Slip basting (*see page 125*) ensures a perfect match but is more time-consuming. You can also use basting tape for matching and holding layers together (*see page 220*).

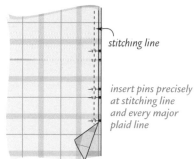

*stitching line*

*insert pins precisely at stitching line and every major plaid line*

---

**Q** My fabric has a large one-way design; how do I make sure the pattern matches at the seams?

**A** Choose a simple style with minimal seamlines. Follow a "with nap" layout after determining the best position for the design on your body. Don't place large motifs over the bustline or on the full thigh or buttocks. Center obvious large-scale designs vertically, so the design is balanced on the body. Once you determine the best positioning for the pattern pieces, place them so that the hemline edges are in the same location on the fabric. To match and secure them for sewing, see the next question.

# Q I'm making draperies from a large-pattern one-way floral. How do I cut and match the seams?

A Home-decor prints are carefully engineered for matching, and they have extra-wide selvages for seaming. To ensure a perfect match, use fusible web tape:

1. Cut the panels so the upper edge of each one is in the same location in the print. In large repeats, you will lose some fabric length; make sure you have enough fabric yardage to allow for this before cutting.

2. On one of the two panels, turn under and press along the edge of the printed design. Flip the panel and position and fuse a strip of fusible-web tape to the turned seam allowance, close to the pressed edge. Remove the protective paper.

3. Position the folded edge along the print on the second panel, matching it precisely, and securely fuse in place.

4. Open the folded seam allowance on the inside and stitch along the fold: a perfect match!

*Note:* If you don't want to use fusible web, slip basting (*see page 125*) is a more time-consuming alternative. Use basting tape on fine fabrics to match designs in garment projects. Remove the tape after stitching.

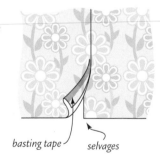

*basting tape*  *selvages*

# Napped and Pile Fabrics

Some of the most luxurious fabrics owe their beauty and soft hand to a napped or pile surface. Corduroy, velvet, velveteen, velour, and fleece are the most popular napped fabrics and are widely available in woven and knit versions. Their textured surfaces require special layout and handling, and some special sewing and pressing techniques. Many of them are easily damaged with pin and needle marks and misplaced stitches.

- - - - - - - - - - - - - - - - - - - - - - - - - - - - - - - -

Q **What is nap and why does it matter in cutting layouts?**

A Napped and pile fabrics have raised surfaces. The texture reflects light differently when held in different directions, creating a noticeable color variation that can be distracting. To avoid color variations in the finished project, these fabrics require "with nap" layouts, with the lower end of all pattern pieces pointing to the same end of the fabric.

- - - - - - - - - - - - - - - - - - - - - - - - - - - - - - - -

Q **What's the difference between a napped fabric and a pile fabric?**

A Napping brushes and raises the surface on knit and woven fabrics to add texture and warmth (the raised fibers trap air). Pile fabrics such as velvet, velveteen, and corduroy are made by incorporating extra yarns in the weaving and then cutting them to add depth to the surface. They reflect light differently, just as napped fabrics do, and require special handling during cutting, layout, and sewing.

**Q** **Are there general guidelines for design choice when using pile and napped fabrics? How about for the layout and cutting of these fabrics?**

**A** Keep the following in mind when picking a design, to ensure cutting ease and accuracy:

* Begin with a simple design with minimal vertical seaming (avoid numerous gores and princess seaming).

* Avoid tightly fitted styles, to prevent seam strain and stress wrinkles that may be difficult to remove.

* Decide which direction the pile should run (*see* Pile Up or Down? *below*) and use chalk to draw arrows pointing toward the bottom on the wrong side along the length of the selvage. Use them to guide your "with nap" pattern placement so that all pieces are positioned in the same direction.

* Do the layout on a single fabric layer placed wrong side up on your cutting surface, to avoid creeping, wiggling, and shifting. It's very difficult to pin the pattern to the pile side and maintain accuracy while cutting, so this requires extra care if you decide to cut with the pile or napped side up.

### PILE UP OR DOWN?

To determine your favorite pile direction, stand in front of a mirror and drape the fabric around your neck with selvages hanging vertically. You will see that one side has a slightly richer look, the other a softer, subtler look. Choose the one you like the best.

* When cutting on a single layer, make duplicate pattern pieces to make layout easier and avoid cutting errors, such as cutting two right fronts!

* Use fine pins in the seam allowances only to avoid pin scars in pile fabrics. Pattern weights are an acceptable alternative to pins. Remove pins as soon as you have marked the fabric pieces as needed.

* Mark only what is necessary. Choose from chalk marking, snip marking, tailor tacks, thread tracing (with silk thread to avoid crushing the pile), or air-soluble marking pens — or the best combination of these for the design you are sewing.

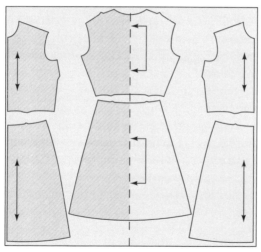

*with nap, single-layer layout (wrong side of fabric facing up)*

*SEE ALSO: Marking Tools and Methods, pages 165–174.*

**Q** How do I prevent the seam layers from creeping and scooting under the presser foot while stitching on these fabrics?

**A** First, make a 10"-long test seam on two layers of fabric.

* Consider fabric type (knit or woven) and fabric weight when selecting the machine needle (*see pages 52–53*).

* Begin with a stitch length of 2.5mm (12 spi) or 4mm (8 spi) on heavy fabrics such as wide-wale corduroy.

* Reduce the pressure on the presser foot a bit. Decrease in small increments as needed for smooth feeding of both layers. If the top layer shifts toward you as you stitch, decrease the presser-foot pressure. Using a roller foot or a walking foot also helps the layers feed together without shifting (but make sure these don't leave tracks on the pile side of the finished seam).

* Loosen the top tension a bit.

* Stitch *with* the smooth nap direction, not against it, to keep the layers from shifting because they are rubbing and fighting each other. That may require not following the guidelines for directional staystitching (*see pages 104–105*).

* Use taut sewing (*see pages 101–102*).

* Check the finished test seam. It should be smooth and pucker-free.

**Q** How do I avoid damaging or flattening the nap or pile when pressing while I sew?

**A** Less is best. Overpressing flattens the surface and causes unwanted shine. Place a thick, velvet-surfaced terry towel or a scrap of the actual fabric right side up on the ironing board. (Bind or serge the edges to control raveling and shedding). Or, invest in a special needleboard or velvet-surfaced cloth designed specifically for pressing pile fabrics. The pile sinks into the needles so the surface is not flattened with the iron.

* Test-press on scraps to determine the best iron temperature. Examine samples to determine how much pressure you can exert on the iron without damaging the nap, and to see if steam is safe and effective. Some of these fabrics can take a normal press without damage, while others may require steaming and finger-pressing only.

* Press from the wrong side only; steam from the right side, without placing the iron on the napped or pile surface, and use your fingers to work steam into stubborn areas if needed.

* Use the flannel side of a seam roll (*see page 37*) when pressing seams open, to avoid seam imprints on the outside.

* Keep any pressing with an iron to a minimum on finished garments. Instead, freshen pile garments after wear by hanging in a steam-filled bathroom and allowing to dry thoroughly before placing in the closet.

# Q How do I finish the seams and hems in pile fabrics? They ravel and shed.

# A Much depends on the kind of fabric you are using. Here are some pointers to keep in mind:

* Plain seams, pressed open, are the best choice for most napped fabrics; serged seams are the best for knit pile fabrics.

* You can serge-finish the separate seam edges to control raveling and shedding, but take care when pressing to avoid imprinting the serging stitches on the outside, especially on lightweight and silky fabrics.

* For a safer, lightweight finish, bind the seam edges with nylon tricot binding (*see page 269*).

* If the garment is fully lined, seam finishing is probably not necessary, but you might want to stitch or zigzag ⅛" from the seam edges before inserting the lining to stop any further raveling.

* Nylon tricot binding is a nice finish for the raw edge of a hem allowance on light- and medium-weight fabrics.

* Serge-finishing hem edges on corduroy is an excellent alternative. Finish hems and seams on knit pile fabrics following the guidelines for knit hems on pages 206–208.

# Q What's the best way to sew a zipper in a pile fabric?

# A In luxurious velvet, velour, and velveteen, it's often easier to do the final topstitching by hand, using the prickstitch (*see pages 123–124*). Use silk thread for almost invisible

stitches. An invisible zipper is also an excellent choice (*see pages 408–414*). In fleece outerwear fabrics, standard machine applications are sturdy and easy to do.

---

**Q** How do I prevent puckered seams in pile fabrics?

**A** Puckered seams are often a sign of too much pressure on the presser foot. Reducing the tension on the needle thread may also help, as well as using a walking foot or engaging the even-feed feature, if you have one on your machine.

---

**Q** I don't have a walking foot. Are there any methods to help overcome the challenge of shifting layers when sewing on pile fabrics?

**A** If taut sewing (*see pages 101–102*) doesn't work, try these remedies:

* Place a strip of tissue paper or soft embroidery stabilizer between the seam layers to keep them from fighting each other while you stitch; tear away from the stitches carefully.

* "Baste" seams with closely spaced pins (every ¾" to 1"), placed perpendicular to the seamline in the seam allowance to avoid pin "scars." Remove as you reach them.

* Use silk thread to hand-baste the layers along the seamline and then again ¼" from the first row in the seam allowances. Stitch immediately and remove the basting.

* Use a stop-and-start stitching method. Stitch for a few inches, then stop with the needle down, and raise the presser foot to release pressure on the fabric. Lower the foot and continue in this manner to the end of the seam.

---

**Q** I overpressed my velvet skirt in a few spots and the pile is flattened and shiny. Is there a way to fix it?

**A** Overpressing pile fabrics often results in permanent damage. You may be able to restore the nap by filling it with lots of steam from the iron and brushing the pile with your hand or a soft brush. On washable fabrics, you can try lightly misting with water and then using a soft brush to raise the nap. Test both strategies on purposely overpressed fabric samples first.

---

**Q** My pattern calls for topstitching, but on my test sample, the presser-foot left marks. Is there a way around this or should I abandon the topstitching?

**A** It's wise to avoid topstitching on pile and napped surfaces, but sometimes it is a necessity around necklines, collars, and front edges. To eliminate the presser-foot tracks (and feed-dog marks on the bottom layer), place the work between two layers of tissue paper or embroidery stabilizer that you can tear away after the stitching is complete.

# CHAPTER SIX

# Interfacings and Linings

Most garments and some home-decor projects require an additional layer of fabric to add body and to support the intended shape of the finished project. Inner-support options include interfacing, underlining, lining, and interlining. Most garments have interfacing somewhere. Jackets and coats, as well as fitted skirts, dresses, and bodices in ball and wedding gowns, are also often lined. Underlining is an alternative to a slippery lining; it adds body and lines a garment in one operation. Knowing how and when to use these methods and materials to support fabrics is essential to creating projects that will hold their shape and wear well for their lifetime.

# Interfacing

Interfacings add shape, stability, and structure to a sewing project. They are available in an array of fabric types — knit, woven, nonwoven, and weft insertion — and as sew-in or fusible interfacings. "Fusibles" are bonded permanently to fabric, using an iron. Choose from an array of weights to produce results that range from soft and fluid support to quite stiff shaping.

- - - - - - - - - - - - - - - - - - - - - - - - - - - - - - - -

**Q** Where is interfacing used?

**A** Sew-in interfacings are basted to the garment edge on the inside before the construction begins. Fusible interfacings are usually applied directly to the facings instead. (Neither will show on the outside of the finished garment.) In addition to necklines, front- and back-opening edges, and the armholes in sleeve-less garments, interfacing is also used to add body, shape, and a bit of firmness to design details, such as waistbands, collars, cuffs, front bands and tabs, welts, flaps, pockets, and buttonholes. In tailored coats and jackets, you'll find interfacing adding weight and support to hemline edges too.

*white areas show where interfacing can be applied beneath fabric*

# Q What are the characteristics of each type of interfacing?

# A Consider the qualities of these major types as they relate to the fabric you are using and the desired results.

**Woven.** A lightweight fabric with lengthwise and crosswise threads and some give in the crosswise direction; cut edges will ravel; lightweight muslin and batiste are good examples; organdy and silk organza are good woven choices for lightweight and/or sheer fabrics; a few fusible versions are available, but most are sew in.

**Nonwoven.** A paperlike fabric that is a web of man-made fibers bonded together; some are completely stable (they have no give), but many have multidirectional stretch; edges do not ravel; cutting with the grain is unnecessary unless the specific interfacing has give only in the crossgrain; lightweight versions are good for knits and for soft shaping in woven fabrics; available in sew-in and fusible versions and a wide range of weights.

**Knit.** Soft, fluid, tricot knit interfacing in light and medium weights; has crosswise give; stable in the lengthwise direction; great for knits but also offers soft shaping without crispness in wovens; available as a fusible only; does not ravel; use to completely interface/underline woven fabrics that need more body.

**Weft insertion.** Knit interfacing with threads interlaced in the crosswise direction through the knit loops for crosswise stability; has bias give like a woven; more drape than a woven interfacing, less than a knit fusible; available in light to tailoring weights; excellent in knits and wovens; does not ravel. *Note:* Warp-insertion interfacings are similar, but the threads interlace through the vertical loops, so the fabric has crosswise give.

**Q** **Are there any guidelines for selecting the best inter-facing for my project?**

**A** Some patterns suggest appropriate interfacing types and weights for specific fabrics. Consider the following in your selection process:

* Care requirements should be compatible with the intended method of care for the finished item. It's okay to use interfacing of different fiber content than the fabric.

* Choose an interfacing that's lighter than the fashion fabric, so it doesn't overwhelm or change the character of the fabric.

* *Remember:* Fusibles form a bond with the fabric, giving firmer results than a sew-in of the same fabric. If in doubt, choose a lighter-weight fusible. You can add another layer of lightweight interfacing if a single layer isn't enough.

* Sew-in interfacing is best for sheer and open-weave fabrics. Select skin-tone interfacings for the least show-through. Silk organza and bridal tulle are often the best choice for these fabric types.

* Fusible knit interfacings are the best choice for knit fabrics because they have similar stretch. They are also excellent for wovens for soft shaping. Weft-insertion interfacings have some give.

* Fusibles are excellent for fabrics that fray. They hold fabric threads in place along cut or trimmed edges — a nice plus when trimming and clipping facing seam edges, particu-larly on fabrics that ravel excessively.

Q Which is better: a sew-in or a fusible interfacing?

A A sew-in interfacing usually doesn't affect the hand or change the character of the fabric like a fusible does. A fusible adheres to the fabric, making it somewhat stiffer after application. As you gain experience with different types, follow personal preferences. Whenever possible, I choose a fusible; it's fast, easy to apply, and stays put inside the garment when fused correctly. On fabrics that can't take the heat and/or moisture, plus the pressure that is required for fusing (*see next question*), use a woven or nonwoven sew-in interfacing.

- - - - - - - - - - - - - - - - - - - - - - - - - - - - - - -

Q So, what types of fabric cannot take the heat and pressure required for fusing?

A Use a sew-in interfacing for fabrics that are highly textured, silk and rayon velvets, napped, beaded or sequined, and highly heat-sensitive. In addition, fusibles are not appropriate for open-weave fabrics and laces that will reveal the interfacing. Fusing is not advised (and frequently doesn't work)

233

for metallics, faux fur, or real leather or suede. However, you can use a fusible with synthetic suede (but not synthetic leather).

If you are in doubt about using a fusible, do a test-fuse sample on a scrap. You may be surprised to find that fusibles work on some corduroys, as well as on cotton velvet and velveteen, as long as you don't press from the right side.

---

**Q** **How do I decide if a sew-in or a fusible is the best choice for a fabric that can take either type?**

**A** Place a layer of sew-in interfacing between two layers of the fashion fabric and drape it over your hand to see how it feels. Is the result crisp enough? Drapeable enough? Flexible enough? Stable enough? For a collar, shape the layers around your neck; for a cuff, wrap the layers around your wrist.

To choose the best fusible interfacing, test-fuse your choice(s) on the actual fabric. Preshrink the interfacing(s) (*see next page*) and fuse as directed (*see page 236*). Cut 3" squares of each one you're considering. Fuse to a piece of fabric that is large enough to fold over the interfacing so you can feel all three layers. For washable garments, launder your test sample to see how it holds up. Save your test-fused samples in your sewing notebook (*see page 48*), noting the brand name of each one.

It's wise to keep a variety of interfacing types and weights on hand so you can test, compare, and choose the best one for the project. My stock includes 5-yard cuts (I buy on sale) of my favorites.

# Q What do I look for after fusing?

A After fusing, examine the fabric's right side for dots of fusible resin bleed-through or unsightly puckers or wrinkles. Feel it to make sure the results are firm enough, but not too firm, for the intended area. If the fusing is unsatisfactory with the general fusing method described on pages 236–238, experiment with more steam, less steam, a lower or higher iron temperature, a damp press cloth, or a dry iron until the bond is firm. If you can't get a firm bond on your fabric no matter what you try, select a sew-in.

# Q How do I preshrink interfacings?

A Be sure to read the bolt end or the plastic interleafing that comes with the interfacing yardage for suggestions about preshrinking. Follow these guidelines:

* It's not necessary to preshrink nonwoven, *sew-in* interfacings such as Pellon.

* Steam-shrink nonwoven (Pellon-type) *fusible* interfacings, as described in step 3 of the fusing process on page 237.

* Launder washable woven sew-in interfacings as you will launder the garment. Polyester nonwoven interfacings do not require preshrinking.

* Wet-shrink fusible woven, knit, and weft-insertion interfacings (*see next question*). These have a plastic resin on one side that melts and bonds with the fabric. Preshrinking eliminates the possibility of shrinkage while it is being

fused in place with the heat of the iron. Bubbles and puckers usually result if the interfacing has not been preshrunk before applying heat or steam to activate the resin.

---

Q **How do I wet-shrink fusible interfacings?**

A Follow these easy steps:

1. Unfold and carefully immerse the yardage in a sink full of hot water and leave until the water has cooled.
2. Squeeze, don't twist, out the excess water. Roll the interfacing in a terry towel to remove additional water and drape it over the shower rod to drip dry. Never wash these interfacings in the washer or dry them in the dryer!

---

Q **How do I apply fusible interfacing so that it stays put in the garment throughout its lifetime? I've had it come undone in some of my projects.**

A Always read the directions that come with the interfacing. Fusible interfacings usually require four things for a permanent fuse: *heat* and *steam* from your iron (some may not require steam), *pressure* from your hand on the iron, and adequate fusing *time*. The following steps outline a standard fusing method that works for most fusibles, but you may find the manufacturer's directions for a specific interfacing varies from these in one or more ways. Be sure to ask for and save a copy of the fusing directions for each interfacing you like in your sewing notebook (*see page 48*).

1. Preshrink interfacing by wet-shrinking (*see previous question*) or steam-shrinking it before fusing (*see step 3*). Cut the pieces using the pattern pieces provided (usually the corresponding garment pattern piece: the collar pattern, for example). *Note:* Directions in patterns, books, and on manufacturer's sheets often suggest trimming away all but ⅛" of the seam allowances on fusible interfacing pieces to eliminate bulk. I *never* do this. It's time-consuming, and I love having it in the seam allowance to control raveling at interfaced edges that must be trimmed after stitching.

2. Adjust the iron temperature to the wool setting (which works on most fabrics). Place the fashion fabric wrong side up on the ironing board and press, to warm it up and to make it more receptive to the fusible, as well as to remove any wrinkles. Be careful not to stretch it out of shape.

3. Position the interfacing, fusible granules down, on the wrong side of the fabric. If you didn't wet-shrink the interfacing to preshrink it, steam-shrink it by holding the steam iron just above the interfacing and steaming it. Move from area to area on large pieces. Watch carefully, and you will see the interfacing draw in a bit (shrink) from the heat and steam. Trim any fusible-interfacing edges that extend past the fashion-fabric edges *before* fusing, to keep interfacing from attaching to your pressing surface.

4. Steam-baste by lightly pressing from the center out to the cut edges, for about a second in each area. *Do not slide the iron;* lift and place in each new location.

5. Evenly dampen the press cloth (but not to dripping wet), if moisture is required in the manufacturer's instructions. Place on top of the interfacing. Place the iron on top and bear down firmly with both hands on the iron to apply the needed pressure. Count the number of seconds recommended for the interfacing: 10 to 15 seconds or more for most. Lift — don't slide — the iron to the next location, making sure the iron overlaps the first fused section by at least ¼".

6. After fusing the entire piece, turn it over and fuse from the right side, using a press cloth to protect the fabric surface. Allow to cool completely; while the fusible resin is warm, it can be reshaped, so take care to keep it flat and wrinkle-free until dry and cool.

7. Check the bond. If it's not firmly bonded, repeat the fusing process.

### INCREASE THE PRESSURE

If you're having trouble bearing down on the iron for the amount of pressure needed, lower your ironing board a bit so you can use your body weight to exert additional pressure on the iron.

Q How do I attach a nonfusible woven or nonwoven interfacing?

A Cut out on the grain, just as for fashion fabric, and use pinking shears to trim away ½" along the inner edges (the ones that won't be caught in a seam) so they won't show past the inner finished edge of the facing. Baste to the wrong side of the garment pieces after staystitching (*see pages 104–105*) and before you begin the construction. To glue-baste, dab glue stick (or apply tiny dots of fabric glue) along the raw edges of the garment piece on the wrong side and smooth the interfacing in place. Keep the glue away from the stitching line. Use your fingers to make sure the two adhere, and allow to dry.

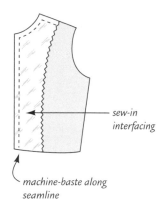

*sew-in interfacing*

*machine-baste along seamline*

Q Is it okay to use more than one type of interfacing in a garment?

A Yes, I do this often. Choose the best one for the desired finished effect in each location where interfacing is needed for support.

## Q How do I attach interfacing along a fold line?

A You have two choices. Either catchstitch the cut edge along the garment fold line, or hand- or machine-baste along the fold line, if the interfacing extends past it. The catchstitching remains in the garment. The basting is removed after the garment is assembled, and the edges are topstitched to secure the interfacing.

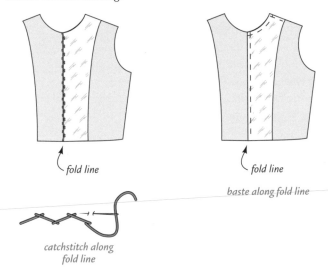

fold line

fold line

baste along fold line

catchstitch along
fold line

- - - - - - - - - - - - - - - - - - - - - - - - - - - - - - - - - -

## Q How do I prevent the inner edge of fusible interfacing from showing as a line on the outside of the garment?

A Whenever possible, apply the interfacing to the facing, *not* to the garment. If you must apply directly to a garment section, pink the inner edge to make it less visible. Or, in some garments (jacket fronts and fitted bodices, for example), you may interface the entire garment piece for added support, which prevents interfacing shadow-through to the right side.

---

Q **I don't have a large enough piece of fusible interfacing for my project, but I do have scraps. Can I piece it?**

A Yes, I do this often. It's best to pink the edges where two sections meet, rather than overlapping them, for a smooth, flat join. This is a great way to use up scraps at midnight when the stores aren't open and you want to sew! Store small pieces flat so you can use them for this purpose.

---

Q **What's the best way to store fusible interfacing?**

A It's impossible to press it to remove wrinkles or creases before cutting the required pieces. Roll it on a tube (from wrapping paper or paper towels, for instance). Preshrink the interfacing as directed on page 235, so it's ready when you're ready to sew — unless you will be steam shrinking it (*see page 237*). If the tube you are using isn't long enough, carefully fold the interfacing lengthwise with fusible resin inside. Tuck a copy of the manufacturer's instructions inside the tube. Cut a square of the interfacing to attach to a reference sheet for your sewing notebook (*see page 48*), along with the interfacing name and fusing directions.

**Q** There is a brown buildup of fusible resin on my iron soleplate. How do I get it off?

**A** It's almost impossible to avoid this. You might have dropped a scrap of interfacing, resin side up on the ironing board; or sometimes the fusible "bleeds" onto your press cloth and transfers to something else when you use it the next time. Keep a tube of hot-iron cleaner handy for removing buildup; look for it in the fabric-store notions department. Follow the directions on the tube. One important precaution: Open the window for ventilation and locate the iron away from a smoke alarm.

To prevent the iron from picking up fusible resin, make sure the ironing board is swept free of any interfacing and fusible-web crumbs. I use an adhesive lint roller to clean off the fusing space. Reserve a new press cloth for fusing and write "this side up" on one side, using an indelible ink pen. Keep that side facing you when you fuse, as some fusible resin can bleed through to the wrong side of the press cloth during fusing.

- - - - - - - - - - - - - - - - - - - - - - - - - - - - - -

**Q** After fusing my interfacing, I notice blisters in the fashion fabric. In some places it seems like the interfacing has actually separated. Can I fix this by re-fusing?

**A** Probably not, particularly if this becomes noticeable after the garment is completed and has been cleaned or laundered. Blisters and separation are the result of improper fusing technique and can sometimes result from attempting to fuse interfacing to a fabric that resists fusing. The finish on the fabric may be the problem in this case. Sliding the iron while fusing can also cause this problem. Blisters point out the need to choose fusibles carefully, always testing first, and then ensuring optimum fusing conditions as outlined in the question about applying fusible interfacings on page 236.

---

Q **My fused sample has a lot of puckering and bubbling. What happened?**

A The fabric or the interfacing shrunk during the fusing, as a reaction to the heat of the iron. If the fashion fabric is bubbled, the interfacing is the culprit — and vice versa. To avoid this in your garment, see the question about how to pre-shrink interfacings on page 235.

---

Q **I've stopped using fusibles because the resin appears to seep through to the surface of my fashion fabric and shows up as small dots. What causes this?**

A For this very reason, I avoid using dot-resin fusible interfacings on smooth-surfaced fabrics, particularly light-weight and light-colored ones. I usually use an interfacing with flakes of resin, which results in an overall pattern that doesn't strike through in an obvious way. This is just one more reason to test several fusible interfacing choices in order to choose the best one for your fabric. Reserve dot-resin fusibles for thicker and more firmly woven fabrics where strike-through is not going to be a problem.

**Q** **Is it possible to remove fusible interfacing if I'm not happy with the results?**

**A** You can try, but it can be tedious and may not work, especially with delicate or loosely woven fabrics or knits. Test first in a small section. Hold the steam iron close to the interfacing for several seconds to soften the fusible resin. Try to gently peel it away from the fabric while it's warm. If you can't lift and pull easily, warm it for an additional 10 seconds and try again. Continue in this fashion until it comes away easily — or give up. If you are successful but can see or feel fusible residue on the fabric, dampen a piece of muslin or similar fabric, position it on the fabric, press, and peel away immediately. Continue this process with clean fabric scraps until you have removed all residue.

# Line, Underline, or Interline

In addition to the support of an interfacing, some garments require a lining, underlining, or interlining — or a combination of these.

**Q** **What's the difference between lining, underlining, and interlining?**

**A** A **lining** is usually cut from a durable but smooth fabric with a somewhat slippery hand, so it's easy to slip in and out of the finished garment. A lining adds a bit of support and covers the seam allowances and any other inner construction, such as the pocket bags inside a coat or jacket. Linings add a feeling of luxury, protect the fabric from body oil, and in skirts and dresses, eliminate the necessity of wearing a slip. They take some of the wearing strain, improving wrinkle-resistance and wear. Antistatic lining fabrics help eliminate garment cling.

Sew the lining as a separate "garment" to match the size and shape of whatever you're making (a skirt or pants, for example), and "catch" it in the waistline seam and around a zipper. In coats and jackets, the lining is attached to the facings. In a jacket, it's attached to the lower hem allowance, but usually hangs free at the bottom edge inside a skirt, pants, dress, or coat. For some fabrics, adding a lining means that seam finishing is unnecessary on the fashion fabric; however, the lining may require seam finishing to control raveling in garments where the lining is loose at the bottom edge.

An **underlining** is usually cut from a lightweight, nonslippery woven fabric and attached to each garment piece *before* any sewing is done. Then the two pieces of fabric are treated as one during the construction. Choose this method to enhance the performance (as in adding body or cutting down on wrinkles) and/or appearance (change the color) of the fashion fabric. The underlining can also double as a lining, or in some cases, you may want to line the garment as well. Sometimes, you can use a lightweight fusible interfacing as the underlining. When a garment is underlined, you may not need to interface it; that's a decision only you can make by handling the underlined fabric to determine if it adds enough body at the edges.

An **interlining** is a thin layer of fabric (cotton flannel, for example) added to the lining fabric for a coat or outerwear jacket for warmth. The two pieces are treated as one during the lining construction. Sleeves are usually not interlined, as the extra layer can make them too tight and uncomfortable.

- - - - - - - - - - - - - - - - - - - - - - - - - - - - - - - - -

**Q** What, why, and when should I underline?

**A** Underlining is most often used in pants, skirts, fitted dresses, and some jackets and coats. Make sure the underlining fabric is lighter weight than the primary fabric in your project, so it doesn't dominate the primary fabric. It should have comparable fluidity. Knits are usually not underlined, but if you must underline, see the next question for options. Consider underlining if you want to:

* Cushion seam allowances so they don't show on the right side. The extra layer of fabric helps eliminate seam-edge imprinting.

* Help prevent wrinkling. Underlining will cushion stress-folds and wrinkles during wear so they drop out more easily on the hanger. It's a good way to control wrinkling in linen garments.

* Protect the skin from uncomfortable (scratchy) fabric. However, a lining may be a better choice if you are super-sensitive, since it covers the seam allowances, too.

* Strengthen and increase the weight of loosely woven fabrics to prevent sagging and stretching. Because it's caught in the seams, it's the first layer to take the wearing stress.
* Help prevent baggy knees in pants and "rump spring" in skirts and pants.
* Alter the color of a lightweight see-through fabric or eliminate the see-through quality of a sheer fabric.
* Improve the weight of a lightweight fabric to make it more compatible with the design you are sewing. (It's usually better to choose a different, more appropriate fabric, but sometimes adding an underlining is the only option.)

- - - - - - - - - - - - - - - - - - - - - - - - - - - -

Q **What kind of fabric is best for underlining?**

A Underlining affects the hand and drape of the fabric, so choose accordingly. Cotton or cotton-polyester batiste or lightweight broadcloth are good choices for most woven fabrics. For fine fabrics, such as wool crepe, silk organza makes a lovely underlining. On knits, fusible weft-insertion or knit interfacings are the best choice because they have inherent stretch but add support. Yes, you can use an interfacing as an underlining! Tricot bathing-suit lining might be the perfect underlining choice for stretch lace, to add modesty and retain the lace's stretch. You can be creative when choosing an underlining to create the desired finished effect and wear qualities.

# Q How much fabric will I need for an underlining?

A I purchase the same amount as the garment requires and preshrink it using the appropriate method (*see page 190*). I often have a bit left over, but it's good to have on hand when I need a woven interfacing. If it's 100-percent cotton, I can use the extra for press cloths, too.

- - - - - - - - - - - - - - - - - - - - - - - - -

# Q How do I attach an underlining?

A Preshrink the fashion and underlining fabrics. Cut the pieces from the fashion fabric and only the main garment pieces from the underlining fabric; transfer all construction marks. Underlining is not used in facings, waistbands, and detail areas that will be interfaced, unless you are using it to alter the color of a lightweight fabric. Attach each piece of underlining to its matching fashion fabric, with wrong sides facing, using basting stitches or glue basting. Treat the two fabrics as one during the construction.

*Note:* If you are using a fusible interfacing for the underlining, refer to the interfacing fusing directions on pages 236–238.

- - - - - - - - - - - - - - - - - - - - - - - - -

# Q Glue basting? What's that?

A It's the fastest way to add an underlining to the garment pieces, ensuring that the underlining is slightly smaller than the outer fabric, so it fits smoothly around the body curves. Think of a garment as a cylinder; each layer inside the next must be slightly smaller to fit smoothly without wrinkles. You'll need *permanent* fabric glue that dries soft and flexible (not a glue stick).

1.  Cut the fashion fabric pieces and the matching underlining pieces. Transfer all construction marks to both fabrics, but mark darts or tucks on the underlining right side *only*.

2.  Place the fabric piece right side down on the ironing board. Position the underlining right side up on top of it and steam-press the layers together.

3.  Lift one lengthwise edge of the underlining and apply tiny dots of glue to the fashion fabric. Smooth the underlining in place in the glue. Repeat on the opposite edge.

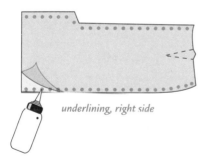

*underlining, right side*

4.  *While the glue is still wet,* fold the piece in half toward the center, and then make one more fold. You will notice small bubbles of excess interfacing forming. Use your hands to gently scoot the excess past the cut

edge. Pat into place and allow the glue to dry with the fabric still folded. When you unroll the piece, there will be a slight curve in it — ready to fit around your curves. Trim the excess underlining close to the fashion fabric's raw edge.

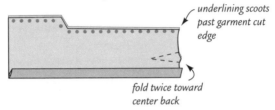

*underlining scoots past garment cut edge*

*fold twice toward center back*

5. Machine-baste through the center of any darts or tucks, extending the basting at least ½" beyond the inner end to hold the layers together.
6. Sew the garment together, treating the two layers of fabric as one. You can trim the underlining in the hem allowances, allowing ½" to extend past the hem fold for cushioning.

- - - - - - - - - - - - - - - - - - - - - - - - - - -

**Q** How do I apply fusible interfacing as an underlining?

**A** Don't try to fuse interfacing to the entire yardage. Instead, use the "block" method. Cut out each garment piece with extra fabric all around — in a rectangular shape and on-grain. Cut matching interfacing rectangles and fuse in place. Then pin the pattern pieces in place and cut out.

# Q Do I apply an interlining to the lining in the same way?

A Yes, you can glue-baste, or you may want to machine-stitch the underlining to the lining ½" from the raw edges and then trim it close to the stitching to eliminate bulk in the seams. At the lower edge, baste the interlining in place along the hemline fold, using tiny stitches on the garment side and longer ones along the fold line. Trim all but ½" of it out of the hem allowance and leave the basting in the fold line.

---

# Q Which fabrics are appropriate for linings?

A A somewhat slippery, light- or medium-weight fabric is the usual choice for lining. China silk is a lightweight lining for soft jackets, dresses, skirts, and pants. Bemberg rayon lining is my favorite for most skirts, pants, and jackets because it is more breathable than a polyester lining. Silklike synthetic and synthetic/natural fiber blend fabrics, often called "silkies," make wonderful linings, particularly in jackets, where the lining will be more noticeable. For a coat lining, look for a heavyweight, silky-surfaced fabric, such as polyester satin or an acetate satin or twill. Polyester linings wear better than rayon or acetate, so they may be the best choice for a coat or jacket that will receive a lot of wear. Reduce dry-cleaning bills by treating lining with a fabric protector, such as Scotchgard.

*Note:* Linings in knit garments can be cut from woven fabrics to control the stretch or from knit fabrics, which won't affect the stretch. It all depends on your goals.

## LINE BY HALF

You may opt to use a half-lining in a skirt. For added durability, cut the pieces with the lengthwise grain running across the pieces (you can do this for full linings, too). This puts the stronger lengthwise grain across the area that gets the most stress. Cut the lining pieces so they end a few inches below the full hip and serge-finish the lower edge, or make a narrow hem.

# Q How do I add a lining to a skirt or a pair of pants?

A Cut the major garment pieces from the lining fabric. You won't need lining for the waistband or most design details (although patch pockets are often lined, so follow your pattern guide sheet). Construct the lining just as you would the garment, with the same fitting process. Press darts or tucks in the opposite direction than in the garment to stagger the layers and avoid lumps.

For the zipper opening, leave an extra ½" of the seam where it will be inserted unstitched, so it will be easy to clear the bottom of the zipper. Slip the lining into the garment with wrong sides facing and baste together

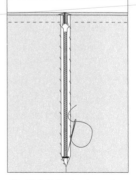

*slipstitch lining to zipper tape*

along the waistline seam. Turn under the raw edges of the lining around the zipper so there is enough room for the zipper to slide by without catching the lining. Slipstitch in place. Finish the waistline and hem the garment. Hem the lining at least ½" shorter than the garment, so the lining won't show at the lower edge.

SEE ALSO: *Line by Half, on previous page.*

Q **My zipper catches the lining edge sometimes. Is there a way to avoid this and make a neat, squared-off finish in the lining around the bottom of the zipper?**

A After ending the lining seam just below the zipper opening, center and fuse a 1"-diameter circle of lightweight fusible interfacing (cut this out with pinking sheers) over the end of the lining's stitching on each side of the seam. Make a 45-degree-angle cut into the seam allowance to the end of the stitching. Then angle down into the lining and make a ¼" cut. Press the seam open, turning down the triangular point as shown on the next page. Slipstitch the lining to the zipper tape, taking two or three stitches in the corners for added security.

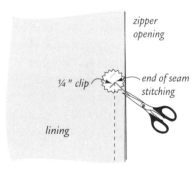

zipper opening

¼" clip

end of seam stitching

lining

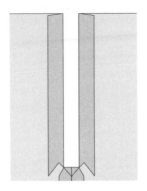 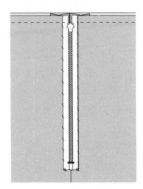

Q **Is there an easy way to line a vest to the edge, instead of facing the vest and hand sewing the lining in place?**

A Yes, the flip lining method is a cinch! (The method in your pattern guide sheet may not match this technique.)

1. Cut out the vest but not the facings. Apply interfacing to the armhole, neckline, and front opening edges. Use the vest pattern pieces to cut the lining. Trim away ¹⁄₁₆" around the neckline, armhole, and front edges of the lining pieces. The lining will naturally roll to the inside of the finished vest instead of peeking out at the finished edges.

2. Assemble the vest by first stitching any darts and the shoulder seams only. Do *not* stitch the side seams. Repeat with the lining.

3. With right sides facing and raw edges aligned, stitch the lining to the vest around the armholes and the neckline edge, ending at the side seam edges. Stitch the lower

edges together in the vest back, as in illustration (A). Trim, grade, clip, notch, and press the seams (*see pages 282–284*).

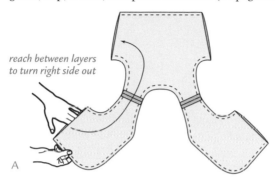

*reach between layers to turn right side out*

A

4. Turn the vest right side out by reaching in one side seam and pulling it through the shoulder. Press the edges. If you wish, you can under-stitch the seams as far as you can comfortably reach into the shoulder area, as in illustration (B).

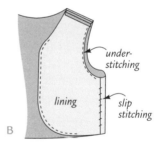

*under-stitching*

*lining*

*slip stitching*

B

5. Pin and stitch the vest side seams, beginning and ending on the lining 1" above the armhole and 1" past the lower edge. You will be sewing in a partial circle inside the vest; take your time and pin well to keep the pieces in position. Press the seam open.

6. Turn in the seam allowance on the vest front and slip-stitch to the vest lining; press.

**Q** How can I prevent the lining in my pants from crawling up my legs (due to static electricity)?

**A** Add French tacks (also called swing tacks) to link the hems. Using a needle with a single waxed-and-pressed thread (*see page 389*) or topstitching thread, hide the knot between the hem allowance and the garment at the inseam, and take a small backstitch through the hem allowance. Take a small stitch in the lining hem allowance, opposite the first stitch, leaving 1" of slack in the thread. Make several more stitches of the same length and slack in the same location. To finish, work close (but not tight) blanket stitches (*see page 124*) over the threads that form the swing tack. End by taking several stitches in the lining hem allowance. Repeat at the outer seam to securely hold the lining hem in place. *Note:* French tacks are essential in lined coats. Make one at each side seam.

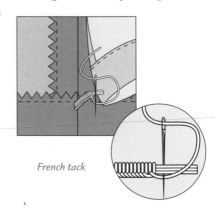

*French tack*

# CHAPTER SEVEN

# Seams and Seam Finishes

Sewing two layers of fabric together to make a seam is the foundation of every other sewing technique. The type of seam and how you finish it depend on two things: the fabric and the desired result. Some seaming methods result in seams with completely finished edges. Others leave the edges exposed, requiring a finish to prevent raveling or to improve the appearance inside unlined clothing. Here you'll find the most commonly used seams and seam finishes, as well as how to cut and apply binding, and stitch and press enclosed seams.

# Basic Seams and Finishes

Plain, French, and flat-fell seams are the three most common machine-stitched seams. Serged seams are popular for knit fabrics, but machine-made seams are also appropriate for these fabrics. Plain seams require additional finishing when the fabric is woven and the cut edges tend to ravel. French and flat-fell seams are completely finished inside and out.

---

**Q** What is the standard seam allowance?

**A** In most garment patterns from commercial companies and independent designers, the standard seam allowance width — the distance from the cut edge to the stitching line — is ⅝". It allows a bit of "letting-out" room for fitting. Patterns designed for knits only may have ¼"- or ⅜"-wide seam allowances. The seam allowance for most home-decor sewing projects is ½", but sometimes only ¼" wide. Read your pattern guide sheet for the correct seam allowance.

---

**Q** How do I make a plain seam?

**A** Adjust the machine for the correct stitch length and tension for your fabric (*see pages 86–87*) and thread it with the appropriate thread in the needle and bobbin.

1. Pin the pieces together, with notches and construction marks matching. Place pins across the seamline with the pin heads to the right so you can remove

them while stitching. Space them 2" to 3" apart. If you are a beginner, it may help to hand-baste (*see page 123*) until you are a bit more experienced at handling fabric layers at the machine.

2. Position the fabric layers under the presser foot, aligning the cut edge with the appropriate seam-allowance mark engraved on the machine's needle plate. Lower the needle ⅝" from the upper cut edge of the fabric pieces and lower the presser foot.

3. Hold onto the threads behind the foot and backstitch to the cut edge. Stitch forward for an inch or so on top of the backstitching and release the threads. Stitch to the other end of the seam, removing pins as you reach them, *before* stitching over them. At the end, backstitch for about ½". (Remove basting if necessary.)

4. Press along the stitches to set them into the fabric for a clean, sharply pressed seam. Press open for a plain seam, or in the direction specified for other seam types.

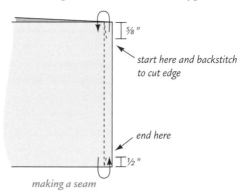

⅝ "

start here and backstitch to cut edge

end here

½ "

*making a seam*

> **TIP**
>
> Hitting a pin with the needle will damage the sewing machine needle, the pin, and the fabric. If you hit one, stop and change the needle to avoid the possibility of snagging the fabric. Discard the damaged needle.

**Q** Are there any other ways to begin and end a seam besides backstitching?

**A** Adjust the stitch length to 1.25 to 1.5 mm (16 to 20 stitches per inch) and stitch the first ¾" of the seam. Then, readjust to the normal stitch length needed for your project. Stop ¾" from the lower end of the seam, change back to the shorter stitch length, and complete the seam. These tiny stitches are less likely to come undone (but they are difficult to remove if you make a stitching error).

----

**Q** What is a "scant" seam allowance?

**A** Stitch in the seam allowance ¹⁄₁₆" or a thread or two away from the actual stitching line. For a scant ⅝" seam, stitch halfway between ⅝" and ½". You can adjust the needle position one small step to the right and then guide the raw edges along the ⅝" mark engraved on the needle plate.

# Q How do I prevent the seam-allowance edges from raveling?

# A Choose from several standard machine and serger finishes:

* Pink individual seam allowances (A) with pinking shears (*see page 23*). Pinking helps disguise edges so they don't imprint and show on the outside like straight edges. This finish is appropriate for most fabrics, including knits (even though they don't ravel).

* Stitch and pink the edges (B) on woven fabrics. The straight stitching stops any further raveling. Before pinking, stitch ¼" from each seam allowance raw edge with a slightly shorter-than-normal stitch.

* Clean-finish individual seam allowance edges (C) in light- and medium-weight fabrics. Turn under and press ¼" on each seam allowance edge; stitch ⅛" from the turned edge. Use this method on straight seam edges only.

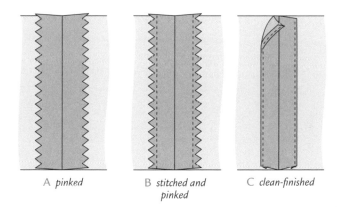

A *pinked*      B *stitched and pinked*      C *clean-finished*

* Zigzag close to the raw edges (D) on woven fabrics. Use a plain, three-step, serpentine, or over-edge zigzag stitch, adjusted for a medium width and length so the edge doesn't curl or tunnel up under the stitches. Adjust the thread tension as needed (*see pages 86–87*). Stitch close to *but not over* the raw edge.

* Serge-finish (E) for the most ravel-proof finish. Serged (also called overlocked) edges are encased in thread loops so they don't ravel. This is my favorite fast finish for unlined garments. It can be used on most fabrics. (*See* Common Serger Seams *on page 273*.)

* Machine over-edge (F) using the blindstitch or other built-in over-edge stitch. Check your manual for stitches and settings.

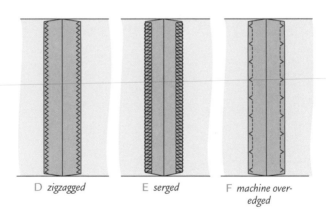

D *zigzagged*          E *serged*          F *machine over-edged*

* Make a double-stitched seam with a second row of straight or zigzag stitching close to the first through both seam allowances, as shown on page 203. Trim close to the second stitching; press the seam to one side.

* Bind raw edges with ready-made bias binding (G), following package directions, or with custom-cut binding. The Hong Kong finish (H) is lovely for both straight and curved seam edges on unlined garments on medium- and heavyweight fabrics (*see next question*). Bias tricot binding is a lightweight alternative (*see page 269*).

* Hand-overcast the raw edges (I). First, machine-stitch ⅛" from the raw edges with the machine adjusted for a longer-than-normal stitch length (8 spi). Use the stitch length as a guideline for making evenly spaced stitches of equal length.

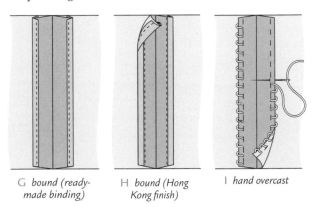

G *bound (ready-made binding)*   H *bound (Hong Kong finish)*   I *hand overcast*

# Q How do I sew a Hong Kong finish?

A Use true-bias strips of a lightweight fabric, such as China silk or fine cotton batiste, in a matching or contrasting color.

1. Cut 1½"-wide true-bias strips (*see next question*) and join pieces with bias seams (*see page 268*); press seams open.

2. With raw edges even, stitch a bias strip to the right side of each seam allowance ¼" from the edge. Take care not to stretch the bias. Turn the strip over the raw edge to the underside of the seam allowance; press lightly.

3. Stitch-in-the-ditch of the seam (*see page 112*), close to the binding, catching it on the underside of the seam allowances. Trim the binding edge close to the stitching (bias won't ravel).

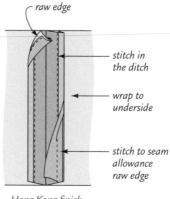

raw edge

stitch in the ditch

wrap to underside

stitch to seam allowance raw edge

*Hong Kong finish*

# Q How do I cut true-bias strips for binding?

A Accurate cutting and careful handling are essential. To cut a few strips, follow the steps below. If you need several yards, try the continuous bias-strip method (*see question on page 267*).

1. Straighten the cut edge of the fabric so it is true and perpendicular to the selvage edges. Fold the fabric on the true 45-degree diagonal with the cut edge parallel to or even with the selvage; press.

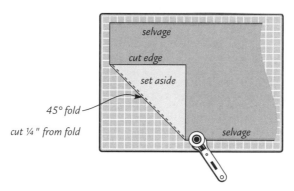

2. Place an acrylic rotary ruler on the fabric and trim away ¼" at the folded edges. Remove the cutaway triangle and set aside to use if you need additional strips.

3.  Using the cut edge as your guide, carefully rotary-cut bias strips of the required width. Take care not to stretch the fabric or the strips.

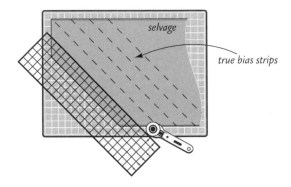

*selvage*

*true bias strips*

Q How much fabric will I need for several yards of bias strips for Hong Kong finishing seams?

A As a rule of thumb: 1 yard of 44"/45"-wide fabric will yield approximately 30 yards of 1¾"-wide bias binding, 16 yards of 2¾"-wide bias binding, or 14 yards of 3¾"-wide bias binding. If you need a lot of binding, you may prefer to use the continuous bias cutting method. In that case, calculate the required size for the fabric square you'll need:

1.  Cut-strip width × needed length in inches = fabric area needed (Example: 2" × 200" = 400 square inches)

2.  Use a calculator with a square-root function to determine the square root of the fabric area needed and round up to the nearest inch. (Example: square root of 400" = 20" square of fabric)

# Q How do I cut one continuous strip of bias from a piece of fabric?

A Here's my favorite method:

1. Rotary-cut a large square of fabric with straight-grain edges all around. Place a straight pin at the center of each of two opposite edges of the square. Cut in half diagonally.

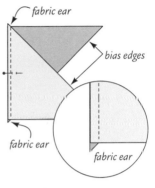

*fabric ear*

*bias edges*

*fabric ear*

*fabric ear*

2. Pin the resulting triangles together with pins matching and the bias-cut edges crossing each other. Stitch ¼" from the raw edges. Press seam open.

3. With a sharp pencil, draw cutting lines on the wrong side, parallel to the long bias edges of the parallelogram. Space them according to the desired

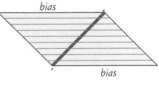

*bias*

*bias*

finished binding width for double-layer or single-layer binding, as you prefer.

4. With right sides together and raw edges even, pin the two short, angled edges together to form a tube, offsetting the seam one width of the marked binding strips, with a tail of fabric extending at each end of the seam. Pin where each set of lines meets, so they match and the cutting line will be continuous around the tube. It will have a twist in it (not shown). Using a 1.25 to

1.5 mm stitch length (16 to 20 spi), sew ¼" from the raw edges; press seam open. Use dressmaker's shears to cut around the tube on the marked lines to end up with one long strip of bias binding.

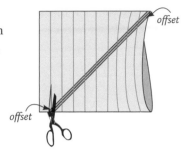

## Q How do I make a bias seam?

A Even though the ends are angled when you cut true bias strips, it's easier to join the ends for perfect seaming with this method. Place two strips with straight ends at precise right angles to each other on a rotary cutting mat. Draw a 45-degree-angle stitching line that intersects the edges of the lower strip. Stitch on the line and trim ¼" from the stitching. Press the seam open.

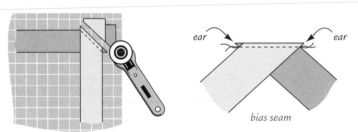

bias seam

**Q** Is there anything else I can use for a bound-edge finish?

**A** Bias tricot binding is a wonderful substitute. It's sheer and lightweight and available in a few basic colors and two different widths. To bind an edge in one step, tug on the binding to determine which way it curls so you can wrap the raw edge with the strip curling around it. Straight-stitch or zigzag in place. Use this product for a lightweight casing (*see pages 331–335*).

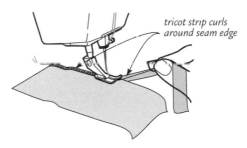

*tricot strip curls around seam edge*

- - - - - - - - - - - - - - - - - - - - - - - - - - - - -

**Q** When should I use a French seam and how do I make one?

**A** French seams are narrow seams that completely enclose the raw edges. Use them when sewing with sheers, laces, and lightweight or delicate fabrics, and for straight or nearly straight seams. You may be able to use them on a gently curved edge.

1. Place the fabric pieces *wrong sides together* and stitch a ⅜"-wide seam, not the standard ⅝". Trim both seam allowances to a scant ¼".

269

2. Press to set the stitches and press the seam open. Don't skip this step, as it will make the following steps easier.

3. Fold the pieces, right sides facing with the first seamline precisely at the edge and press. Stitch ¼" from the edge. Press the seam to one side.

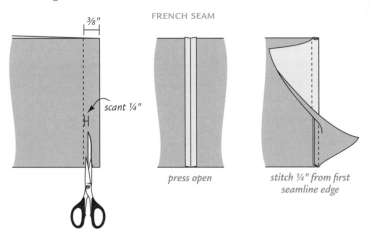

FRENCH SEAM

3/8"

scant ¼"

press open

stitch ¼" from first seamline edge

---

# Q What is a flat-fell seam and why would I use it?

A This seam is stitched twice, creating a strong seam with no exposed raw edges. It's the classic seam for jeans but is also appropriate for completely reversible garments, unlined coats and jackets, and sportswear items. The hallmark of success is a flat seamline on the wrong side and an even-width, topstitched welt on the right side.

# Q How do you make a flat-fell seam?

A Accurate stitching and careful pressing are essential when following these steps:

1. Place the pieces *wrong sides together* and stitch a standard ⅝"-wide seam. Press the seam open. Trim one of the seam allowances to a scant ¼" wide.

2. Turn under and press ¼" at the raw edge of the wider seam allowance. Turn the wider seam allowance over the narrow one and press so the resulting seam is ⅜" wide. Pin or baste and stitch close to the pressed edge.

FLAT-FELL SEAM

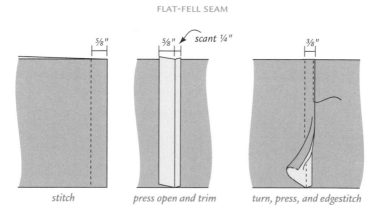

stitch     press open and trim     turn, press, and edgestitch

**Q** My jeans have seams that look like flat-fell seams on the right side, but the raw edges are visible on the inside. What seam is that?

**A** It's a mock flat-fell seam, a fast and easy substitute for a true flat-fell seam.

1. Sew the seam with *right sides facing*, press the stitching to set the stitches, press open, and then press *both* seam allowances to one side (A). On fabrics that ravel, serge or zigzag the raw edges together, or pink them. On heavy fabrics, trim the underlying seam allowance to ¼" to eliminate bulk (B).

2. On the right side of the project, use the edgestitching foot to stitch close to the seamline through all layers (C). Switch to the regular presser foot and use the edge of the foot as your guide for straight topstitching parallel to and ¼" to ⅜" from the first stitching.

MOCK FLAT-FELL SEAM

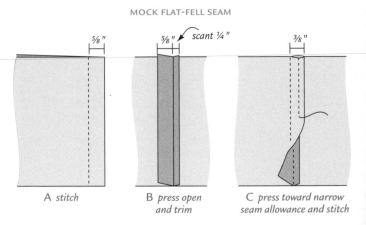

A *stitch*

B *press open and trim*

C *press toward narrow seam allowance and stitch*

## COMMON SERGER SEAMS

| Type of Seam | Best Used for |
|---|---|
| 3-thread overlock 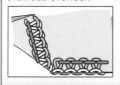 | Construction seams in stretchy knits; seam finish on raw edges of pressed-open plain seams |
| 4-thread overlock 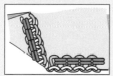 | Construction seams in knits and wovens; best choice for durable seams in sports-, mens-, and childrenswear |
| Flatlock (2- or 3-thread)  | Construction seams in stretchy knits (activewear and lingerie); visible on outside of garment; has loops on one side, "ladders" on reverse |
| Rolled edge (2-thread) 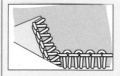 | Very narrow seams on sheer fabrics for narrow fine-line finish (in place of French seam) |

*Note: Some sergers are capable of other seams that incorporate a chainstitch with the overlock stitch, which creates a very stable, nonstretchy seam.*

## ZIGZAG OPTIONS

| Type of Zigzag | Best Used for |
|---|---|
| Simple zigzag | Finish on single or double seam-allowance layers; satin stitching (*see page 115*); gathering over cord (*see page 331*) |
| Multistitch zigzag | Same as for simple zigzag; narrow the stitch width to control fabric fraying |
| Basic overlock (over-edge) or substitute blindstitch (*see page 312*) | Stretch stitch for lightweight knits and fine wovens; overcast raw edges with point of the zigzag at or near seam-allowance edge; attach elastic (*see page 337*) |
| Double overlock | Overcasting knits and wovens; stitching and finishing ¼"-wide seam allowances |
| Super stretch | Seaming ¼"-wide seams on super-stretch (e.g., swimwear) fabrics; applying raw-edge appliqués; decorative stitching |

Q **Are there any machine stitches that finish seam edges like a serger does?**

A Zigzagging is a very common edge-finishing stitch, along with the serpentine multistitch zigzag. Most zigzag machines offer one or more "stretch" stitches that create seams similar to overlocked serger seams. Some were designed specifically for knit sewing, but you can also use them to control raveling on single seam layers of wovens for a nonravel seam finish. Choose from those shown in the Zigzag Options on the previous page, and consult your machine manual for the ideal stitch settings. Test on scraps first. Twice-stitched seams like those shown for sewing on knits (*see page 203*) are also a good substitute for serged seams.

## Special Seaming Challenges

Sewing curved seams and adding piping between seam allowances offer special sewing challenges.

**Q** My pattern has curved seamlines. Are there any special handling techniques?

**A** Fitting the convex and concave pieces of a curved seam together smoothly, without puckers or pleats, takes patience and preparation.

1. Use a shorter-than-normal stitch length (1.25 to 1.5 mm or 16 to 20 spi) to staystitch the concave section a scant ⅝" from the raw edges to reinforce the seamline. Clip to the stitches every ¼" to ½" between the notches that were marked on the pattern (the deeper the curve, the closer the clips should be).

2. Place the convex and concave curved pieces together with right sides facing and notches matching. Spread the clipped edge to match the unclipped edge, adding more clips if necessary, so it is easy to match the two

raw edges precisely. Pin. With the clipped side facing you, stitch along the seamline, just **inside** the reinforcement stitches in the seam allowance.

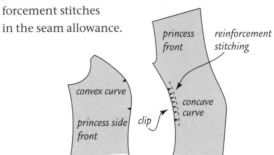

3. Press the curved area of the seam open over a pressing ham (*see page 37*), notching out fullness in the seam allowance if needed to make it lie flat. Finish the seam edges as desired. On fabrics that ravel, you may want to treat the clipped edges with a tiny amount of liquid seam sealant.

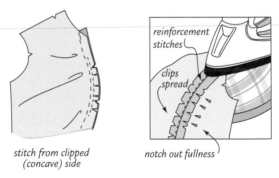

*stitch from clipped (concave) side*

*notch out fullness*

PRESS OPEN OVER HAM

**CONVEX OR CONCAVE?**

Which is which? If you cup your fingers, you create a "cave" inside your fingers and palm; that's a concave curve. The outside curve of your other cupped hand is a convex curve that fits into the cave. Just remember the concave and the rest is easy!

**Q** What about stitching two curved layers together that are the same shape?

**A** Shorten the stitch length to 1.25 to 1.5 mm (16 to 20 spi). For accuracy, guide the cut edge along the seam guide on the needle plate and stitch slowly, watching the edge as you guide it. *To avoid distortion, never stretch a curved seam edge while you stitch.* On extreme curves, you may need to stitch a few stitches, stop, lift the foot, adjust the edge with the seam guide, and then continue in this start-stop-adjust fashion.

*SEE ALSO: Enclosed Seams, pages 282–286.*

**Q** How do I add piping or cording to a seam?

**A** Both piping and cording have a flange to include in a seam allowance. They are common in home-decor items but are also a nice touch at the edge of a collar or around a simple neckline, tucked into a faced edge. Either purchase ready-made or make your own. To add it to a seam, follow these steps:

1. Pin- or hand-baste the piping to the seam allowance of one layer of the seam, with the piping seamline along the project seamline. The outer edges of the piping fabric or the cording flange may not be aligned with the project's cut edges. *Do not stretch* the piping or the fabric.

2. Adjust the zipper foot to the right of the needle; if possible, adjust the needle position so it will stitch just inside and to the left of the stitching that holds the piping materials together. Use a contrasting thread in the bobbin and machine-baste the piping in place. Don't catch the cord in the stitching.

3. With right sides facing and the piping basting stitches facing you, pin and stitch the two layers together. Stitch just inside the basting. It may feel like you are "crowding" the cord while you stitch, but doing this ensures that the basting won't show on the right side of the finished seam. It's not necessary to remove the piping basting.

4. Trim and grade (*see pages 282–283*) as needed and press lightly.

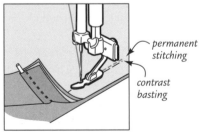

*permanent stitching*

*contrast basting*

*adding piping or cording*

**Q** **Are there any special tricks for applying piping around curves and corners?**

**A** Clipping the piping seam allowance will help you to gently ease the piping around the curve as you baste it in place in the seam allowance. Shorten the stitch length for smoother stitching. Use the normal stitch length when stitching in straight lines. On corners, pin-baste the piping to the first edge and stitch to within an inch of the corner. Adjust the piping down to the corner, and clip the seam allowance almost to the piping stitching; pin-baste the remainder of the piping in place. Use a shorter stitch for the 1" before and past the clipped corner, and then return to normal to complete the stitching.

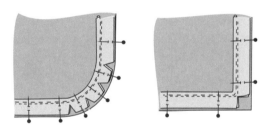

*clip piping seam allowance to ease around curves and corners*

---

**Q** **How do you neatly join piping ends when the piping encircles the edge of a sleeve or a pillow?**

**A** Leave at least 1½" of the piping free at the beginning. Stitch around the perimeter, then near the place where you started, stop and undo the piping stitches. Cut the cord inside to butt up to the first end. Leave at least 1" of fabric beyond the cut end to turn under and over the butted ends. Trim the turn-under to ¼". Complete the stitching.

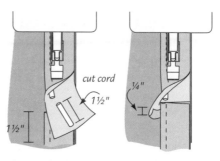

*butt cord ends and turn under excess fabric*

---

Q How do I match intersecting seams and eliminate bulk where seams cross, such as at the waistline, shoulder, or underarm?

A Press and finish seam edges before you sew the two garment sections together. Use a fine needle to hold them securely with seamlines perfectly aligned. *If the seam allowances were pressed to one side,* adjust so the two allowances lie in opposite directions to nest together for a perfect match and eliminate a distracting and thick bump. *If seams were pressed open,* place a fine pin or needle pin through all layers at the outer edges of the seam allowances, to keep them from getting pushed out of place while stitching. After stitching, reduce bulk by clipping the seam allowances at an angle from the

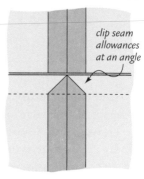

*intersecting seams*

seam edge to the stitching line. Do this whether the crossing seam will be pressed open, pressed toward the garment in one direction, or enclosed inside a facing.

- - - - - - - - - - - - - - - - - - - - - - - -

Q **The machine jams when I start stitching, and I end up with a messy bunch of stitches on the underside of my seam. What's wrong?**

A Those birds' nests are a real plague and often happen because the feed dogs don't have much to grab onto at the beginning of a seam. Check the threading and make sure the bobbin thread is engaged in the tension mechanism. When you start a seam, pull enough top and bobbin thread behind the presser foot to grasp firmly. As you begin to stitch, hold onto them to give the feed dogs a bit of traction.

For lightweight fabrics, change to a straight-stitch throat plate (*see pages 16–17*). If you don't have a straight-stitch plate, consider investing in one. For a quick fix, place two layers of Scotch Magic Tape or masking tape over the zigzag hole and run an unthreaded needle up and down to pierce a hole in it. Clean any adhesive residue on the needle with rubbing alcohol. Remove the tape when you're ready to zigzag.

SEE ALSO: *Lead On!, page 97.*

Q **Is there an easy way to rip out machine stitches without damaging the fabric?**

A On the bobbin-thread side of the seam, use a sharp seam ripper or small, sharp scissors to lift and snip every fifth or sixth stitch along the seam. Flip the piece over and pull the thread. It should lift away easily in one piece, leaving only small thread tufts on the reverse to remove. Run a piece of masking tape over the seamline to pick up these tufts, or use a lint roller, a small foam paintbrush, or a pink pencil eraser to whisk them away. There are other ways to unstitch a seam, but I find this method the fastest, easiest, and safest.

## Enclosed Seams

Enclosed seams require careful sewing and turning so that the seamline rolls slightly to the inside, rather than to the outside, of the garment. Trimming and grading, clipping, notching, and careful pressing are essential for smooth finished edges that lie flat. You'll use these techniques to apply facings at the neckline and armhole edges of sleeveless garments, as well as when attaching facings to waistlines or creating cuffs, collars, and pocket flaps.

**Q** **What is trimming and grading?**

**A** Trimming and grading removes some of the seam allowance in enclosed edges at necklines and armholes, and on collars, cuffs, and pockets. To trim an enclosed seam, cut away at least half of a ⅝" seam allowance. To grade an enclosed seam, trim the seam and then trim the layers to staggered widths, with the seam allowance that lies closest to the garment left *slightly wider* than the remaining layers; this provides a bevel so the edges don't imprint or make a visible ledge on the right side. For a double-layer seam, trim to ¼" and ⅛".

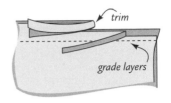

Don't worry about raveling on the trimmed seams. The edges will be enclosed, understitched (*see question on pages 284–285*), and perhaps topstitched. Before turning and pressing, clip inward (concave) curves, spacing them ¼" apart in highly curved sections, farther apart in flatter areas of the curve. Also trim away excess fabric at points and corners.

---

Q **How do I turn a curved enclosed edge so it is smooth and free of lumps?**

A On concave neckline and armhole curves, clip to the stitching line every ¼" or so to help the seam lie flat when you turn the facing inside. On outward curves of a collar, notch out V-shaped sections along trimmed and graded seam

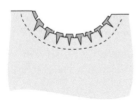

*clip inside (concave) curves*

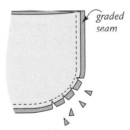

*notch out fullness on outside (convex) curves*

283

allowances, so the excess fabric can't double up on itself when turned (which would create a lumpy finish with "pokey" edges). Use pinking shears to make quick work of notching trimmed seams. *Remember:* Clip inward curves and notch outward curves.

---

**Q** I'm afraid to clip and notch enclosed seams on loosely woven fabrics. Any advice?

**A** Stagger clips and notches to avoid weakening the seam. Notch or clip only one layer, then move ¼" away and repeat on the other layer of the seam.

---

**Q** How do I prevent finished facings and the faced edges of collars and cuffs from rolling to the outside along the pressed edge?

**A** Understitch enclosed seams to attach the seam layers to the facing (or the lining), making it easy to press a flat edge. The stacked-and-stitched layers weight the facing so it turns naturally to the inside, creating a soft roll of the fashion fabric so the facing doesn't show along the edge. Here's how to understitch:

1. Stitch the seam, press flat along the stitching to set the stitches, and then trim, grade, and clip (or notch outward curves along) the seam.
2. With the seamline under the presser foot and the facing to the right, stitch through all layers close to the

facing's seam edge. Adjust the needle position or use your edgestitching foot for better control.

3. Use your fingers to spread the layers along the seam-line as you sew, to make sure the facing is completely flat. Stop periodically to make sure the seam allowance layers are under the facing.

4. After understitching, turn the facing to the inside and press. The understitching makes the pressing struggle-free!

*Note:* On collars with square corners or sharp points, you will only be able to stitch partway into the point along each of the three edges.

seam stitching

under-stitching

understitching

facing

---

Q How do I understitch a blouse or jacket with turn-back lapels?

A Understitch on the garment side above the point where the lapel turns onto the garment (lapel roll) and on the facing side below the point of the roll. Secure the threads at the point of the roll by drawing them between the layers inside the facing, and tie off.

Q **How do I stitch an enclosed seam in a pillow cover so the pillow corners will be square and filled out?**

A On the wrong side of one pillow cover, chalk-mark the intersecting seamlines at each corner. Pin the two pieces together and stitch; when you are within a few inches of the seam intersection, begin tapering inside the line. Pivot and reverse the tapering. For a really plump pillow, use a pillow form slightly larger than the finished pillow cover or stitch wider seams when sewing the pieces together. You can also tuck bits of polyester fiberfill into pillow corners to help plump them out.

## Collars

Collars require the support of interfacing, plus trimming, grading, clipping, and notching as described in the previous section. Here you'll find a few additional tips for preparing collars. Attach them to the garment neckline and finish as directed in your pattern guide sheet.

Q **What type of interfacing should I use in a collar?**

A Interface the upper collar *and* the undercollar layer with fusible interfacing, if possible (although not on sheer or show-through fabrics). When *both* layers are interfaced, they can be handled the same way and are less likely to stretch out of shape during sewing. On light- and medium-weight fabrics, I use a lightweight fusible interfacing on both so they have the same hand and handling. On medium- and heavyweight fabrics, I use a medium-weight interfacing on the upper collar and a softer interfacing on the undercollar (also called the collar facing in some patterns).

- - - - - - - - - - - - - - - - - - - - - - - - - - - - - - - - - -

**Q** How do I make sure my collars are smooth, with flat outer edges and points (or curves) that lie flat?

**A** After applying the interfacing, trim a scant ⅛" from the outer edges of the undercollar, tapering to nothing at the collar's outer edge as shown. This helps it roll to the underside on all three enclosed edges. When you pin the smaller undercollar to the upper collar, gently force the raw edges to match. Stitch with the undercollar facing you so the feed dogs help ease the upper collar to the slightly smaller undercollar. Trim, grade, clip, and turn as described on page 282. Understitch (*see question on page 284*) *before* you turn the collar right side out and press. Otherwise, press the seams open on a point presser

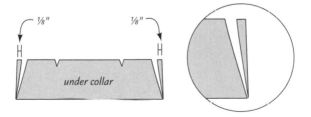

(*see page 40*) to make it easier to turn and press, and so the undercollar doesn't roll out at the edge.

If your pattern provides separate pattern pieces for the upper- and undercollars, compare them. You may find that the undercollar is already a bit smaller. However, for heavier fabrics, it's a good idea to trim the undercollar as described on the previous page.

- - - - - - - - - - - - - - - - - - - - - - - - - - - - - - - - -

**Q** I always end up with lumpy points and corners that don't look square on the finished collar. What to do?

**A** Don't pivot sharply when stitching around the point. To make room for the trimmed seam allowances:

1. Mark the seam intersections where you would pivot. Stitch toward the point, stopping ½" from the intersection with the needle down.

2. Shorten the stitch length a bit and continue stitching, stopping shy of the seam intersection. With the needle in the fabric, raise the foot, pivot halfway, lower the foot and take a stitch or two across the point to the next seamline. Stop, pivot, and stitch the next ½". Return to the normal stitch length and continue to within ½" of the next corner. Repeat with the second point or corner.

two small
stitches

Carefully trim to remove as much of the seam allowance as possible. On very sharp points, trim as close as possible to the stitches and taper the trimming on either side of the point. Trim far enough into the seam on each side of the point, so the two seam allowances don't overlap inside and create a lumpy, knobby point when turned. Turn right side out and press.

---

**Q How do I press an enclosed seam in a collar (or cuff)?**

**A** For a smooth and easy turn, press the seam open after trimming and clipping it (*see the questions about trimming and clipping on pages 282–283*). This  may seem strange, but it makes turning the enclosed edge (right along the stitching) so much easier. Use a point presser to reach into the point or corner (*see page 40*). For rounded edges, place the piece on the ironing board and use the point of the iron and your fingers to coax open one seam allowance and press.

**Q** How do I turn sharp points in collars without making a hole in them?

**A** Don't use scissors or anything else with a sharp point. Invest in an inexpensive bamboo point turner. You can use the curved end of it to help shape enclosed curves, too. Other alternatives include a wooden bamboo skewer, filed to a dull point with an emery board, or a chopstick.

- - - - - - - - - - - - - - - - - - - - - - - - - - - - -

**Q** How can I keep collar points from curling away from my shirt?

**A** First, make sure you've followed the directions on pages 287–288 for trimming the undercollar a bit smaller. In addition, you can weight the points by adding a small triangular patch of lightweight fusible interfacing to each point on the upper collar before you sew the upper collar to the undercollar.

## Face It or Bind It

Facings finish the shaped raw edges of armholes and necklines, as well as opening edges on jackets, coats, shirts, and blouses. They are cut as separate pieces and are shaped like the garment edge. On straight-grain edges, such as the front opening edges of a jacket with a jewel neckline, a facing is often cut as an extension to the pattern piece. Neckline facings are typically used to hide raw edges on a collar. In some cases, you can substitute a bias binding for a facing, adding a neat designer finish and detail around the neck and/or armholes.

**Q** If the facing is a separate piece, how do I prepare and attach it to the garment?

**A** Interfacing is essential to control stretch in the garment and the facing edges. Apply a fusible interfacing of the appropriate type and weight to the wrong side of the facing piece(s). (*See pages 236–238.*) If you prefer a sew-in interfacing, attach it to the garment (*see page 239*) before applying the facings. To attach a facing to a closed neckline (as in a tank top) or armhole, follow the steps below. *Note:* Apply interfacing and finish the edges of cut-in-one facings as described here for separate facings. Follow your pattern directions for folding and stitching them in place.

1. Staystitch (*see pages 104–105*) the garment edges that will be faced.

2. Stitch the front and back facing pieces together at the shoulder seams (and underarm seams for armholes), press open, and trim the seams to ¼". Finish the outer unnotched edge of the facing, choosing from finishes listed in Edgy Options, on page 294.

3. With right sides facing and seam allowances matching, pin and stitch the facing to the edge. Press the stitching to set the stitches.

4. Trim, grade, and clip the seam and then understitch. (*See the question on enclosed seams on page 282.*) Turn the facing to the inside and press. Tack the facing edges in place at the seam allowances.

**Q** How should I tack facings in place?

**A** You can use a few whipstitches (A) or a cross-stitch (B) to tack the edges to the seam allowances. I prefer to stitch-in-the-ditch (C) whenever possible. To do so:

1. Turn facings to the inside and pin in place.
2. On the outside, begin stitching at the faced edge in the seamline; sew to within ½" of the inside edge of the facing.
3. Stitch slowly, taking care not to jump the ditch into the garment itself. Use shorter-than-normal stitches on light-weight fabrics to hide the stitches better (C).

Topstitching also keeps facings in place — if it is appropriate for the project.

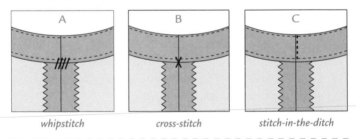

*whipstitch*                    *cross-stitch*                    *stitch-in-the-ditch*

**Q** How do I substitute a bound edge for facings on the neckline and armholes of a simple shell blouse or tank top?

**A** Cut out the front and back pieces, following the pattern tissue. *Also cut the facings* to support the neckline shape and keep it from stretching. Apply a lightweight fusible inter-facing to the wrong side of the facings and then stitch them together at the shoulder seams, trim the seam allowances to ¼", and press open.

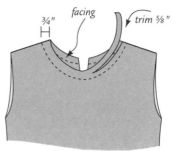

1. Stitch and press the garment shoulder seams and place the facing on the garment *with wrong sides facing* and raw edges even. Pin. Accurately machine-stitch ¾" from the raw edges. Trim ⅛" from the stitching to remove the entire seam allowance.

2. Decide how wide you want the binding; ¼" is standard. Multiply by 10 to determine the cut width for the binding strip. Cut a true-bias strip (*see pages 265–266*) of this width, making it long enough to fit around the neckline if possible; seaming bias strips for a bound neckline is *not* recommended because you want the finished binding to be smooth and seam-free.

3. With wrong sides facing and raw edges even, fold the binding strip in half lengthwise. Press carefully to avoid stretching. Using rotary cutting tools, carefully trim the folded strip to measure 4 times the desired finished binding width. For ¼" finished binding, that would be 1". For best results, hand-baste the layers together ¼" from the raw edges.

4. Pin-baste the binding to the neckline edge with raw edges even, stretching the binding slightly at the inside (or concave) curves (*see page 277*) to make it fit. Stitch ¼" (or other

desired finished width) from the raw edges. Press to set the stitches.

5. Turn the binding toward the seam allowance and then to the inside over the edge. The folded edge should sit just past the stitching line on the

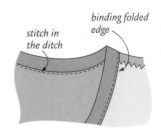

stitch in the ditch

binding folded edge

---

### EDGY OPTIONS

To finish facing inner edges, choose from these options:

* **Stitch and pink** the outer edge of fabrics that won't ravel or aren't prone to excessive raveling. Pinking helps "blur" the edge so it doesn't show from the right side.
* **Clean-finish** by turning under and pressing ¼" along the outer edge, then edgestitching in place.
* **Bind the edge** (hems, too) using the Hong Kong finish (*see page 264*) for a professional ravel-free finish, especially nice on unlined jackets. This finish is bulkier than the others; use on medium to heavy fabrics.
* **Use a serger.** With a 3-thread medium-width and length overlock stitch, serge from the right side. For easier serging, leave one seam open on armhole and neckline facings. Stitch the open seam after serge-finishing the edge.

inside. Pin in place, making sure the binding is an even width on the right side. Press lightly and hand-baste in place. With a zipper foot adjusted to the left of the needle, stitch-in-the-ditch of the seam (*see page 112*) on the right side to secure the binding on the inside.

*Note:* For less bulk when binding a knit garment, use a single-layer strip, cut 4 or 5 times the desired finished width. Finish one edge with overlocking or a pink-and-stitch finish (*see pages 261–262*). Apply as directed earlier, disregarding step 3.

- - - - - - - - - - - - - - - - - - - - - - - - - - - - - - -

Q How do I prevent faced V- and wrap-front necklines from stretching and gaping?

A This happens due to the bias in the cut edge; it can get stretched during stitching. You can stabilize the edge and make it hug your body to eliminate gaping with a simple taping procedure *before* you attach the facing:

1. After staystitching (*see pages 104–105*), cut two lengths of preshrunk woven seam or twill tape 1½" longer than the stitching line on the pattern from the shoulder edge to the point of the V. On the wrong side, center one piece over the stitching line with one end even with the cut shoulder edge and the excess extending past the point (A). Repeat with the other piece (*see illustration on next page*).

2. Draw each tape at least ⅛" past the cut shoulder edge (up to ½" for a very full bustline). Pin at the shoulder, and then pin the remainder of the tape in place, evenly distributing the ease above the point (B). If you're unsure of the

amount to adjust for your figure, pin the front to the back at the shoulders and try it on. Adjust the amount of tape draw-up if necessary.

3. Stitch ½" from the raw edge, beginning at the point of the V. Before sewing the shoulder seams, place the front facing in place on the garment, then trim the facing shoulder edge so it matches the garment shoulder edges.

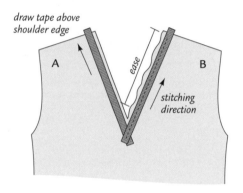

*draw tape above shoulder edge*

A

*ease*

B

*stitching direction*

---

**Q** My pattern calls for a facing, but my fabric is sheer and I don't want the facing to show through. What can I do?

**A** For sheer and semisheer fabrics and openwork fabrics, such as lace, try cutting the facing from a solid-color sheer fabric. Test the color beneath the sheer. Often a skin-tone sheer is a good choice. For interfacing, try skin-tone tulle or silk organza instead.

# CHAPTER EIGHT

# Hems and Hem-Edge Finishes

As with seams, the raw edges on hems require a ravel-free finish for long wear and a neat finished appearance inside. Unless you want the hemline or hem stitching to show as a decorative effect, the finished hem should be almost invisible from the right side. Hems can be sewn by hand or machine.

# Selecting the Right Finishing Method

Examining ready-to-wear clothing for hemming techniques can provide quick guidelines for choosing hems and finishes appropriate for your sewing projects. Choose from a variety of hand-sewn and machine-stitched hem techniques, discussed in the answers that follow.

- - - - - - - - - - - - - - - - - - - - - - - - - - - - - - - -

**Q** **What's best? A hand-sewn hem or a machine-stitched one?**

**A** The old home-sewing standard of hemming exclusively by hand has gone by the wayside. That doesn't mean you won't do any hand hemming, however. Today's sewers often opt for machine finishes wherever possible, to save time and create garments with finishes that mimic readymade clothing (to avoid a "homemade" look).

It's a good time investment to add some hemming stitches to your arsenal of hand-sewing stitches (*see* Common Hem-Edge Finishes *on pages 302–305*). You'll need them for some fabrics and designs. For example, a wide machine-stitched hem on a velvet sheath would create a bulky finish with an obvious hemline on the outside — definitely not in keeping with the garment's dressy look. A hand-sewn hem, or one done with a carefully adjusted machine blind hem, would be a better choice. Hemming yards and yards of chiffon by hand would be a lovely finish but would require lots of time. Doing a rolled edge on the serger or by machine is faster and easier.

# Q What are the basic steps to follow when hemming?

A First, decide on the appropriate hem and hem-edge finishing methods for the style and the fabric — often the same seam-finishing method you've used throughout the garment. (*See pages 261–264.*)

1. Determine the desired finished length and mark the hem fold line. The width on the pattern is only a guideline; change it as needed for your project and preferences. Mark the hemline so it is the same distance and parallel to the floor all around (except on asymmetrical designs). Decide on the width of the hem (*see* Hem-Width Guidelines *on page 308*). Turn up the hem allowance and press. Trim any excess hem allowance to the width required for the chosen hemming method.

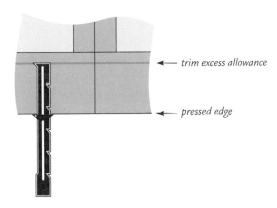

← *trim excess allowance*

← *pressed edge*

2. Finish the hem's raw edge, choosing from the basic seam finishes: pinked; pinked-and-stitched; serged or zigzag finishing; clean finished; bound (*see pages 261–263*).

3. Turn and press the hem allowance to the inside and sew in place, using the chosen hand-sewing or machine-stitching method.

4. Press the completed hem from the inside and from the outside as needed, taking care not to make a hem-edge imprint on the right side. Use a press cloth if necessary to protect the fabric.

------------------------------------------------------------

Q How do I make sure the hemline is even all around on skirts, dresses, coats, and pants?

A Put on the undergarments and the shoes you plan to wear; both affect the hemline. If the garment is bias-cut or very flared, allow it to hang at least 24 hours before marking the hem. (Fold finished bias-cut skirts and dresses to prevent long-term stretching).

* **For pants,** turn up the suggested hem allowance all around and pin in place. Try on and adjust as needed before pressing and trimming the hem allowance.

* **For other garments,** have someone use a hem marker to place pins all the way around at the desired finished length.

**Q** **How do I determine the best skirt/dress length for my figure?**

**A** A good, safe length for a straight skirt on most figures is in the "shadow of the knee" — the spot where the calf curves in toward the back of the knee. With fuller styles and softer fabrics, a skirt can be slightly longer or shorter and still be flattering. Find your three best lengths: near the knee, in the calf area, and near the ankle. If you wear a variety of heel heights, determine the best lengths with each one. Coats should be hemmed at least 1" to 2" longer than skirts and dresses.

1. Stand in front of a full-length mirror, wearing shoes with the average heel height you wear most often. Hold a piece of fabric in front of you, draped to the floor.

2. Gradually raise the fabric to several different locations on your leg and notice that as you raise the hemline up and down, your leg will look thicker or thinner at different spots. Find the spot in each of the three areas (knee, calf, ankle) where the fabric doesn't hit the fullest part. Measure and make note of these lengths in your sewing notebook (*see page 48*) so you can make sure your pattern pieces are of sufficient length when doing future pattern adjustments before cutting.

---

SEE ALSO: *Fitting Adjustments, pages 143–155.*

## COMMON HEM-EDGE FINISHES

Hem-edge finishes provide an anchor for the permanent hand or machine stitches that will hold the hem in place; they also stop

| Edge Finish | | | Fabrics |
|---|---|---|---|
| Turned-and-stitched | | | For crisp sheers and most lightweight fabrics |
| Pinked-and stitched | | | Best for fabrics that ravel little or not at all, including knits of all weights |
| Overlocked (3-thread serger) | | | All fabric weights and types |
| Zigzagged | | | Woven fabrics that may ravel |

the fabric from raveling. Check the chart below for illustrations
and pertinent information on finishing hem edges.

| Basic How-To |
| --- |
| Turn under ¼" at raw edge. (Machine-stitch for a clean-finished seam if desired; see pages 261–263). Turn under remaining hem allowance. Press and pin. Machine edgestitch in place or hem by hand with invisible slipstitch (*see page 314*). Also see the question on shirttail hems, page 309. |
| Stitch ⅜" from hem allowance raw edge, then pink the raw edge. Machine-topstitch along stitching or blindstitch between layers, or use catchstitch or blindstitch (*see pages 314–315*). |
| Use silk, rayon, or cotton embroidery thread in the loopers so stitches are less likely to imprint on the right side of lightweight and hard-surfaced fabrics. Topstitch or hand-sew the hem in place with a blindstitch (*see page 315*). |
| Use a wide, medium-length zigzag to stitch close to (but not over) the edge. Trim close to stitching if needed. Machine topstitch or hand-sew in place with a blindstitch (*see page 315*). |

| Edge Finish | | Fabric |
|---|---|---|
| Bound | | Medium- and heavy-weight fabrics |
| Serged narrow rolled edge | | Lightweight and sheer fabrics, such as chiffon; use woolly nylon thread in the lower looper to help stubborn fabrics roll |
| Seam tape (polyester woven, not bias tape) | | Fabrics that ravel; not for sheers |
| Hand overcast | | Fabrics that ravel; use if sewing machine or serger is not available for finishing the edge using one of the other methods |

Use Hong Kong seam finish (*see page 264*), or bind the edge with ready-made bias tape or nylon tricot binding (*see page 269*). Top-stitch in place just below the binding seamline or use a hand hemming stitch between the layers.

Adjust the serger for the rolled-edge stitch with lightweight thread (rayon or cotton embroidery thread) in the needle and upper looper. Trim away excess hem allowance at the desired finished length. Allow the knife to trim a thread or two only along the trimmed edge as you serge. On very sheer fabrics, use a 2-thread rolled edge for a lighter, more supple edge.

Machine-baste ¼" from the upper raw edge of the hem allowance. Place seam-tape edge along the stitching and machine-stitch in place. Then hand sew the seam-tape edge in place, or stitch between the layers, as shown at left, for a bound hem.

Hand stitch over the raw edge; use a hand-sewn tailor's hem to secure the hem allowance to the garment. (*See also overcasting directions on page 263.*)

**Q** **Is there a standard best length for pants, trousers, slacks, culottes, and jeans?**

**A** Fashion and heel height dictate the right length for the most flattering look. Below are a few style guidelines. With the exception of tapered pants, try to make the legs long enough to cover the top of the shoe down to the heel; otherwise, the pants will look too short.

* Narrow, tapered pant legs must be a length that will clear the top of the foot. Make them as long as possible without wrinkles on the top of the foot.

* Straight-leg pants and trouser styles should touch, if not "break" slightly, on the top front of the shoe.

* Wide legs should go almost all the way to the floor; otherwise, they appear too short.

* Shorts, cropped pants, and culottes should hit your leg in an attractive location, as discussed in the guidelines for skirt hems in the previous question.

*tapered leg*  *straight leg*  *full leg*

slight "break"

306

**Q** How do I determine how wide the finished hem should be?

**A** The suggested hem allowance is usually designated on the pattern pieces and/or in the pattern guide sheet. Consider fabric weight, the available length for the hem, and your sewing preferences. In addition to the information in the chart on page 308, consider the following:

* The straighter the edge, the wider the hem allowance can be. The more it curves, the narrower it should be.

* Very full skirts in soft or sheer fabrics can take a wider hem (unless the edge is curved); extra weight in the hem helps the skirt hang better.

* Narrow hems are best for light- to medium-weight fabrics.

* Use a narrow, machine-stitched hem to minimize stretching and sagging on soft and stretchy knits. (*See the questions on knit hems on pages 206–208.*)

- - - - - - - - - - - - - - - - - - - - - - - - - - - - - - - -

**Q** What are the best hem finishes for home-decor items such as napkins and tablecloths or curtains and draperies?

**A** It's best to hem napkins and tablecloths with a rolled-edge serger hem or a narrow double hem. (*See the next question on shirttail hems.*)

Hem unlined curtains and draperies with double hems, to weight them so they hang straight. Side hems on draperies are usually cut 2" to 3" wide and finish to 1" or 1½". Bottom hems in medium- and heavyweight fabrics are cut 6" wide, and finish to 3". They can finish to 4" or even 6" on sheers.

For the best finish, hem the sides first and then the bottom edge. To make a double hem, turn and press the total hem allowance, then turn the raw edge in to meet the fold, and press. Machine-stitch close to the inner folded edge using an edgestitching foot if available; you can also use the blind-hem stitch and presser foot to stitch the hem (*see page 312*). Side hems in lined draperies are single layer and are sewn to the lining panels and topstitched in place.

## HEM-WIDTH GUIDELINES

| Garment/Silhouette | Recommended Width |
| --- | --- |
| Straight skirts/dresses | 1½"–2" |
| Full skirts/dresses, dresses with straight-cut bottom edge, culottes | 2"–4" for turned and stitched; depends on fabric weight and desired effect |
| Flared skirts and dresses (A-line shapes; gored) | 1½"–2" |
| Bias-cut skirts | Narrow (⅛"–⅜") hem |
| Coats | 2"–3" |
| Pants, trousers, shorts | 1½" |
| Narrow-legged pants | 1" at most; may be faced instead |
| Jeans | Narrow double-turned hem |

## Q What is a shirttail hem? How do I make one?

A A shirttail hem is a very narrow hem used to finish shirts, as well as napkins, tablecloths, and other home-decor items. Use a serger or make a twice-turned hem by machine:

**Serger shirttail hem.** Serge-finish the raw edge using a medium to wide, medium-length 3-thread overlock stitch. Turn the serged edge up along the needle thread and topstitch in place. This is a quick-and-easy hem with less bulk than a twice-turned hem.

**Machine shirttail hem.** If necessary, trim the hem allowance to ⅝". Machine-baste ⅝" from the cut edge and use the basting as a guide to turn and press the allowance to the inside. Turn the raw edge in to meet the fold and press. Stitch close to the inner edge, using an edgestitching foot if available. For a smooth turn on curved shirttail hems, use a pin to lift and pull the basting stitches to draw up the excess fullness in the curves.

You can also purchase a special hemmer presser foot that will roll and stitch the hem in one operation. It takes a little practice to get the hem started into the foot.

*serger shirttail hem*

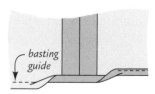

*machine shirttail hem*

309

Q I don't have a serger to make a rolled hem. Is there an alternative to hand hemming?

A Use a very narrow machine hem to mimic the serger rolled edge. Determine the desired length on the garment and trim any excess hem allowance, leaving only ⅝" for the hem.

1. On seams that will be crossed by the hem fold, trim the ends at an angle to eliminate bulk. Machine-stitch ½" from the trimmed edge. Turn under and press the hem allowance; on curved edges, clip the raw edge down to the stitching, if necessary, to facilitate turning.

2. Adjust the needle position to the right so that the inner edge of the right-hand toe of the presser foot is aligned with the hem edge. With the fabric right side up, stitch close to the folded edge. On the wrong side, trim the hem allowance close to the stitching.

3. With the garment *wrong side up*, turn the stitched-and-trimmed edge and stitch again on top of the first stitching. Press as needed from the wrong side.

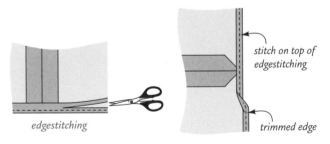

*edgestitching*

stitch on top of
edgestitching

*trimmed edge*

**Q** How do I make a wider topstitched hem on pants and skirts?

**A** Use a topstitched hem for straight, not curved, hems; it's often used on knits. Machine-stitched hems may have one or two rows of stitching.

1. Trim the hem allowance if needed, allowing an extra ½" for turn-under on woven fabrics if you don't have a serger.

2. **For woven fabrics:** Serge-finish the raw edge, or turn under and press ½" along the raw edge. Turn up the hem, press, and pin in place. **For knits:** Serge-finish the edge, or pink, turn, and press the hem allowance.

3. Stitch close to the inner turned edge or just inside the inner edge of the serging. On sportier styles, stitch ¼" from the first stitching in the hem allowance. To topstitch the hem with a twin needle (*see page 57*), machine-baste the hem in place with a contrasting thread in the bobbin and then stitch with the twin needle from the right side with the left-hand needle just to the right of the machine basting.

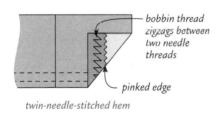

bobbin thread zigzags between two needle threads

pinked edge

*twin-needle-stitched hem*

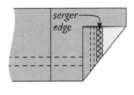

serger edge

*parallel rows of topstitching*

# Q How do I make a blind hem by machine that doesn't show on the right side?

A After preparing the hem allowance, including finishing the upper edge as desired, hand- or machine-baste the hem to the garment ¼" from the hem-allowance edge or just below the edge-finish stitching. (Choose the blindstitch for woven fabrics or the stretch blindstitch for knits, if these are available on your machine.) Use thread to match the fabric for the most invisible stitching, or try invisible monofilament thread (*see page 71*). To adjust the blindstitch for your fabric, prepare a 6"- to 10"-long hem mock-up and follow the hemming procedure outlined below:

1. Select and adjust the blindstitch-setting stitch width and length for the fabric thickness. Test the stitch on your hem mock-up. Attach the blindstitch foot.

2. Fold the hem allowance back against the right side of the garment along the basting and place under the presser foot with the soft fold of the garment against the right toe or the center blade of the foot.

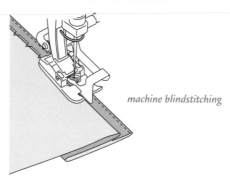

*machine blindstitching*

3. Stitch along the fold, catching only a few threads of the fold with the left swing of the needle. To end the stitching, leave thread tails to tie off securely.

4. Open the hem sample and press from the right side. The straight stitches should lie next to and never catch the fold. If the stitches are too long and visible, they will form a visible tunnel or pull along the stitching in a way that won't press flat. Adjust the stitch so the zigzag stitch doesn't bite so far into the fold before stitching the project hem.

---

Q **Can I use strips of fusible web to turn up and secure a hem without stitching?**

A I prefer to use one of the hand- or machine-stitched hem techniques, but a fused hem comes in handy now and then. Be aware that it is a *permanent* hem. Use lightweight fusible web for hemming to keep the edge light and flexible. Test on scraps first. Fusible, even when it's lightweight, stiffens the edge somewhat.

1. Finish the hem-allowance edge first to prevent raveling if required. If no finish is required, pink the raw edge to help disguise it from the right side.

2. Rotary-cut (*see page 25*) narrow strips of fusible web or use precut fusible tape. Apply it to the wrong side of the hem allowance *just below the edge-finishing stitches*. Remove the protective paper, position the hem allowance on the inside, and fuse in place. Make sure it is permanently fused along the entire circumference.

# Q If I don't want to machine-stitch, what are my choices for hand hemming?

A Functional stitches used for hand hemming should be almost invisible and pucker-free on the right side of the garment or project. Following are descriptions of the basic hand stitches, along with when to use and how to make them.

**Slipstitch.** This almost invisible stitch is commonly used for sewing hems in place. It is also used along turned edges, such as the inside edge of a waistband or 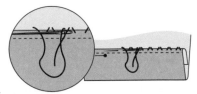 a continuous lap opening for a shirt cuff. It's also used when sewing patch pockets in place by hand. Work from left to right with the folded edge facing you. Slip the needle into the fold and then take a tiny stitch opposite where the thread exits the fold; catch only one or two threads of the garment fabric for the most invisible stitch. Slip the needle back through the fold for about ¼" before emerging to make the next stitch.

**Catchstitch.** This stitch is usually made over a raw edge to hold it to the fabric layer beneath it. It is worked from left to right, creating a little "catch" where the thread 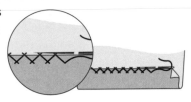 overlaps as the stitch is made, creating a strong stitch. It's often used for hemming and for holding facings in place and for a stronger version of the blindstitch done between fabric layers *(see next entry)*.

314

**Blindstitch.** (Also called tailor's hemming stitch.) This stitch is worked from right to left between two fabric layers. When the stitch goes through the garment layer, it catches only a thread or two. The stitch through the hem layer can be longer for added strength. To turn this into

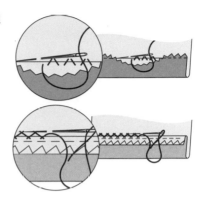

a tailor's hemming stitch, use the catchstitch as described on page 314. With either stitch, it is advisable to take a small backstitch or two in the hem allowance after every sixth stitch. This ensures that the entire hem will not come undone if you catch something in the stitches and they break.

# Solving Problems

**Q** The upper edge of the hem allowance is fuller than the garment. How do I handle the excess?

**A** Trim the hem allowance to the desired finished width and machine-baste 3⁄8" from the hem's raw edge with the wrong side facing you. Turn and press the hem allowance in place along the fold, matching the seamlines. Pin near the upper edge. Use a pin or needle to lift and pull up the basting stitches every few inches to draw up the fullness. (Be careful not to pull up too much ease.) Tuck clean white paper between the layers to avoid edge imprinting and steam out fullness in natural-fiber fabrics by holding the steam iron just above the eased edge. Allow to dry. Finish the raw edge as desired (*see pages 261–264*) and hem with the desired stitching method.

*hemline fold*

---

Q How do I avoid lumps at the pressed lower edge of a hem?

A Trim the seam allowances to ¼" in the hem allowance only, thus staggering the bulk when the hem is turned. Also remove excess at the foldline by clipping up at an angle. If it is a French seam (*see page 269*), serged (*see page 262*), or twice-stitched (*see page 202*), make a clip or twist the seam at the hemline fold so that it lies in the opposite direction in the hem allowance.

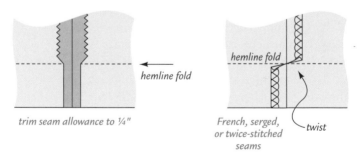

*hemline fold*

*trim seam allowance to ¼"*

*hemline fold*

*French, serged, or twice-stitched seams*

*twist*

# CHAPTER NINE

# Shaping to Fit

Making clothing requires cutting flat pieces from fabric, then using seams, darts, gathers, pleats, and tucks to shape them to fit the body. Learning how to stitch and press darts is key to molding fabric to hug body curves in fitted and semi-fitted styles. Gathers, pleats, tucks, and elastic applications offer additional ways to adjust fullness in specific pattern designs to fit it to the body contours at the waist, wrist, neckline, and ankles. These shaping methods are commonly used in home-decor projects, too.

# Darts

Stitching darts (tapered and stitched folds) is the classic technique for making a flat piece of fabric fit smoothly over body contours at the hip, bust, waist, upper back, and elbow. They are essential in clothing when the fashion is for body-fitting garments, such as straight skirts, fitted pants, figure-skimming sheath dresses, and fitted jackets, skirts, vests, and blouses.

---

**Q** Where are darts most commonly used?

**A** In general, darts extend from the waistline up or down to point to the fullest part of the body — the bustline or tummy, for example — and end about ½" to 1" before the fullest part of it. They may also be used in the side seam for the bust, at the elbow in a fitted sleeve, and at the back shoulder. The larger the curve, the farther away from the fullest part the dart should end, to place the fullness in the garment over the fullness of the body curve. Misplaced darts place fullness in the wrong place and look puckered at the point. Avoid puckered points and misplaced fullness with careful placement, stitching, and pressing. Transfer darts to the fabric pieces following the marking guidelines on pages 170–172.

---

**Q** How do I stitch a dart that doesn't have an unsightly pucker at the point?

**A** If you didn't use dressmaker's carbon to transfer the dart marking, mark a solid stitching line as follows:

1. Fold the fabric right sides together with the marks matching. Pin through the layers perpendicular to the stitching line.
2. Begin stitching at the wide end, backstitching to the cut edge; remove pins as you reach them.
3. Within ½" of the dart point, shorten the stitch to 1.5 mm (16 spi). Take the last few stitches so they lie along the folded edge as shown. Continue stitching along the edge and then off the point for several stitches.
4. Raise the presser foot and draw the point of the dart toward you, then insert the needle — with the thread chain still intact and with a little slack in it — into the dart a bit above the point. Set the stitch length to 0 and take several stitches in place to create a knot in the edge of the dart, as in illustration (A). Clip the threads close to the fabric. For a double-pointed dart, use the same process but stitch in two steps from center to the points, as shown in (B). Overlap the stitches at the center starting point.

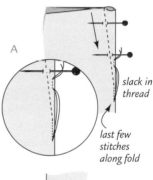

A

slack in thread

last few stitches along fold

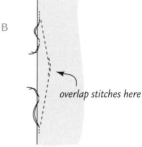

B

overlap stitches here

**Q** If I don't chainstitch and backstitch at dart points, how do I secure the stitches?

**A** Tie the two threads together in an overhand knot, and work it carefully down the thread so that it lies at the dart point. Clip the thread ends and add a drop of seam sealant for added security.

– – – – – – – – – – – – – – – – – – – – – – – – – – – –

**Q** How do I press a dart?

**A** Check the fit before you press, then follow these steps to maintain the contour and shaping that darts create:

1. Beginning at the wide end, press the dart flat to create a crease at the fold and set the stitches into the fabric. Stop pressing at the point to avoid creasing the garment beyond the point.

2. Place the dart over the contour of a pressing ham and use your fingers and the point of the iron to turn it in the direction specified on the pattern guide sheet. Tuck a folded piece of white paper between the dart and the garment, and press (*see illustration on page 42*). Avoid placing the weight of the iron on the dart edges, to prevent them from imprinting on the fabric's right side. On extreme curves, clip the dart and press it open (*see next question*).

Q Is there a way to eliminate the dart thickness in thick fabrics?

A Slash the dart through the center fold, ending within ½" of the point and clip the curved areas as needed so you can press the seam open. Press the points flat on wider darts or to one side on skinny darts.

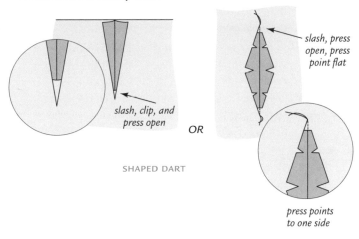

slash, clip, and press open

OR

SHAPED DART

slash, press open, press point flat

press points to one side

- - - - - - - - - - - - - - - - - - - - - - - - - - - - -

Q Does it matter in which direction a dart is pressed?

A Pattern guide sheets usually specify the pressing direction. In general, press horizontal darts down and vertical darts toward the center. For a more youthful-looking bustline, press horizontal bust darts up toward the neckline, rather than down as usually directed. If the fabric is bulky, it's okay to slash and press wide darts open in any location.

**Q** Is it okay to change a dart to gathers for more ease?

**A** This is a great idea when fitting the front of a straight skirt or fitted pants over a full, rounded tummy. For best results, loosen the needle tension, set the machine for a basting-length stitch, and stitch from the right side between the two dart lines. Pull on the bobbin thread to draw up the ease to fit, distributing it evenly. Do the same on a back shoulder seam to eliminate the dart (*see easing illustration on page 328*).

- - - - - - - - - - - - - - - - - - - - - - - - - - - - - - - -

**Q** How do I make sure the bust darts are in the correct location?

**A** You'll need two accurate body measurements:

1. From the center of the shoulder to your bust point (in a well-fitting bra).
2. From bust point to bust point.

Measure your pattern in these same places and mark your bust point on the tissue with an X.

Look at the darts on the pattern. They should point to and stop ½" to 1" short of your bust point. (You may find a bust-point X on some pattern tissues, but it may not match where yours is.) Adjust darts as needed for a better fit, *before* you cut fabric, then check the location in the fabric as you sew. You may need to fine-tune the bust-point positions as you go along, as they may be a bit too low in knits and other fabrics with lots of give.

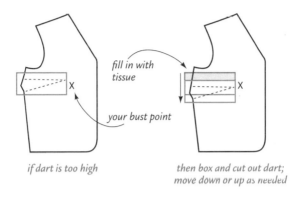

*if dart is too high*          *then box and cut out dart; move down or up as needed*

To adjust a pattern the easy way, draw a box around the dart, cut it out, and move it up or down, in or out, so the point is correctly positioned. It should be neither too high, too low, nor too far toward the center or away from it. Adjust so the fullness at the end of the dart will be where it is needed. Tuck a piece of pattern paper behind the hole that is left, and tape in place.

## Tucks and Pleats

Tucks and pleats draw in and control fullness. They provide a decorative or more tailored look, when gathers are too soft for the desired effect. They require folding and straight stitching; if your work is not precise, errors multiply quickly with multiple pleats or tucks and adversely affect final fit and appearance. Careful marking (*see pages 165–174*) sets the scene for accuracy. Because they involve multiple layers of fabric, pleats and tucks are most effective in light- to medium-weight fabrics.

# Q What's the difference between tucks and pleats?

A **Pleats** are fabric folds designed to control fullness in a variety of ways, determined by the way they are folded, stitched, and pressed. Most types, other than those that release into soft fullness, require a sharp press along the length of the pleat fold. Pleats are deeper than tucks, providing design ease to flow over body curves.

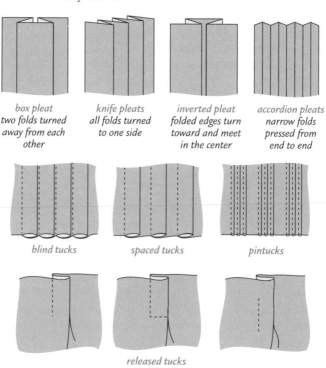

*box pleat*
two folds turned
away from each
other

*knife pleats*
all folds turned
to one side

*inverted pleat*
folded edges turn
toward and meet
in the center

*accordion pleats*
narrow folds
pressed from
end to end

*blind tucks*

*spaced tucks*

*pintucks*

*released tucks*

**Tucks** are narrow folds of fabric. They may be stitched partially or along their entire length. The stitching may be visible on the outside or may be done from the inside to control the fullness, as in the waistline tucks in trouser-style skirts and pants. When partially stitched, inside or out, they are called released tucks. Make tucks and pleats following the directions specified in your pattern guide sheet.

-------------------------------------------------------------------

**Q** **Any tips for sewing perfect tucks?**

**A** Here are a few tips for perfectly spaced and stitched tucks:

* Mark the tuck fold lines accurately. Use a see-through plastic or acrylic ruler and a water- or air-soluble marking pen or fine-line chalk marker (*see* Marking Tools and Methods *on pages 165–174*).
* Check the pattern tissue for the correct stitching width from the fold.
* Use a straight-stitch presser foot and needle plate for better stitch quality and accuracy.
* Press each tuck before stitching, to crease an edge to follow when stitching (but not if you used a marking pen, as iron heat often sets these inks).
* Place pins perpendicular to the pressed edge.
* Stitch all tucks in the same direction and with the needle thread always on the side that will show when the tuck is pressed in the correct direction. (There are often visual differences in the stitch quality on the bobbin side.)

✳ Press along the stitching line to set the stitches and then press to one side. Lightly press from the wrong side to avoid tuck-edge impressions on the right side of the tucked area.

- - - - - - - - - - - - - - - - - - - - - - - - - - - - - - - - - - - -

**Q** How do I handle seams inside the fold of the pleats in my skirt when making the hem?

**A** Determine where the uppermost edge of the hem allowance will fall and clip the seam allowances to the stitching at that location. Clip at the hemline fold and remove excess fabric in the hem allowance by trimming the seams to ¼". Notch out wedges in the seam allowance at the hemline fold for a flat hem fold there (A). Turn and complete the hem with the desired method. On the inside of the garment, edgestitch the hem allowance through the layers at the pleat edge (B).

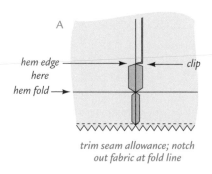

A

hem edge here ⟶ ⟵ clip

hem fold ⟶

trim seam allowance; notch out fabric at fold line

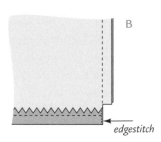

B

edgestitch ⟵

**Q** Is there a way to keep pleats pressed and hanging straight, for easier pressing during the garment's life?

**A** After hemming, stitch close to the inside folded edge of each pleat on the inside as shown in the hem allowance in the previous question. Continue along the length of the inside crease, so it's edgestitched from end to end. Press again from the outside, tucking fabric strips between the pleat edge and the fabric to avoid edge imprints.

- - - - - - - - - - - - - - - - - - - - - - - - - - - - - - -

**Q** How do I press crisp pleat edges in fabrics made of synthetics or synthetic blends?

**A** After pressing with the steam iron, with the paper strips still in place, immediately replace the iron with a tailor's clapper (*see page 37*) and bear down for several seconds. The cool wood will absorb the steam and train the edge to remember its crease. Allow the fabric to cool completely before moving it. You can set creases in pants legs in the same manner.

## Ease and Gathers

When you sew together two layers of fabric of unequal lengths, you will need to ease or gather the longer layer to fit the shorter one. Pin and stitch carefully. This will ensure eased areas with no obvious tucks, and gathered areas with the fullness evenly distributed.

# Q What's the difference between easing and gathering?

A Gathers are obvious in the finished piece; for instance, gathers are the defining detail in a dirndl skirt. Ease can also be worked into a seam without obvious gathers. There is often a *slight ease* in back shoulder seams to provide a bit of extra room to accommodate the natural back shoulder curve. Shirt sleeves with a flat cap may have a bit of ease between the notches. Set-in sleeves (*see pages 359–367*) require *moderate* ease to create a smooth rounded cap or *extensive* ease for styles with obvious gathers (often found in little girls' dresses).

---

# Q How do I handle minimal ease, like what's needed in the back shoulder?

A The ease is usually in a defined area: between a set of notches, dots, or other construction marks. Match the notches first, then the ends of the seam, and pin. Match the center of the larger edge to the center of the smaller edge and pin. Then use a few pins in each section to evenly distribute the fullness (this is called "easing to fit"). Stitch, removing pins as you reach them.

Experienced sewers often use minimal pins and sew with the eased side down, so the feed dogs can help with the easing. The goal is a smooth seam without puckers in either layer of the fabric.

*easing at the shoulder seam*

**Q** How do I prevent little pleats from being caught in the easing or gathering?

**A** Standard directions for gathering suggest machine-basting on the seamline and then again ¼" away. This gives you *no* control over the gathered fabric *below* the seamline. Adjust the standard method slightly by using three rows of machine basting.

1. Adjust machine for a long stitch and loosen the upper thread tension by one or two settings to make it easier to draw up the fullness.

2. Machine-baste ¼", ½", and ¾" from the raw edges.

3. Draw up all three bobbin threads from each end of the stitching, adjust the gathers evenly, and pin the gathered piece in place on its companion piece.

4. *Stitch from the gathered side,* ⅝" from the raw edges (halfway between the two lower basting rows) so you can see what you're doing. The lower row of stitches prevents the fullness from getting caught in the stitches.

5. After stitching, check the seam from the right side, clip any machine basting that is visible below the seamline, and remove any visible stitches.

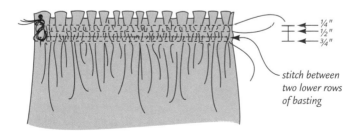

¼"
½"
¾"

stitch between
two lower rows
of basting

## LET THE FEET DO IT

You may be able to purchase a **gathering presser foot** for your machine. It can gather a piece of fabric separately and/or gather it while you stitch it to its companion piece. If you do a lot of home-decor sewing or make garments with yards of ruffling, you may want to invest in the **ruffler attachment** that creates tiny pleats, rather than gathers, to draw in excess fullness. Follow the directions that come with the foot or ruffler.

**Q** How do I prevent the gathering thread from breaking while I'm drawing up the gathers?

**A** Be sure to decrease the upper-thread tension. Divide the expanse to be gathered into smaller sections, like quarters or eighths, so the threads are not overly stressed while you pull them. Do the same on the piece to which it will be sewn. For the machine basting, use topstitching thread in the needle and bobbin.

1. Adjust the machine for a long stitch. Machine-baste as described in the previous question, beginning and ending at the division marks and leaving a long thread tail at each end each time you start and stop.

2. Pin the fabric to be gathered to the piece to which you're attaching it, matching the division marks. Working one section at a time, draw up the gathers to fit, pin securely, and tie off the threads at both ends, or wrap them in a figure 8 around the last pin in the

section. Adjust the gathers evenly, keeping the gathers perpendicular to the cut edges. I stroke gathers with the point of a pin to adjust them evenly. Place lots of pins perpendicular to the stitching to control the gathers.

3. Stitch from the side with gathers. Every few inches, stop, raise the presser foot to release pressure, and lower again to continue stitching.

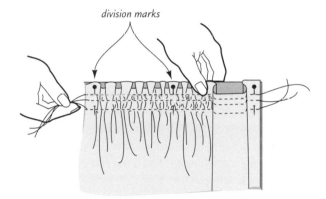

*division marks*

### CORD IT

On long expanses in home-decor items, you can zigzag over a heavy thread or cord without catching it with the needle so it can slide freely under the stitches. Pull on the cord and slide the fabric along the cord to create the gathers. Adjust the fullness evenly, pin to the corresponding piece, and stitch.

## Q Is there a formula for determining how long a fabric strip should be to make a gathered ruffle?

## A The fuller the ruffle, the richer the look. Measure the distance along or around the edge where you attach the ruffle. Use the directions below to determine the cut length and width, and cut the ruffle strips. You may need to join several strips for the total required length. (*Use bias seams as shown on page 268.*)

* **For lightweight fabrics,** multiply that measurement by 3.
* **For medium-weight fabrics,** multiply by 2 or 2½.
* **For a single-layer ruffle,** cut the desired finished width plus one seam allowance and ½" for a shirttail hem (*see page 309*). If you prefer, cut away ½" as you serge-finish one edge with a narrow rolled edge (*see page 310*).
* **For a double-layer ruffle,** cut the strip twice the desired finished width plus two seam allowances. Fold the strip in half lengthwise with wrong sides facing and press.

# Elastic Applications

Elastic is either stitched directly to fabric to draw up fullness or inserted through a casing: a fabric tunnel stitched in place at the elastic location. Casings are most commonly used at the waistline, neckline, wrists, and ankles. They may be included in the pattern piece as a turn-under allowance, or they may be created with an additional layer of fabric. Elastic can also be attached directly to the fabric without a casing.

# Q How do I choose the right elastic for my project?

A Most packaged elastic includes recommendations for use, along with the correct application methods, but you'll also find assorted elastic types available on large reels to purchase by the yard. Below are the basic types:

* **Braided.** Lightweight with a slight rib; easily identified because it narrows when stretched and returns to its original width when the tension is relaxed; use in casings at waistbands, leg openings, sleeve edges, and around necklines; good choice for swimwear; use in casings only, as it loses stretch if you stitch through it.

* **Knitted.** Doesn't narrow when stretched; use for casings and direct elastic applications; softer than braided and woven types; resists curling; comfortable next to the skin; use in casings or stitch directly to the fabric.

* **Woven.** Has visible crosswise and lengthwise ribs, and resists curling; very strong and thicker than other types; does not narrow when stretched and isn't affected by stitching through it; use in casing or stitch directly to the fabric; use for home-decor and apparel.

* **Transparent.** Made of polyurethane (meaning it is rubber-free); strong; stretches three to four times its original size with great recovery; use only for direct applications; stretch several times before using to ensure good recovery after it's applied; chlorine-resistant; won't fall apart if nicked by scissors, pins, or serger blades; good for swimwear, aerobic wear, and lightweight knits where other elastic types might be too bulky.

Specialty elastics are made with one of the first three methods and are enhanced for special sewing applications and wearing comfort. The most common are listed below:

* **Pajama.** Soft and flexible; can be stitched directly to the fabric for nonbulky application.

* **Lingerie.** Usually ¼" to no wider than ⅝" with a picot loop on one edge that peeks out at the finished edge after it is sewn to the fabric's right side and flipped and stitched in place on the inside; lace-patterned elastic is also available in a variety of motifs and widths for lingerie sewing.

* **Nonroll.** Resists rolling and twisting; a special favorite for waistband casings; can also be stitched directly to the fabric; choose mesh style for light- and medium-weight fabrics and heavier ribbed versions for heavier fabrics.

---

**Q** Should I preshrink elastic?

**A** It's a good idea to preshrink all types, except for transparent elastic, before you measure and cut the required lengths. If the application method you choose requires stitching through the elastic, preshrinking is not necessary.

---

**Q** How do I make a casing?

**A** When a turn-under casing allowance is included on the pattern pieces for pull-on pants and skirts, follow the directions in the pattern guide sheet (*see pages 130–131*).

Sometimes elastic is required in the garment interior (at the waist or within a sleeve, for example) where there is no edge to turn for the casing. Solution: Add a piece of fabric wide enough to accommodate the elastic you've chosen, plus ⅝" which allows ¼" turn-under allowance, plus a little ease room for the elastic. Ready-made bias tape with edges already turned is a common choice, but you can also use a strip of lightweight fabric, ribbon, or tricot-knit binding of the appropriate width for the elastic. *Note:* If you are using tricot-knit binding or ribbon, you won't need turn-under allowances on the long edges.

1.  Cut the casing material 1" longer than the garment area to which it will be stitched. Turn under and press ½" at each short end and edgestitch. Turn under and press ¼" on the long edges.

2.  Position the prepared strip on the garment in the casing location with the turned ends meeting, usually at a seamline. Stitch ⅛" from the long edges.

3.  Insert the elastic, adjust the fit, and lap and stitch the elastic ends securely.

To create a casing at a shaped edge, apply bias tape or self-fabric bias binding (*see page 265*) as for a facing, leaving an opening for the elastic insertion. Turn to the inside, press, edgestitch, and insert the elastic as described above. It's not necessary to close the opening.

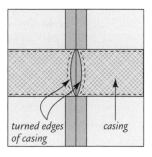

*turned edges of casing*     *casing*

**Q** What's the best way to join the ends of elastic in casings?

**A** Choose from the following options:

* Overlap the ends and stitch in the X-box pattern shown on page 346, and trim the excess elastic close to the stitching.
* Butt the ends after trimming away all excess and use a wide zigzag or serpentine stitch to join the ends.

- - - - - - - - - - - - - - - - - - - - - - - - - - - - - - -

**Q** How do I apply elastic directly to the garment when there is no casing?

**A** Use narrow knitted or woven elastic and cut it 8 percent shorter than the length of the garment where it will be applied. Your pattern may specify the length to cut. Adjust the machine for a long, narrow multistitch zigzag (or substitute two rows of straight stitching) and use a ballpoint needle.

**For a waistline application with a zipper opening at center front or back.** Divide the elastic and the garment location where it will be stitched into eighths; mark with pins or marking pen. Pin the elastic to the garment with marks matching and ½" extending at the opening edges. Stitch in place, stretching the elastic to fit between the marks. (Turn under the elastic ends and whipstitch to the zipper or seam allowance at the opening edges.) On shorter expanses, such as at a sleeve edge, quarter-mark the elastic and the garment, and apply in the same manner.

**For elastic in the interior of a sleeve.** Apply to the sleeve *before* you stitch the underarm seam. It's easier than applying it in the round.

**For a garment without an opening.** Overlap the ends and stitch together in the X-box pattern (*see page 346*) to make an elastic circle before pinning and stitching in place.

To apply directly:

1. Adjust the machine for a straight stitch (slightly longer than normal), zigzag, or three-step zigzag stitch adjusted for medium width and length. Insert a ballpoint or stretch needle. Test on a scrap and adjust the thread tension if needed.

2. Quarter-mark the elastic and the garment edge or area to which you are stitching the elastic. Pin the elastic to the garment at the marks only and then stitch with the elastic facing you; stretch it to fit as you go.

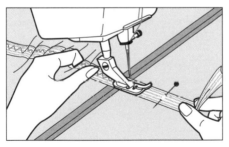

*stretch elastic to fit between quarter marks*

**Q** Is there an advantage to using a casing instead of stitching elastic directly to the garment?

**A** It's much easier to adjust the elastic for a perfect fit in a casing, and it also makes it possible to adjust or replace worn elastic later. Stitched-on elastic is difficult to remove and stitching through elastic does weaken it somewhat.

- - - - - - - - - - - - - - - - - - - - - - - - - - - - - -

**Q** How do I prevent popped stitches in the casing stitching on knits?

**A** Hand-wrap (don't machine-wind) woolly nylon thread onto the bobbin. Don't stretch it as you wind. Use regular thread in the needle. Adjust the machine for a narrow zigzag stitch. With the casing allowance pinned in place and facing you, stretch the casing as you stitch it in place. The stretchy thread in the bobbin will be on the right side of the garment and will prevent popped stitches.

SEE ALSO: *Casings, pages 345–349.*

# CHAPTER TEN

# Waistlines, Pockets, and Sleeves

Waistbands require special attention for a smooth, comfortable fit. Pull-on styles require a casing with elastic to control the fullness. Included here are methods for both. Learning to set in a classic sleeve is essential for great-looking results. Applying cuffs can add some special challenges. Patch pockets and flaps are a common detail on jackets and shirts; inside pockets show up in many garment styles. Details like these require careful preparation and stitching methods.

# Waistbands

The classic straight-cut waistband is the most prevalent and traditional waistline finish for pants and skirts. Adding interfacing ensures long and comfortable wear, as well as an attractive fit.

- - - - - - - - - - - - - - - - - - - - - - - - - - - - - - - -

Q **Can I simply cut a straight-grain strip of the correct length and width instead of using the pattern piece?**

A Yes. Unless your waistline measurement is precisely the same as the one for your size in the pattern sizing chart, you will need to customize the length anyway. You might prefer a wider or narrower waistband than the pattern provides. Fabric thickness affects the fit and the necessary length of the waistband strip. Use the following method to customize the waistband for your preferences, fabric, and garment style:

1. Determine the waistband cut length: Add 6" to your waistline measurement for seam allowances, lapping at the opening edge, and extra for fitting adjustments. You'll trim the excess later (*see step 5 on page 342*).

2. Determine the waistband cut width: Refer to the pattern piece. Standard waistbands finish to 1¼". To change that, multiply the desired finished width by 2 and add 1¼" for seam allowances.

3. Cut the waistband strip using these measurements. If possible, cut it so one long edge is along the selvage. If you can't include the selvage, cut the waistband strip on the straight grain and serge-finish or bind one long edge with bias tricot (*see page 269*).

**Q** **Does it matter which grainline I use when cutting the waistband?**

**A** With interfacing to control stretching, this isn't an essential consideration. Corduroy wales, striped fabrics, and rib weaves should be cut with the lengthwise grain along the length of the band. For napped fabrics, the lower edge of the waistband should be cut in the same nap direction as the garment, so there is no color or shading variation.

---

**Q** **What should I use for waistband interfacing?**

**A** For a smooth, stiff waistband, look for a sew-in, nonroll waistband interfacing sold by the yard. For softer bands, choose a fusible nonwoven waistband interfacing and follow the manufacturer's application directions.

---

**Q** **How do I attach the waistband using a sew-in, non-roll interfacing?**

**A** This method requires a straight waistband strip, with one long edge cut along the selvage. Cut the waistband extra long, as directed in step 1 on the previous page, for enough length to ensure a good fit.

◄— interfacing
◄— basting
◄— selvage

1. Machine-baste along the seamline at the long unfinished edge. Position one long edge of the nonroll interfacing along the stitching on the wrong side, with the interfacing covering the seam allowance. Edgestitch.

2. Fold the fabric around the interfacing to simulate a finished band and wrap around your waist. Adjust to fit, allowing at least 1" of wearing ease. Mark the waistband where it comes together in front on both halves of the waistband. This will be the center front or back.

3. Remove the interfaced waistband and mark the center front or back halfway between the marks. With right sides facing and center fronts and backs matching, pin the band to the garment waistline edge with pins parallel to and right along the edge of the interfacing. *Note:* When pinning the band to the garment, you should find it necessary to gently ease the curved raw edge of the waistline to the straight edge of the band.

4. Turn the band to the inside and try on to test the fit. Adjust, using some of the excess waistband as needed for more room. After testing the fit, stitch right next to the interfacing, removing pins as you reach them.

5. Trim the ends, leaving at least 1⅝" for the underlap or overlap and seam allowance on one end, and ⅝" for a seam on the other end. Trim away ⅝" of the interfacing at each end of the trimmed band (the waistband will be impossible to turn and press otherwise). Fold the band with right sides facing and the long edge (selvage, serged, or bound) of the band extending ⅝" below the waistline seam.

6. Stitch a scant ⅝" from the end that will lap (A) and trim the seam to ¼"; clip the corner. At the remaining end (B), stitch a scant ⅝" seam to allow room for the bulk of the

seam in the finished band. Trim and clip the seam; press
open on a point presser (*see page 40*). Turn right side out
and press.

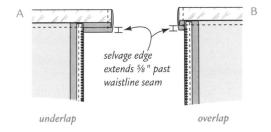

*selvage edge
extends ⅝" past
waistline seam*

*underlap*          *overlap*

7.  Pin the band in place with pins perpendicular to the
    seamline on the right side. At the lapped section, turn
    the seam allowance under with the folded edges parallel.
    Clip just past the zipper tape and treat the cut edge with
    liquid seam sealant. Stitch-in-the-ditch from the right
    side to secure the remainder of the underlayer.

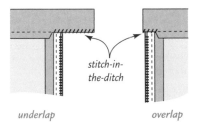

*stitch-in-
the-ditch*

*underlap*          *overlap*

**Q** **Is there an easy way to make belt loops without the need to stitch and turn a narrow tube?**

**A** Yes. This is also the easiest way to make narrow straps for dresses and narrow ties for drawstring waistline casings. Each loop should finish slightly longer than the finished waistband width to allow room for the belt to slide comfortably. Here's what you do:

1. Add two ⅝" seam allowances to the desired finished length to determine how long to cut each one. Multiply this by the number of loops needed and cut a strip that length and four times the desired finished width, which is usually ¼" or ⅜".

2. Fold the strip in half lengthwise with wrong sides facing and press. Turn the raw edges in to meet the fold and press. Stitch close to both long edges. Cut the strip into the required lengths for your belt loops and attach to the finished waistband, or position and baste to the waistline before applying the waistband.

3. After completing the waistband, zigzag-finish the short end of each loop. Turn under ¼" and pin loop even with the upper waistband edge. Stitch in place, backstitching across the loop edge for added security.

*easy belt loops*

# Casings

Cut-on, turn-down casings (facings that are cut as part of the garment piece) are the classic method for fitting the waistline of a pull-on skirt or pants.

- - - - - - - - - - - - - - - - - - - - - - - - - - - - - - - -

**Q** **What is a casing?**

**A** It's a fabric tunnel with elastic or a drawstring that draws in and controls fullness. It's made with a turn-under allowance or with a separate strip of fabric to create the tunnel. Casings are commonly used at skirt and pants waistlines, the lower edges of sleeves, some pant legs, and in peasant-style necklines. They are a common component in knit activewear.

- - - - - - - - - - - - - - - - - - - - - - - - - - - - - - - -

**Q** **How do I create a turned casing for elastic at a waist-line edge?**

**A** The width to turn under on a garment with a cut-on casing is indicated on the pattern pieces and is designed to finish to ¼" wider than the elastic. If you have elastic that is a different width than indicated in the pattern, adjust the finished width of the casing before cutting the pieces.

1. On woven fabrics, turn under and press the raw edge of the casing allowance (usually ¼" or ½"). Serge-finish (*see page 262*) the casing's raw edge on knits and heavy wovens, or bind woven edges with bias tricot seam binding (*see page 269*).

2. Turn the casing under along the casing fold line indicated and press. Stitch close to the inner turned edge of the casing, leaving a 2"-long opening. Stitch close to the upper pressed edge. On skirts and pants, begin and end the stitching so the opening is close to the center back seam or one of the side seams.

2" opening

3. Insert the elastic and overlap and stitch the ends.

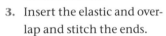

---

# Q How do I insert elastic in a casing and join the ends?

**A** Attach a bodkin or large safety pin to one end. Draw it through the casing, grasping it through the fabric so you can push and pull it along. To join the ends, overlap, pin, and try on to check and adjust the fit. Trim excess, allowing 1" of overlap. Lap the ends and stitch and X-box as shown; for firm, thicker elastic, you can butt the ends and stitch them together with a wide zigzag stitch. After joining the ends, pop them into the opening and complete the casing stitching at the opening.

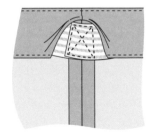

**Q** I've seen elastic waistbands with multiple rows of elastic. How do I achieve that look?

**A** Substitute two or more pieces of ⅜"-wide elastic for the single elastic. Make ½"-wide stitched tunnels. You may need to adjust the width of the cut-on casing to accommodate the elastic width and number of pieces you want.

1. Leave an opening in one of the seams as shown (A). Clip the seam at the casing fold line, press the seam open, and fuse the seam allowances in place with narrow strips in the casing opening area for easier elastic threading.

2. Turn under and press the casing allowance; edgestitch the upper and lower folded edges as for a standard casing (*see step 2 on the previous page*), and then stitch the channels. Cut each piece of elastic to fit your waist, plus 1".

3. Work all pieces through the casing at the same time for even fullness in all rows (B). Adjust the fit, overlap ends, and secure with stitching. It's not necessary to close the opening in the seam.

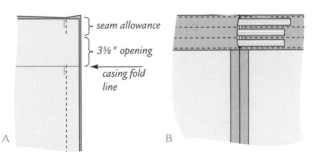

seam allowance

3⅝" opening

casing fold line

A                                    B

# Q Can I convert a pattern with an elastic casing to one with a drawstring?

A Yes! Make two buttonholes in the garment in the area that will lie on top of the turned casing allowance. Space several inches apart where you want the drawstring to emerge. Stabilize the buttonhole area first with a strip of fusible interfacing applied to the garment's wrong side. Make button-holes long enough to accommodate the width of the drawstring with a little ease. Turn and stitch the cas-ing in place. Insert the drawstring through the buttonholes.

*make buttonholes
for drawstring*

---

# Q Can I adjust a fitted skirt or pants pattern so it has an elastic casing instead of a fitted waistband?

A Yes, but it is not recommended for heavy fabrics. Don't mark or stitch darts. Instead, cut the side seams straight up from the fullest hip. For 1"-wide elastic, add 2⅝" above the waistline seamline (not above the upper edge of the pattern) for the fold-over casing. Proceed with the casing as directed on pages 345–346.

**Q** The elastic in my finished casing is curled over on itself. How can I prevent this from happening?

**A** Here's something you can do with any elastic casing: After inserting the elastic and lapping and stitching the ends, try the garment on again and adjust the fullness around the waist, with the side seams and the center front and back seams in the correct position on your body. Use safety pins to secure the casing layers to the elastic 1" from each seam on each side of the seamline. Stitch-in-the-ditch (*see page 112*) through the elastic from the upper to the lower edge of the casing.

- - - - - - - - - - - - - - - - - - - - - - - -

**Q** Whenever I try to pull elastic through a casing, the pin gets caught under the seam allowances. How can I prevent this?

**A** Here are three options:

* Trim the casing turn-under seam allowance to ¼", ending the trimming ⅛" from where the lower edge of the casing will lie. Machine-baste the seam allowances in place ⅛" from the seamline on each side of the seam. After inserting the elastic, remove the basting.
* Trim the seam allowance as directed above and use ¼"-wide fusible web strips to fuse them to the fabric.
* If the seam is serged, twist it carefully (don't clip) at the upper fold line for the casing, so each half goes in the opposite direction. Baste in place, insert the elastic, and remove the basting.

# Patch Pockets and Flaps

The most popular patch pockets and flaps have square or rounded corners. Take time to prepare them correctly to ensure sharp points or smooth curves.

- - - - - - - - - - - - - - - - - - - - - - - - - - - - - - -

**Q** **How do I make a patch pocket with evenly rounded lower corners?**

**A** First, snip-mark (*see page 169*) the hemline fold at each end of the pocket, remove the pattern, and then:

1. Cut and apply tricot-knit fusible interfacing (*see page 269*) to the wrong side of the pocket, to stabilize the cut edges, prevent pocket sag, and line the pocket. Finish the upper raw edge of the pocket with clean finishing, zigzagging, or serging (*see pages 261–263*).

2. Turn the hem allowance to the pocket's right side along the hemline marks, and stitch each short end. Adjust for a basting-length stitch and stitch ⅝" from the pocket's outer edges from hem edge to hem edge. Machine-baste ½" from cut edges in the curved areas.

3. Trim seams to ¼" in the hem's seam allowances and clip the corners. Press on a point presser (*see page 40*). Trim the remaining allowance around the pocket to ⅜" with pinking

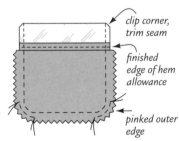

clip corner, trim seam

finished edge of hem allowance

pinked outer edge

shears to automatically notch out excess in the curves.

4. Turn the hem right side out and press. Topstitch the hem's lower edge in place from the right side, or slip-stitch in place from the wrong side.

5. Use the basting as a guide to turn under and press the pocket's raw edges and gently draw up the basting in the curves to control the fullness.

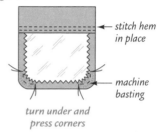

→ *stitch hem in place*

→ *machine basting*

*turn under and press corners*

6. Pin the pocket in place on the garment's right side. Stitch to the garment using one of the following methods:

   * Edgestitch no more than ⅛" from the turned edges.
   * Edgestitch and then topstitch ¼" from the edge-stitching (you can use a widely set twin needle to do both rows at once).
   * Use a blindstitch (*see page 315*) or appliqué stitch and monofilament thread (*see page 71*).
   * Slipstitch in place (*see page 314*) so no stitching shows on the pocket surface.

7. Remove the basting stitches, if you can see them, at the outer edge of the pocket.

Q **How do I neatly begin and end the stitching on the pocket?**

A If you are topstitching and edgestitching, leave long threads to draw to the inside and tie off securely. Add a drop of seam sealant or glue to the knots for security. If you are edgestitching, reinforce the upper ends of the pocket by stitching a small triangle as shown below. Draw threads to the inside to tie off. Other options include using a narrow zigzag stitch or bar-tacking at the upper ends of the pocket.

*stitched triangle*

*narrow zigzag for ½ "*

*¼ "-long bar-tack by hand or machine*

*interfacing for stability*

Q How do I make neat corners with crisp, nonbulky points on pockets with square corners?

A Machine-baste precisely ⅝" from the pocket edges to be turned. Stitch off the ends to avoid puckered corners. Press under the corners or points precisely at the stitched intersections, and trim the pressed allowance to a scant ¼". Turn the adjoining edges under along the basting with the pressed edges meeting.

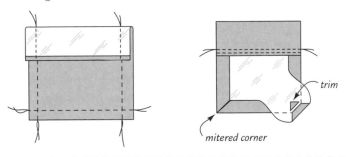

trim

mitered corner

---

Q How do I bar-tack?

A Drop the feed dogs (or cover them with an index card and lower the needle through it several times to punch a hole). Adjust the machine for a zigzag stitch (0 stitch length and medium to long stitch width). Take several stitches in place, then pull threads to the inside and tie off. To bar-tack by hand, take several stitches in place, and then do a buttonhole stitch (*see page 394*) over the threads but not into the pocket. Draw the thread to the underside and take several stitches in place to end the stitching.

## MAKE IT ROLL

To prevent the lining from showing at the pocket edges, carefully trim away ⅛" along the lining outer edges (excluding the upper edge). When you pin the lining to the pocket with right sides facing, make the raw edges meet, and pin. Stitch with the lining side up so the feed dogs will help ease the slightly larger pocket to the lining. When you trim, press, and turn the pocket right side out, the lining will naturally roll to the underside because it's slightly smaller than the pocket.

Q My patch pocket has a separate flap. How do I prepare and attach it?

A For easier stitching and a flatter application, cut the facing from fashion fabric or from a lightweight lining fabric. Apply lightweight interfacing to the wrong side of the flap.

1. Trim ¹⁄₁₆" from the outer edges of the flap facing, to make it slightly smaller and make it pull slightly to the underside of the finished flap. With right sides facing and raw edges even, pin the facing to the flap, easing the flap to the lining if necessary. Stitch from the lining side, but begin and end precisely ⅝" from the upper cut edge of the flap.

2. Trim the seam to ¼" (using pinking shears at curves), clip square corners, and press the seam open, as shown for

enclosed seams on page 289. Turn right side out and press.
Machine-baste a scant ⅝" from the raw edges.

3. Pin the flap to the garment with the basting along the flap positioning line. Stitch just inside the basting at the ⅝" stitching line. Backstitch at each end.

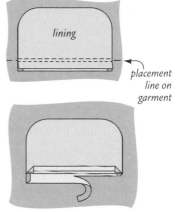

*placement line on garment*

4. Lift the facing layer of the seam allowance and trim close to the stitching.

*trim flap's seam allowance only (close to stitching)*

5. Complete in one of the following ways:

   * **For a raw-edge finish:** Stitch again through all layers ¼" from the first stitching and trim the facing layer close to the second stitching.
   * **For a finished edge under the flap:** Turn under and press ¼" on the facing seam allowance, turning in the ends at an angle if not already shaped that way. Edgestitch in place.

6. Turn the flap down along the stitching line and press, using a tailor's clapper to make a firm, sharp edge (*see page 41*). On thick or stubborn fabrics, slipstitch the upper corners of the flap in place for about ¼".

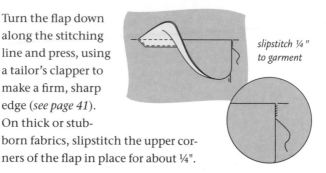

*slipstitch ¼" to garment*

---

**Q** How do I make sure that both lower curved edges of my patch pockets are the same shape?

**A** Trace the pocket shape along the seamline onto heat-proof template plastic or the matte side of some freezer paper. Position the template on the wrong side of the pocket (press in place if using freezer paper). Turn the pocket edges against the template edge and press.

---

**Q** How do I prevent the upper edges of patch pockets from stretching out of shape?

**A** Place the pocket-interfacing pattern piece with the grainline arrow along the crosswise (stretchiest) direction of the interfacing to place the stable direction of the interfacing along the upper edge. Don't use all-bias nonwoven interfacing in pockets, because there is no stable nonstretchy direction.

# In-Seam and Slant Pockets

Trousers, pants, and skirts often feature in-seam or slant pockets. Here are a few tips for easier sewing and a better fit.

---

**Q** **How do I prevent in-seam pockets from stretching at the folded or stitched edge, so they don't buckle?**

**A** Stabilize the opening edge to prevent pocket "gaposis." Cut a piece of seam or twill tape (*not* bias tape) 2" longer than the opening (this will be marked on the pattern tissue with dots). Position and stitch the tape to the pocket along the fold line or along the seamline if pocket is to be sewn to the garment. Follow pattern directions to complete the pocket.

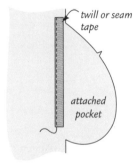

twill or seam tape

attached pocket

Taping can be used to stabilize other seams. It's often used in the shoulder seams in stretchy fabrics, as well as on the wrong side of the opening edges for an invisible zipper, to prevent stretching and buckling.

---

**Q** **How do I prevent slant pockets from gapping out from the body? Mine never lie flat against the body curves just below the waistline seam.**

**A** Machine-baste the pocket-edge lining to the front of the garment with right sides facing, stitching ½" from the raw edges. Cut a piece of woven seam or twill tape (*not* bias tape) the length of the pocket-edge seamline on the pattern tissue. Center over the basting; pin at the bottom end only. At the upper end, use a vanishing-ink pen to mark on the lining: a dot on the tape and another dot ¼" above it. Gently pull the tape until the dots match; pin in place. Distribute the fullness between the pins and pin. Stitch permanently. Finish the pocket as directed in your pattern guide sheet. The turned-and-pressed pocket edge will cup into your hip curve and won't stretch out of shape during wear.

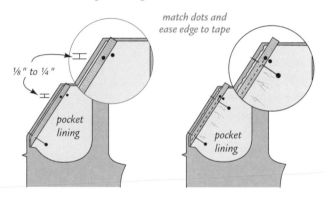

match dots and
ease edge to tape

⅛" to ¼"

pocket
lining

pocket
lining

---

**Q** Even when I stabilize trouser-pocket seam edges with tape, they gap. Any suggestions?

**A** Because the slant edge is straight and the body curves, it may still pull away from the body. Edgestitch and/or top-stitch the upper 2" of the pocket to the garment layer beneath the pocket edge. That should do the trick if you taped the seam first. *(See the next question.)*

**Q** When I sew the inside pocket layers in slant-pocket designs, there's often an unsightly pulling on the outside of the garment. How do I prevent that?

**A** It happens due to cutting and/or stitching inconsistencies. The fix is simple. Place the skirt or pant leg right side up on a flat surface and pin the pocket edge to the underlayer. Then fold the leg or skirt section back to expose the pocket layers. Don't be surprised if the cut edges don't match; *pin them together as they lie*. If you force the edges to match, it causes the buckling. Pin carefully and stitch as pinned. Trim excess before finishing the seam edges together with zigzagging, serging, or pinking.

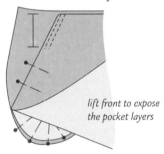

*lift front to expose the pocket layers*

*pin as layers lie; don't force to match*

## Set-In Sleeves

Set-in sleeves offer their own set of sewing challenges. A smoothly set sleeve at the edge of the natural shoulder is the sign of careful sewing and demonstrates a good understanding of how to handle ease. Extra tips not included in the standard pattern guide sheet are covered in the following questions.

## SLEEVE OPTIONS

A smoothly set sleeve requires careful handling to avoid puckers and pulls that scream "homemade." The flat-capped shirtsleeve offers fewer sewing challenges and is reserved for looser-fitting and more casual styles, including T-shirts.

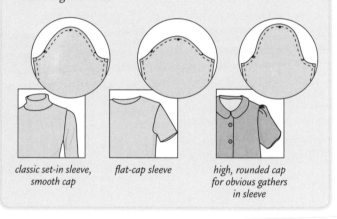

*classic set-in sleeve, smooth cap*

*flat-cap sleeve*

*high, rounded cap for obvious gathers in sleeve*

Q **What's the significance of the single and double notches on the pattern piece of the sleeve cap?**

A Mark these carefully! Double notches identify the back armhole on the garment and sleeve. The back half of the sleeve has more ease; the back armhole accommodates the outer curved shape of the back. The front section doesn't need as much ease because the armhole is hollow (an inward curve). If you set the sleeves in backward, the sleeves won't hang straight, and it will be difficult to stitch the sleeve to the garment.

**Q** **How do I set in a smooth sleeve? Mine always have little puckers caught in the stitching.**

**A** The following method helps distribute the ease better than the standard way and is appropriate for smooth-cap and gathered-cap set-in sleeves.

1. Snip-mark (*see page 169*) the notches and the dots at the sleeve cap and those halfway between the notches. Snip the corresponding marks and notches on the garment pieces.

2. Machine-baste ¼", ½", and ¾" from the raw edge of the sleeve cap, beginning and ending each row of basting ½" beyond the front and back armhole notches on the sleeve cap. Do this *before* stitching the sleeve's underarm seam. Three rows of stitching,

*machine-baste ¼", ½", and ¾" from edge*

instead of the two called for in most directions, provide better control and smoother results. On needle-sensitive fabric (velvet, for example) place this ease stitching ⅝", ½" and ¼" from the raw edge.

3. With right sides facing and the sleeve cap's wrong side facing you, match snip marks at the front and back armhole and pin the sleeve into the armhole. Match and pin the underarms. Pin at the outermost edge of the

*no ease ½" on each side of dot*

shoulder seam allowances to keep easing out of the top 1" of the sleeve cap.

4. Beginning at one set of notches, carefully draw up the gathers, using your fingers to smooth the gathers along the sleeve cap until it fits from the notch(es) to the shoulder seam. Use a few pins to hold temporarily. Repeat on the other half of the sleeve. Be very careful not to draw the gathers too tight. When the sleeve cap fits the armhole, tie off the basting threads securely at each set of notches, or wrap them around the pins in a figure eight.

5. Working on half the sleeve cap at a time, smooth out the easing so the sleeve cap is smooth; use as many pins as necessary to control the ease and notch snip marks. On natural-fiber fabrics such as wool, cotton, silk, or linen, try steam-shrinking the gathered sleeve cap. (*See* Shrink It! *on page 364.*)

6. Machine-baste the sleeve into the armhole, stitching from the sleeve side, so you can see the pins and control the ease. Remove pins as you reach them. Try on for fit. Make any required changes before permanently stitching the sleeve from the garment side, next to the machine basting. Begin stitching at the notches, stitch around the underarm to the next notches and back around to the notches where you started. Overlap the first few stitches and, without stopping, gradually taper the stitching so you are stitching ⅛" from the first stitching into the seam allowance, tapering back into the original stitching when you reach the opposite notch(es) to reinforce the underarm seam.

7. Trim the seam allowance from notch to notch *in the armhole only*. This section of the seam allowance "stands up" inside the garment, but the remainder of the seam allowance sits under the sleeve cap to help fill it out for a rounded appearance. If you wish, zigzag or serge the trimmed seam in the underarm area. To prevent raveling in the seam allowances, zigzag or serge them together.

## A WORD ABOUT DOTS

On most garments, the dot at the top of the sleeve matches the shoulder seam. On others, where the shoulder seam is dropped forward, as in garments with yokes, it will not match the shoulder seam, but the pattern will have a shoulder dot to mark for matching. There will also be a dot in the underarm area of a 2-piece sleeve for matching to the garment side seam.

# Q How do I press a set-in sleeve?

# A Finish the seam-allowance edges as desired, then:

1. Use only the tip of the iron to set the armhole stitching. Press only in the seam allowances and don't move the tip of the iron into the cap itself.

2. Use your fingers to push the seam allowances into the sleeve cap where they act as a filler.

3. Place the sleeve cap, right side out, over a pressing ham (*see page 37*) and steam it. *Don't press it flat with the iron.* Use your fingertips to caress the steam into the fabric and shape a rounded cap. *For shirts or jackets* with dropped shoulders and a flat sleeve cap, set the stitches and then press the seam allowance toward the sleeve. Topstitch through all layers if desired.

## SHRINK IT!

On natural fibers, use the steam iron to shrink out some of the sleeve cap. After completing steps 4 and 5 of setting in a sleeve (*see page 362*), remove the pins and place the sleeve cap over the curve of a pressing ham (*see page 37*). Hold the steam iron above it to steam thoroughly. Allow to dry completely before pinning the sleeve into the armhole.

# Q Can I sew a sleeve into an open armhole instead of making set-in sleeves?

A Setting a sleeve into an open armhole is usually reserved for flat-capped sleeves like those in shirts and T-shirts, where sleeve-cap ease is minimal. In more closely-fit garments with normal armholes, the sleeve cap must be higher and rounder, requiring more ease. Because of a looser fit under the arm, the flat-cap sleeve can be sewn first, and then the side and sleeve seams can be stitched in one operation.

You can sometimes use a modified flat-cap method to sew in a standard set-in sleeve. Ease-stitch, adjust the ease, and pin the sleeve into the open armhole as for a flat-cap sleeve. Stitch only from notch to notch in the sleeve cap. *Then* stitch and press the underarm seam in the sleeve and the side seam in the garment. Complete the sleeve's armhole stitching from notch to notch under the arm.

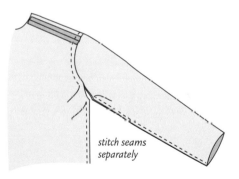

*stitch seams
separately*

**Q** I set-in the sleeves without puckers, but when I put on the garment, sometimes there are wrinkles in the front or back armhole. How do I get rid of them?

**A** The fullness in the sleeve cap is in the wrong place on your body, usually due to an overly erect back or rounded posture. To get rid of the wrinkles, release the stitching from notch to notch, and move the fullness as needed: toward the shoulder in front, if the problem is rounded posture, or in back for erect posture. Adjust smoothly, pin, and baste the sleeve in place to check the look and fit before stitching permanently.

*shift some fullness toward shoulder*

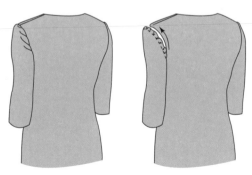

*shift some fullness toward shoulder*

**Q** I set-in the sleeves, but the armhole seam does not line up with my shoulder — it hangs over the edge. Can I take a deeper seam all around to make it fit better?

**A** No. The garment is too wide from the neck to the outer edge at the shoulder. If you take in the seam of the sleeve and the garment together at the shoulder, you'll lose the round shape of the cap and it won't fit your shoulder. Remove the sleeve from the armhole, try on the garment and assess the shoulder-seam length. Making sure that you leave ⅜" seam allowance in the garment beyond the edge of your shoulder, trim any excess at the shoulder, carefully tapering back into the armhole curve at the front and back notches. Repin the sleeve, baste, try on, and adjust again if necessary before stitching.

## Cuffs

Cuffs are cut as one piece or two (the cuff and the cuff facing). Interfacing is necessary for body so the cuff can support buttons and buttonholes — and so it has long-term durability. Before the cuff can be sewn to the sleeve, you must make an opening to allow the cuff to lap over itself and button closed to fit your wrist. Your pattern will include directions for a faced placket or bound opening (continuous lap) in the sleeve for this purpose.

**Q** How should I interface a cuff?

**A** Fusible interfacing is the perfect choice for most cuffs, unless fusing is inappropriate for the fabric. For easier handling, I find it best to interface the entire one-piece cuff or both layers of a two-piece cuff with lightweight fusible interfacing. Contrary to most fusible directions, I *never* trim the interfacing seam allowances; fusible interfacing helps prevent raveling at the cut edges of the trimmed seams. It also helps achieve a flat press along the edges. *Note:* If fusible interfacing won't work on the fabric, use a sew-in interfacing and follow the pattern's directions to attach it to the cuff piece.

SEE ALSO: *Interfacing, pages 230–244.*

**Q** How do I prepare the interfaced cuff to attach it to the sleeve?

**A** **For a one-piece cuff.** Fold the interfaced cuff/facing piece in half and stitch the short ends. Trim seams to ¼", clip the corners, and press open over a point presser (*see page 40*), to set the stitches and make it easy to press sharply along the finished edge after turning the cuff right side out.

**For a two-piece cuff.** With right sides facing, sew the cuff and facing pieces together along the short ends and one long edge. Trim and press as directed for a one-piece cuff. To press the seam open on the long edge, lay the cuff on the ironing board and press one seam allowance away from the other as shown for a collar on page 289.

Q How do I make sure the curved edges on shaped cuffs are the same shape?

A To ensure smooth stitching and identical rounded corners, make a template and mark the curves for stitching. Sew the cuff layers together (*see* Begin in the Middle, *below*). Trim and press as directed for the straight-edged cuff (*see previous page*), but use pinking shears around the curve to notch out excess fullness. Turn and press before attaching as directed for the straight cuff.

## BEGIN IN THE MIDDLE

For truly identical curves on cuffs, pockets, flaps, and collars, stitch in two steps: Beginning at the center of the long raw edges of the cuff, stitch around one corner to the upper raw edges of the cuff. Then stitch the remaining curve in the same way, with the beginning stitches overlapping at the center where you started each half. Approaching the curve from the same direction as you stitch ensures the same shape.

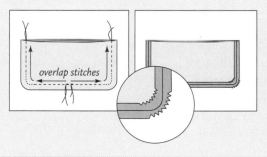

**Q** How do I attach the cuff to the lower edge of the sleeve for the smoothest finish?

**A** The wrapped-cuff application ensures a neat finish at each edge of the vent (the opening at the lower edge of the sleeve). It's not the typical method in standard pattern directions. After preparing the faced placket or continuous lap opening in the sleeve and making pleats or gathering the sleeve's lower edge as directed on the pattern guide sheet, follow these steps:

1. Turn the sleeve wrong side out. With raw edges even and right sides facing, pin the cuff to the sleeve. Match all construction marks. Stitch, taking care not to catch the facing layer of the sleeve in the stitching.

2. At each end of the cuff seam, wrap the facing and the facing's seam allowance snugly around the cuff, with the right side of the cuff against the wrong side of the sleeve. Stitch for 2" along the same stitching. This little "wrap job" ensures a neat finish at the opening edge of the sleeve vent.

   Trim and grade the seam allowance (*see page 282*). Turn the cuff right side out and press the trimmed seam allowance toward the cuff over the end of a sleeve board or seam roll (*see page 38*).

3. Turn the remainder of the cuff/facing seam allowance under so the fold lies along the stitching line. Press and then slipstitch in place.

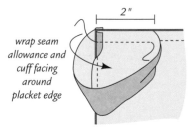

*wrap seam allowance and cuff facing around placket edge*

2"

# CHAPTER ELEVEN

# Fasteners and Closures

Buttons and buttonholes, snaps, hooks and eyes, zippers — all are essential elements in most sewing projects. Some require a bit of handwork, but most can be attached or worked by machine, speeding you along to the completion of your project. With mechanization and computerization, making buttonholes is now a breeze, and buttons and hook-and-eye closures can be machine stitched in place. Lapped, centered, and invisible zippers are easier than ever when you know the sewing tips and tricks included here.

# Buttonhole Basics

You will need the special buttonhole foot that comes with your machine to make beautiful buttonholes. Even though the machine does most of the work, there are still several concepts to understand, so the buttonholes you make fit your buttons and are correctly positioned. Study your manual and practice making buttonholes on fabric scraps until you know the process and are satisfied with the results.

---

**Q** Are there guidelines for selecting the appropriate buttonhole style from the many available on my machine?

**A** The two basic styles are straight-ended and keyhole, but you will find many other options on today's computerized machines. Straight buttonholes may have one or two rounded or pointed ends instead of the standard bar-tacked ends. The round end accommodates shank-style buttons on jackets and coats. Buttonholes designed expressly for knits, called knit or stretch buttonholes, prevent rippled edges. Your machine may have many other styles. The one you choose depends on your preference, as well as what will look best for your fabric/pattern/button combination. Keep the following in mind when planning and making buttonholes:

* Position the standard buttonhole with bar tacks at both ends, vertically or horizontally.
* Position buttonholes with one straight and one round end horizontally, with the round end closest to the opening edge.

* Choose round-end buttonholes for blouses and other garments made of lightweight and loosely woven fabrics; the stitches on these buttonholes control raveling better than buttonholes with straight bar tacks.

* Use shank-style buttons with keyhole buttonholes. To cut the round end open, use an eyelet punch.

---

Q **I measured the button diameter and made my buttonholes ⅛" longer than the buttons, but the buttonholes are too short. What's wrong?**

A Allow for the button diameter *and* its thickness to determine the buttonhole length. Wrap a narrow strip of paper around the button at its fullest point and pin, as shown. Slip the paper off, flatten it, and measure from the fold to the pin. Add ⅛" to come up with the buttonhole length. Make a test buttonhole on scraps of the same fabric combination as the garment area where you will be making the buttonholes. Test how the button fits — it should be neither too snug nor too loose — and adjust the buttonhole length if necessary on another test scrap.

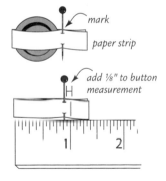

*mark*

*paper strip*

*add ⅛" to button measurement*

Q **What is the best way to mark buttonholes on a project?**

A Careful marking is essential. Buttonholes usually follow the cross- or lengthwise grain, unless they are positioned differently for aesthetic purposes. Horizontal buttonholes extend ⅛" past the center front (CF) or center back (CB) as in (A). Vertical buttonholes lie on the center front or back line where the pieces overlap (B).

On women's blouses, first mark a buttonhole position at the fullest point of the bust, then space the buttonholes above and below at the desired spacing. On garments with turn-back

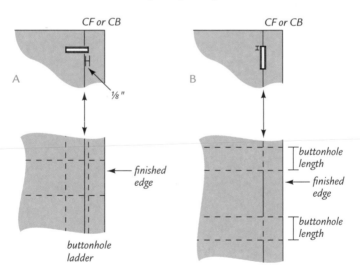

lapels, the first buttonhole is positioned at the point where the lapel breaks at the garment edge.

On many machines, you can set buttonhole length and save it, making it easy to make all of your buttonholes the same. Test on scraps first and then save the setting. If you aren't able to do this, you must mark the buttonhole beginning and ending points on the project. Use tailor's chalk to mark the beginning and ending points for each buttonhole with a straight line at each end and draw a straight line between them to create a "buttonhole ladder." Then machine-baste along the marks or use pieces of narrow masking tape for a more permanent set of marks to ensure the correct placement. Or, draw the ladder on a piece of water-soluble embroidery stabilizer, then pin it to the garment, stitch through it, and carefully tear it away from the finished buttonholes.

---

**Q** **I've misplaced my pattern. How do I position and mark the buttonholes?**

**A** Without a pattern to guide you, check the position and spacing on similar garments that you own, and use them as a guide.

To determine spacing between buttonholes, mark the desired position for the top and bottom buttons; measure the space between and divide by the number of buttons minus 1. For a 5-button closure, divide by 4 to determine the spacing.

# Q Does it matter whether I make horizontal or vertical buttonholes?

# A Follow the buttonhole direction specified on your pattern piece. Horizontal buttonholes take wearing strain and are more commonly used for this reason in blouses, shirts, jackets, and back openings. Vertical buttonholes stitched parallel to the long edges are essential in front plackets (as in menswear shirt styles) for aesthetic reasons. They are usually vertical along the front or back opening edge of skirts that button for the same reason.

- - - - - - - - - - - - - - - - - - - - - - - - - - - - - - -

# Q Do you have any tips for making buttonholes in knit fabrics?

# A Knit fabrics require stabilization to prevent buttonholes from rippling, stretching, or gaping around the button. If the pattern calls for interfacing, make sure the one you choose has little or no stretch in at least one direction. Fusible knit-tricot and fusible weft-insertion interfacings are both stable lengthwise and stretch in the crossgrain.

* **Use the facing pattern pieces to cut the interfacing.** Position the direction with the least amount of stretch in the direction of the buttonhole. If there's no interfacing required, cut patches of interfacing with pinking shears and center the wrong side of the fabric over the buttonhole locations on the wrong side; fuse.

* **Add a layer of machine-embroidery stabilizer** under the garment or between the facing and the garment while you stitch buttonholes to stabilize the area; baste the layers

together around the buttonhole area before stitching. Place a strip of stabilizer on the garment's right side and mark the buttonhole on it. This will keep the top layer of fabric from stretching while you stitch through the layers. Tear away after stitching the buttonhole.

* **Avoid using a dense satin stitch for knits.** Some machines have special buttonhole stitches for knits. Always test-stitch first on the same layers (fabric, interfacing, and stabilizer) to make sure you've chosen the best combination for your knit to avoid rippling buttonholes.

* **Cord the buttonholes** to prevent stretching on very stretchy knits (*see below*).

- - - - - - - - - - - - - - - - - - - - - - - - - - - - - - -

## Q How do I make a corded buttonhole?

**A** Trap a length of topstitching thread or crochet cotton under the buttonhole stitches as you go. Your buttonhole foot may have an extension on the back or front designed to hold the cord in place. Wrap the cord over it and bring the two ends forward. As you stitch the buttonhole "legs," the zigzags should trap the cord *without stitching through it*. Pull gently on the two cords to draw the loop against the bar tack at the buttonhole end. Thread the cord into a large-eyed needle,

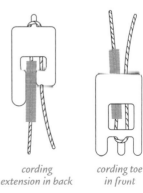

*cording extension in back*

*cording toe in front*

pull to the wrong side between garment and facing, and tie off securely. Trim ends close to the tie-off.

- - - - - - - - - - - - - - - - - - - - - - - - - - - - - -

# Q How do I cut a buttonhole open without cutting the stitches?

A For a clean slice through the fabric layers, use a chisel-like buttonhole cutter and a small wooden block placed under the buttonhole. Carefully position the blade between the buttonhole "legs" and bear down to cut through the fabric layers. If you don't have this tool, slip the point of a pair of sharp sewing or embroidery scissors into the fabric layers near the buttonhole center and cut out to the ends. Using scissors is safer than a seam ripper: it's too easy to slice right past the buttonhole end with a seam ripper. Place a straight pin across each end of the buttonhole before cutting for extra insurance; don't cut over the pin to avoid blade damage.

- - - - - - - - - - - - - - - - - - - - - - - - - - - - - -

# Q How do I make button loops for faced edges that meet at the center front or back?

A Make self-filled (seam-allowance enclosed) tubing for the loops, for all but sheer fabrics.

1. Cut a bias strip 2" to 3" longer than the total length of tubing you need for all buttons and 6 times as wide as the desired finished width/diameter.

2. Trim one end to a sharp point and cut a piece of sturdy string or cord 4" longer than the bias strip. Secure it to the right side at the pointed end of the

strip by stitching through it
several times (A).

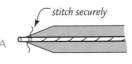

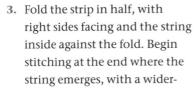

3. Fold the strip in half, with
   right sides facing and the string
   inside against the fold. Begin
   stitching at the end where the
   string emerges, with a wider-
   than-desired seam allowance and tapering into the
   desired finished width (B). Stretch the bias slightly as
   you stitch, to put a bit of give in the seam. This will
   prevent the stitches from popping when you turn
   the tube.

4. Trim the seam allowance so it is equal to the width
   from the stitching line to the fold. Carefully pull on
   the string to turn the tube right side out and use your
   fingers to work the tube back over the string and the
   seam allowance. Cut away the string.

5. Stitch to the garment, following your pattern
   guide sheet.

*Note:* For sheer and thin fabrics, you can leave the seam
allowance wider, since it will require more fabric to fill the tube.

## TEN TIPS FOR BEAUTIFUL BUTTONHOLES

1. Mark placement carefully, so all buttonholes are the same length and distance from the opening edge.

2. Choose the best buttonhole for your project and fabric. Use a stretch buttonhole for knits and a keyhole style for metal-shank buttons on tailored jackets and coats.

3. Match thread color to the garment. For multicolored prints, match the needle thread to the print color in the buttonhole location.

4. Choose cotton or rayon embroidery thread for smooth buttonholes on lightweight fabrics.

5. Loosen the top tension slightly to prevent bobbin thread from showing along the outer edges of the finished buttonholes.

6. Make a test buttonhole on a sample of the same fabric layers as in your garment.

7. Stitch with consistent, moderate speed for stitches of equal density. Don't pull or push the work under the foot. Stitch twice on thick fabrics for a more pronounced buttonhole.

8. Stitch over cord to prevent stretching in knits or to improve the appearance of a buttonhole. (*See page 377.*)

9. Use a stabilizer underneath. On napped fabrics, place a water-soluble stabilizer on top to protect the nap and prevent the buttonhole stitches from sinking into it. Carefully tear away the stabilizer. Residual bits will wash away during laundering.

10. Apply a thin line of liquid seam sealant between the buttonhole legs and allow it to dry before cutting the buttonhole open to control raveling.

# Solving Problems

**Q** How can I keep blouses and shirts from gaping at the bustline?

**A** Re-space the buttonhole placement so there is a button-hole at the fullest point of the bustline, which is the point of most wearing stress. Even more important: Be sure to adjust the pattern to fit your bustline without pulls before you cut. A too-tight fit across the full bust causes "gaposis." If the garment fits correctly, placing the buttonhole at the bustline is a secondary measure to keep the button buttoned. Mark and stitch the bustline buttonhole first and then re-space the others above and below it.

---

**Q** I was careful, but I cut the stitches in one of the but-tonhole legs and it's coming undone. Can I fix it?

**A** Use a seam ripper to carefully cut the stitches on the *back* of the buttonhole and lift away all stitches on the right side. Place a layer of water- or heat-soluble embroidery stabi-lizer under the buttonhole and pin or baste in place. Slowly restitch the buttonhole, making sure the needle swings over the raw edge and that it *doesn't catch the opposite cut edge of the* buttonhole. This requires careful handling while you stitch. Remove the stabilizer, following manufacturer's instructions for the type you are using. You can also use this method to replace stitching on worn buttonholes.

Q I cut into the bar-tack stitches at the end of the buttonhole. Can I repair this mistake?

A To repair, rip out the buttonhole and restitch it as directed on the previous page. Or pin a piece of stabilizer behind the buttonhole, adjust the buttonhole length so the bar-tack stitches end just past the cut end, and stitch the buttonhole again, over the original stitches. Make sure the needle lands between the two rows of buttonhole stitches and into the stabilizer, or you will end up with a closed buttonhole. If you cut through the entire bar tack and into the fabric beyond, repair the buttonhole and then disguise the cut in the garment with beading, embroidery, or small appliqués. Repeat on every buttonhole so this looks planned, rather than the result of an accident.

---

Q When I cut the buttonholes open, the interfacing color shows along the edge. Is there anything I can do?

A Use a permanent-ink marker in a color that matches or closely matches the buttonhole thread, and carefully color the cut edges. When selecting interfacing for areas with buttonholes, choose a light color for light- and medium-colored fabrics and gray or black interfacing for darker ones.

---

Q Is there a way to control raveling along the cut edges of a buttonhole?

A Whenever possible, use a fusible interfacing; it controls the raveling on the layer to which it is fused. Before cutting open buttonholes, particularly on loosely woven fabrics, apply a thin line of liquid seam sealant to the fabric between the two rows of stitching. Allow it to dry completely before cutting the buttonhole open.

---

**Q** Can I fix rippled buttonholes in my knit garment?

**A** Thread a needle with topstitching thread or buttonhole twist; double but don't knot the ends. Slide the needle under one row of the buttonhole stitches, leaving a long thread tail. Make a U-turn, insert the needle, and draw thread under the second row of stitches. Insert the remaining thread tail into the same needle, and slip the needle and threads between the garment and facing layers. Tie off and trim the ends. In the future, consider cording buttonholes in knits as you make them (*see page 377*).

---

**Q** I made a buttonhole in the wrong place; it's not cut yet. How do I get it out?

**A** With great care. Work only on the inside of the garment and use a seam ripper to lift and cut the tiny stitches. Pick out the stitches on the right side. If you can lift a facing and access the stitches, you can try a seam ripper to cut them and then remove the threads on the outside. Or, try inserting a sturdy needle under the stitches and running the blade of single-edge razor over the stitches on top of the needle.

# Button Facts

Today's button selection is vast and colorful. Sometimes buttons are simply functional, but often they are decorative, too. Choosing just the right one can make the difference between an ordinary garment and one that is more interesting. Sewing them in place beneath their corresponding buttonhole (*see the first question on page 386*) is not difficult, but positioning is critical to smooth working and a clean, finished look.

Q **Are there any guidelines for choosing buttons for my project?**

A Check your pattern envelope, under the notions requirements, to determine the correct button size. The two basic styles are flat buttons with two or four holes, and buttons with a metal or plastic loop shank on the underside. You can also purchase button forms to cover with fabric to match or contrast with your project. Make sure that the color, style, weight, and care requirements are compatible with the fabric.

Q **What's the purpose of a shank button other than appearance?**

A The shank holds the button above the surface of the garment, allowing room for thick fabric layers to lie beneath it without stressing the buttonhole. They are most often, but not always, used on coats, jackets, and other projects made of bulky fabrics.

**Q** My pattern envelope specifies ½" buttons, but the ones I want are ⅝". Can I substitute that size?

**A** It's always best to use the size specified; it's okay to change button sizes, but by no more than ⅛" smaller or larger in diameter. The distance from the outermost end of the buttonhole to the garment edge must be at least ⅛" more than half the button diameter to provide plenty of room for the button to lay on the garment. If the button is too large, it may touch or sit over the finished edge, creating a visual distraction.

## BUTTON MEASUREMENT EQUIVALENTS

Buttons are marked with two additional numbers: millimeters and line (from the French word *ligne*).

| Inches | Millimeters | Lines |
| --- | --- | --- |
| ¼ | 7 | 10 |
| ⅜ | 9 | 15 |
| ½ | 13 | 20 |
| ⁹⁄₁₆ | 14 | 22 |
| ⅝ | 16 | 24 |
| ¾ | 19 | 30 |
| ⅞ | 22 | 36 |
| 1 | 26 | 40 |
| 1⅛ | 28 | 45 |

**Q** When I button up, the top layer of fabric always buckles. How do I prevent this?

**A** Even the slightest placement error can create this problem. Mark button positions *after* completing the buttonholes (*see pages 374–375*). To prevent buckling, mark and sew the buttons one at a time. Stop after each button is in place to button it through the buttonhole and check for accurate placement.

1. Lap the buttonhole side of the garment on top of the button side *with center lines matching*. Pin the layers together between the buttonholes.

2. **For vertical buttonholes,** push a pin into the bottom fabric layer ⅛" below the upper end of the buttonhole; lift the top layer carefully, leaving the pin in place. Insert a pin into the fabric at the pin point or use a fine-tip water- or air-soluble marking pen to mark the button-centering position. Center and sew buttons in place at the marks.

3. **For horizontal buttonholes,** insert the pin ⅛" from the end of the buttonhole that is closest to the outer edge of the overlapping layer. Sew the button in place *before* marking the placement and sewing the next one in place.

- - - - - - - - - - - - - - - - - - - - - - - - - - - - - - - - - -

**Q** How do I sew on a button securely, so it won't pop off later?

**A** Follow this procedure for two-hole and four-hole flat buttons. It creates a thread shank or stem that allows space behind the button and limits strain on the buttonhole.

1. Thread a hand-sewing needle. Cut and double a 36" length of thread and knot the ends (*see pages 119–121*). To avoid kinks and knots, the total length should be no longer than 18" after doubling. To make it glide more easily through the fabric and prevent kinking, wax your thread. (*See* Wax It! *on page 389.*)

2. Take a small stitch on the right side, to hide the knot beneath the button. Position the button and take one stitch through the button and the fabric layers, bringing the needle back up through the layers for the next stitch.

3. Place a sewing needle or round toothpick across the button and continue stitching, taking several more stitches through the button and the fabric layers. This secures the button and leaves a short thread shank between it and the garment. For thicker fabrics, use a wooden bamboo skewer, a large square matchstick, or a thick tapestry needle instead of the sewing needle or toothpick. This will lift the stitches away from the button for a longer thread shank.

4. Remove the needle or toothpick, lift the button against the stitches, and you'll find the thread shank. Wrap the needle and thread snugly around the thread (four times or more) to strengthen the shank. Take a few backstitches under the button to secure it.

*toothpick*

# Q Can I sew on buttons by machine, like they do in ready-to-wear?

A This is my favorite method for two- and four-hole buttons, because it's faster and the results are more secure. First, check your manual; your computerized machine may have an automatic button-sewing stitch. Otherwise, follow these directions on any zigzag sewing machine. *Note:* When sewing buttons on thick fabrics, you can use a tailor-tack presser foot (an extra purchase) on top of the button to create a longer thread shank.

1. Mark the button position carefully (*see the first question on page 386*). Center the button over the positioning mark *with the holes in the button parallel to the buttonhole direction.* Use a dab of glue stick on the button back or put a piece of Scotch Magic tape over the button to hold it temporarily.

2. Attach the button-sewing presser foot or the open-toe embroidery presser foot. (If you don't have these, remove the regular presser foot, but be careful not to catch your fingers in the stitching.) Drop the feed dogs (or cover them with an index card taped in place) and adjust the machine for a zigzag stitch width that will reach across the holes in the button without hitting the button and breaking the needle.

3. Place a needle or toothpick over the button between the holes and perpendicular to the stitch direction. Drop the presser-foot lever, even if you are not using a presser foot. Use the hand wheel to take the first stitch, then *slowly* zigzag the button in place with four or more stitches.

On computerized machines, you will end by stitching in place through one hole to secure the button. For mechanical machines, raise the needle after taking the last zigzag stitch and move the stitch-width selector so that the needle is over the right-hand hole in the button. Change the stitch width to 0 and stitch in place several times to make a "knot." For added security, leave a thread tail long enough to thread into a needle.

4. Thread the bobbin thread into a hand-sewing needle, and bring it to the fabric surface under the button. Thread the needle and bobbin thread into the needle and wrap the thread shank. Hand-stitch through the fabric layers and secure with several small stitches.

### WAX IT!

Waxing sewing thread for handwork makes it stronger and helps it glide more easily through the fabric. Purchase a cake of beeswax in the notions department; it often comes in a slotted plastic container that makes it easier to use. Draw the thread through the wax several times, then place it between a few layers of paper towel and press with a warm iron to melt the wax onto the thread. (If you don't press it, the wax tends to rub off the thread as you sew.)

**Q** I don't like shank buttons. Is there a special way to attach flat buttons on thicker fabrics?

**A** Add an extra-long thread shank while you sew the button in place so the buttons fit through the buttonholes and stay buttoned. Use a square matchstick or a bamboo skewer to lift the threads away from the button (instead of a toothpick). For added strength, use topstitching or buttonhole thread and do a buttonhole stitch (*see page 394*) around the thread shank.

- - - - - - - - - - - - - - - - - - - - - - - - - - - - - -

**Q** When I sew with doubled thread, the thread often breaks at the eye. Is there a way to remedy this?

**A** The shredding and breaking is due to strain on the thread. If you cut the thread length and fold it in half, then thread it as one through the eye of a crewel needle, the thread that lies in the needle eye will not break or shred as easily. Be sure to wax the thread (*see page 389*) for strength.

- - - - - - - - - - - - - - - - - - - - - - - - - - - - - -

**Q** The buttons on my coats and jackets often fall off. Is there a way to prevent this?

**A** Reinforce buttons with a small, flat backing button. Place the flat button on the facing side and sew it on at the same time you sew the buttons to the garment's right side.

The added weight of an extra button may be too much. For delicate fabrics, use small, clear buttons or substitute a small folded square of lightweight ribbon or matching fabric between the outer layer and facing, directly under the button, so it won't be seen on the inside of the finished garment.

**Q** I made covered buttons, but the silvery form color shows through the fabric. How do I prevent this?

**A** Press fusible lightweight woven or weft-insertion interfacing to back the fabric, before cutting out the circle for the button cover. It will mask the color of the form.

---

### BUTTON-SEWING TIPS

* Double the thread for hand-sewing buttons to reduce the number of stitches you must take. However, it's usually easier to make neat stitches with a single thread and more stitches.

* Wax thread for button sewing for strength and sewing ease. (*See* Wax It! *on page 389.*)

* Use topstitching thread for heavier fabrics such as wool coatings: it's a bit thicker and stronger.

* Tug gently after each stitch to make sure each one is completed, so there are no stray loops of thread on the back side of the fabric. These are unsightly and not secure.

* Sew an extra button or two to the inside at the bottom edge of your garment, just in case you lose a button. It's easier than digging through your button collection to find a perfect match. (This is often done in ready-to-wear, on men's shirts, and on coats and jackets, so why not do the same?)

# Hook Closures

Choose hooks and eyes (or snaps; *see* Snap to It! *on pages 395–396*) when an inconspicuous closure is required. Hooks are most often used in areas of stress, to secure neckline edges above a zipper or to hold edges that meet as in a cardigan-style jacket. Hook-and-loop tape (popularly known as Velcro) is another closure fastener that is particularly appropriate for many home-decor items.

---

**Q** My package of hooks has loops and straight bars. What's the difference?

**A** Choose the loops (really called "eyes") if the edges of your garment meet but don't overlap, as at the front edges of a cardigan-style jacket. Use the bar when one layer overlaps the other, as on a waistband.

---

**Q** How do I position and sew hooks and eyes?

**A** Position the eye so that the outermost edge lies at, or slightly away from, the finished edge. With doubled and waxed thread (*see page 389*), take a few small stitches in place close to the loops and then make buttonhole stitches (*see page 394*). Catch only a thread or two of the garment in each stitch, and position the beads of the stitches along the outer edge of the loops. Before ending the stitching, slide the needle between the fabric layers, so you can catch the hook in place with several stitches. Make sure none of these stitches show on the garment's right side. To end the stitching, take several small inconspicuous stitches in place.

Attach the hook to the loop to determine the correct position and sew in place in the same manner. You can replace an eye with a thread loop. Some sewers prefer these because they are less conspicuous than a metal eye. Note the extra stitches on the hook and loop to keep them in place (*see the next couple of questions*).

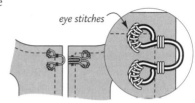

*eye stitches*

*hook and loop positions, so edges meet*

---

# Q What about hooks and bar-style eyes?

A These are preferred on areas that receive a lot of wearing stress: waistbands, for example. Position the hook first on the underside of the overlap, with the loop edge close to the garment edge. Use buttonhole stitches as described for hooks and eyes. To keep the hook really flat, take several stitches over the hook end between the hook and the base. Next, catch the bar in the hook and mark the position of the holes with a nonpermanent marker. Stitch in place.

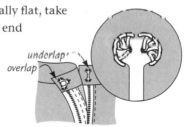

*underlap*
*overlap*

*edges overlap*

You can make an inconspicuous thread loop to replace a metal one in areas that are not under excessive wearing strain. Use a single strand of topstitching thread (or doubled all-purpose thread) that matches the fabric. Sew the hook in place and mark the placement for the loop. Take several stitches in place, just long enough for the hook to catch, and then cover the thread strands with buttonhole stitches as shown, without catching the fabric underneath. Secure the stitching on the outside.

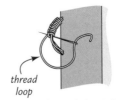

Use the same basic procedure to create belt carriers (use the belt width plus ½"), button loops large enough for the button to slip through easily, and French tacks to hold a lining in place at a garment hem (*see page 256*).

*thread loop*

*buttonhole stitch over threads*

---

Q **Hook closures are uncomfortable at the back of the neck. Is there an alternative closure?**

A Try a hanging snap. Sew the receiver half (or socket) to the left side of the opening above the zipper. Snap the other half into it. Thread a needle with doubled thread and knot. Hide the knot under the facing, then take the thread through a hole in the snap. Take a small stitch in the facing, back through the hole and repeat. Cover the threads with a closely spaced buttonhole stitch.

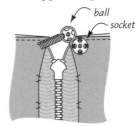

*ball*
*socket*

*hanging snap*

# Q When should I use hook-and-loop tape?

A This is best on loose-fitting garments; otherwise undue strain can cause the tapes to release. Since the tape adds bulk, it is not suitable for sheer or lightweight fabrics. The edge-stitching required to attach the hook-and-loop tape shows on the right side of the overlap, unless you use fusible hook-and-loop tape. When stitching the loop side to the overlap, make sure the bobbin thread is a close match to the fabric color. Stitch the hook half to the underlap. Use a larger sewing-machine needle to easily puncture the tape. Slip a thin piece of cardboard against the edge of the tape to keep the presser foot level while you stitch for the most secure stitch.

---

# Snap to It!

Snaps are used to secure overlapping edges that are not under stress during wear.

---

# Q Does it matter which half of the snap is sewn to the overlap?

A Sew the socket to the underlap — the part of the garment closest to your body — and the ball to the underside of the overlap (*see the illustration on the next page*). Position and sew the ball in place first, using buttonhole stitches, as described for hooks and eyes on page 393. Take a few stitches in place to begin, then cover them with the snap half and sew in place, taking care that the stitches don't show on the outer fabric layer. When moving from hole to hole, slide the needle underneath the snap in the fabric layers. To mark the position for the socket, rub the ball with tailor's chalk and then press it into position on the underlap to transfer the chalk. Center the socket and sew in place.

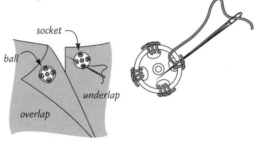

SEE ALSO: *Hanging Snap, page 394.*

# Lapped and Centered Zippers

Don't let the Z-word scare you. With today's methods, installing zippers is much easier than you might think. Choose from a variety of zipper styles and applications: lapped, centered, and invisible are the most common. Zippers are the most common choice for center-front and center-back applications. Occasionally, they are used in a side seam. Adding a zipper to the seam of a pillow cover makes it easy to remove and wash.

## Q How do I choose a zipper from the styles available in the notions department?

## A For most garments, choose a nylon-coil or polyester-coil zipper on a lightweight zipper tape. Other options are:

* For sportswear with an exposed zipper: Look for sports zippers with plastic or metal teeth on a slightly heavier tape. Separating zippers for sportswear are also available.

* For fitted pants cut from medium- and heavyweight fabrics, including jeans: Choose a trousers zipper with metal teeth for strength and to resist wearing strain.

* For a clean-line center-back closure without any visible stitching in skirts, pants, and dressers: Choose an invisible zipper. These leave a long, clean seamline with only a shapely zipper pull exposed at the top.

* For large home-decor projects and outdoor gear: Continuous zipper is sold by the yard; you can customize the zipper to fit by adding a zipper pull and stitching over the coils at the opposite end (*see page 405*) as discussed for shortening zippers. *Note:* You *cannot* use zipper by the yard to make separating zippers for jackets or sleeping bags.

---

## Q When inserting a lapped or centered zipper, how do I work around the bulky zipper pull?

## A The real secret is to purchase a zipper 1" to 2" longer than the opening, so it extends above the cut edge. Then you can move the zipper pull out of the way of the stitching. You cut away the excess later, after unzipping and adding the facing

or waistband to "stop" the zipper (*see
question on page 400 about trimming*).

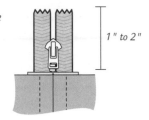

1 " to 2 "

---

## Q How do I insert a lapped zipper?

**A** You will need narrow basting tape for this quick-and-
easy method. It works really well when inserting a fly-
front zipper in trousers or when you must remove and replace
a broken zipper, too.

1. Machine-stitch the seam below the zipper opening
   and press open.
2. Turn under and press the ⅝" seam allowance on the
   side that will lap over the other and ½" on the underlap side (which creates a small pleat at the
   end of the opening).
3. Apply basting tape to the right side of the
   zipper along both long edges. Remove the
   protective paper on the tape on the right-
   hand edge of the zipper (as you look at it).

*basting tape*

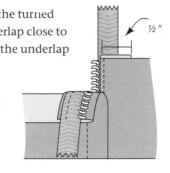

4. Position the zipper with the turned edge of the garment underlap close to the zipper teeth beneath the underlap edge; allow room for the zipper to slide easily. Use your fingers to secure the fabric to the basting tape on the zipper. Edgestitch in place with the zipper foot adjusted to one side to clear the zipper teeth. Remove the tape.

5. Remove the protective paper on the remaining edge of the zipper tape. Position the overlap so the turned edge just covers the edgestitching on the underlap. Finger-press to adhere the zipper tape to the under-side of the overlap.

6. On the right side, align one edge of ½"-wide Scotch Magic tape with the seamline to use as a topstitching guide — or mark the stitching line with a water- or air-soluble marking pen and ruler. Adjust the zipper foot to the right of the needle. Beginning at the bot-tom of the zipper just below the bottom stop, stitch along the tape end, pivot and stitch along the edge of the tape up to the garment raw edge.

**Q** **I used the extra-long zipper as recommended. What do I do with the excess?**

**A** Unzip the zipper and apply the facing (*see page 291*) or waistband (*see pages 340–343*) that your garment requires. Then, *and only then*, cut off the excess zipper.

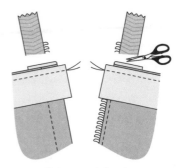

*facing or waistband*

---

**Q** **How do I install a centered zipper?**

**A** This method requires basting tape and ½"-wide Scotch Magic tape. An extra-long zipper is recommended for the easiest application.

1. Machine-stitch the seam below the zipper opening first, backstitching at the lower point of the opening. *Without breaking the stitching,* change to a basting-length stitch (4 mm or longer) and machine-baste the opening closed; press open. Use scissors or a seam ripper to break every sixth stitch or so to make for easy removal later.

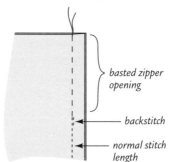

*basted zipper opening*

*backstitch*

*normal stitch length*

400

Attach the zipper foot and adjust the foot to the right of the needle.

2. Apply narrow, double-faced basting tape to *both* outer edges on the right side of the zipper tape, as shown on page 398, for the lapped zipper method. Unzip the zipper. Remove the protective paper on *both* pieces of basting tape. Place the unzipped zipper right side down on one seam allowance with the coil on one half of the zipper just shy of the machine-basted seamline. Finger-press the basting tape to the seam allowance. Zip the zipper and finger-press the other side in place. (Substitute machine- or hand-basting for the basting tape if you prefer.) If you are *not* using an extra-long zipper, the upper stop should be ¾" below the upper cut edge or ¼" below the seamline if the edge has been faced.

3. On the right side of the garment, center ½"-wide Scotch Magic tape over the seamline or mark stitching lines ¼" from the seamline with a removable marker.

4. Attach the zipper foot. *Beginning at the bottom of the zipper below the stop and at the seamline*, stitch along the edge of the tape, pivoting and continuing to the upper end of the zipper. Adjust the zipper foot to the opposite side of the needle and stitch the rest of the zipper. Pull the threads to the inside to tie off securely for a neat finish.

*stitch next to tape in direction of arrows*

5. Remove the tape and the basting tape if you used it. Remove the basting in the seamline and press lightly to set the stitches.

- - - - - - - - - - - - - - - - - - - - - - - - - - - -

**Q** Are there any other guidelines for inserting lapped and centered zippers that will help ensure success?

**A** Review the following list of suggestions for perfect zipper application:

* Preshrink the zipper for items that you intend to wash, unless the woven tape is polyester (in which case pre-shrinking is not necessary). Place the zipper in a measuring cup of hot water and allow it to cool. Air-dry and press if needed. Press to remove creases.

* Choose a zipper compatible with the fabric weight. Zippers with metal teeth are best for sportswear and heavier fabrics. Flexible nylon and polyester coil zippers work with most fabrics. For lightweight fabrics, look for zippers with fine coils and lightweight zipper tape.

### STITCH IT BY HAND

A hand-picked zipper is a wonderful alternative on lightweight fabrics, woolens, and if you simply enjoy handwork. The prickstitches used (*see pages 123–124*) are tiny and all but disappear when you use silk thread in a color that closely matches the fabric.

* Interface the zipper area in lightweight fabrics to add support, so the zipper weight doesn't drag on the placket area. Cut strips of lightweight woven or weft-insertion fusible interfacing the precise width of the seam allowance, and fuse it to the underside of the allowance before inserting the zipper. For knits, try centering a ½"-wide strip over the seamline and fuse in place.

* Match the thread to the fabric as closely as possible, for the most invisible application.

* Finish the zipper-opening seam allowances first; then attach the zipper

* Always stitch both halves of a centered zipper from the bottom to the top to prevent stretching one side of the fabric in the opposite direction from the other, creating diagonal pulls in the finished placket.

- - - - - - - - - - - - - - - - - - - - - - - - - - - - - -

Q **How do I finish the facing around the zipper on the inside of the garment?**

A For a lapped application, turn under the seam allowances, angling as needed to clear the zipper slider; slip-stitch (*see page 314*) to the zipper tape.

*When using a centered application.* For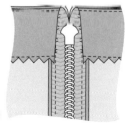
a neat ready-to-wear finish, prepare the garment's upper edge by reinforcing the stitching along the upper-edge seamline for ⅝" on each side of the seamline where you will be applying the zipper. Use a 1.25 to 1.5 mm stitch length (16 to 20 spi) and proceed as shown on the next page.

1. Clip the seam allowances on the seamline, ending at the reinforcement stitches (A). Turn the seam allowance to the inside and press.

2. Assemble the neck or waistline facing, press the seams open, trim the seam allowances to ¼", and then turn under and press the seam allowances at the opening edges (B). Pin and stitch the facing in place.

3. Trim and grade the seam (*see pages 282–283*) and understitch (*see pages 284–285*). Insert the centered zipper as directed on pages 400–402.

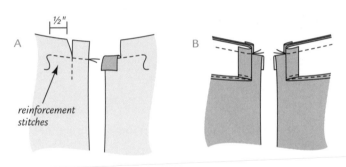

A

½"

*reinforcement stitches*

B

---

Q **There's a gap above the zipper at the upper faced edge. How do I close it?**

A Use a traditional hook with a loop-style eye or a thread loop (*see page 394*). Or try my favorite: a hanging snap (*see page 394*). To avoid gaps in future projects, consider this approach: Buy a zipper that is longer than you need (*as discussed on pages 397–398*). When you zip the zipper in the finished garment, there will be no gap.

# Solving Problems

## Q My zipper is too long. Can I shorten it?

A Yes. The easiest way is to make a machine or hand bar tack over the coil or teeth where you want the zipper slider to stop. Here's how:

1. Use the zigzag or open-toe presser foot, and adjust the machine for a zigzag stitch that will clear the width of the zipped coil or teeth. Drop the feed dogs and zig-zag several stitches. Pull thread tails to the back of the zipper and tie off in an overhand knot. Apply a drop of seam sealant.

2. Cut away the excess zipper below the bar tack using scissors. When cutting metal zippers, take care to cut in between the teeth to avoid damaging the scissors. When inserting the zipper, you will stitch over the coil or teeth in the zipper at the bottom end of the zipper. Use the handwheel to stitch slowly over this area to avoid breaking the sewing-machine needle.

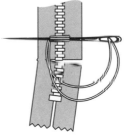

*Note:* You can also do bar-tacking by hand with doubled and waxed thread, or you can sew the bar-type hook from a hook-and-eye closure across the zipper instead.

*bar-tack over zipper teeth*

**Q** Basting tape seems to have gummed up the needle on my machine. Now I'm getting skipped stitches. What should I do?

**A** Use a cotton ball saturated in rubbing alcohol to remove the adhesive buildup that results from stitching through basting tape.

---

**Q** The seam allowance wasn't caught in the topstitching of my lapped zipper. How can I correct it?

**A** Think ahead and purposely cut the seam allowances ¾" wide when you cut out the project. If it's too late for that, you can extend the seam allowance *before* you insert the zipper using woven seam tape (*not* bias tape). Overlap a strip on each seam allowance edge by a scant ¼" and edgestitch in place — do not catch the garment in the stitching. If you've already done the zipper topstitching and it missed the seam allowance, carefully remove the stitching, add the tape extension to that seam allowance edge, and redo the zipper topstitching.

---

**Q** How do I make sure seamlines match when a zipper crosses a waistline or yoke seam?

**A** Before you baste the entire seam, clip the seam allowance of that seam to the stitching 1¼" from the opening raw edges and press open in that area. Trim the clipped seam allowances to ¼". With right sides facing, match the seamlines

and secure with a straight pin.
Machine-baste for 1" above
and below the seamline. Check
from the right side to make sure
they match. Adjust if necessary
before basting the remainder of
the seam in preparation for the
zipper application.

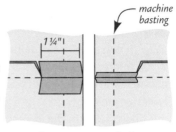

*clip, press open, and trim*

---

Q **Skirt and pants patterns usually call for a 7" zipper.
Is it okay to use a longer one for a longer opening?**

A Yes, particularly if your waistline is small in comparison
to your hips. A longer zipper will make it easier to step
into and out of a garment without breaking the zipper. For
skirts and pants, I allow for an 8"-long zipper opening when I
baste the seam and then use a 9" or 12" zipper and the application method shown on page 400.

---

Q **My zipper seems to hang up on the metal teeth. Is
there any remedy short of removing and replacing
the zipper?**

A Try treating it with a zipper lubricant such as Dritz Ezy-
Zipper Glide, or rub paraffin wax along the teeth. If these
don't work, it's probably time to replace the zipper.

# Q Must I replace a broken zipper or can I fix it?

A It depends on the damage; see the list below. If you must remove and replace a zipper, pay attention to how it was put in. You will need to unstitch a portion of the waistband or waistline facing on skirts and pants and replace it later.

* Missing teeth in the upper two-thirds of the zipper length? Remove and replace the zipper.

* Missing teeth near the bottom? Zip so the slider is just above the area where teeth are missing and shorten the zipper as shown on page 405 to make a new stop.

* Slider off the track on one or both sides? (*See* Back on Track *on the next page.*)

* Missing pull tab? If possible, salvage a pull from the zipper in a discarded garment or add a decorative pull (from the notions department). Otherwise, replace the zipper.

* Zipper won't stay zipped? Remove and replace the zipper in the same manner it was inserted. For a temporary emergency fix, zip the zipper and insert a safety pin through the zipper tapes below the slider.

## Invisible Zippers

When invisible zippers first appeared in the late 1960s, they were a novelty. Now they are the zipper of choice for an uninterrupted seamline with only the teardrop pull showing at the top.

## BACK ON TRACK

Here's how to fix a zipper when the slider has derailed:

* Remove the stitching on both halves at the lower end of the zipper.
* Remove and discard the metal bottom stop.
* Remove the zipper slider completely and then, starting at the top, guide the teeth back into the slider grooves, pushing the slider along the teeth to the lower end. You may need a pin or needle to help you work the slider down the zipper. This technique won't work unless you can seat the slider evenly on the teeth as you go so they will interlock.
* When the slider reaches the bottom, pull the slider up a little to be sure that the teeth are interlocked correctly.
* To make a new zipper stop, see instructions on how to shorten a zipper on page 405.

Q How do I insert an invisible zipper so the coil and zipper tape do not show?

A Unzip the zipper and place it right side down (coil-side up) on the ironing board. Heat the steam iron to the synthetic setting and use your fingers to "unroll" the coil at the upper end. Replace your fingers with the tip of the iron and continue unrolling and pressing the coil all the way down to the zipper pull, so it will lie flat under the tunnels in the special invisible-zipper foot.

*unroll and press coils flat*

An invisible zipper is stitched into a completely open seam *before* completing the seam below the zipper. The adjustable invisible-zipper presser foot has two tunnels on the bottom to hold the coils in the correct position for stitching. Purchase a generic foot or one designed specifically for your machine. Press the zipper tape, not the coil.

1. Carefully machine-baste ⅝" from the raw edge on each half of the garment for placement guidelines. Attach the invisible-zipper foot and center the needle.

2. Beginning on the right-hand opening edge, position the zipper coil as shown, just past the ⅝" seamline into the garment, with the zipper tape in the seam allowance. Pin temporarily so you can lower the presser foot with the pressed coil under the tunnel. *Stitch from the top down,* ending the stitching with backstitching when the foot touches the zipper pull.

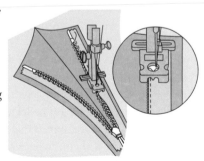

3. Position the remaining half of the zipper on the other half of the opening in the same

manner. Pin and stitch as for the first half of the zipper.

4. Zip the zipper. Pin-baste the seam below the zipper to prevent stretching and distortion while stitching. Adjust the zipper foot to the left of the needle or attach the traditional zipper foot and adjust. If you have multiple needle positions on your machine, fine-tune the needle position to stitch close to but not in the zipper-securing stitches. *Beginning a few stitches above the end of the zipper stitching and a thread or two to the left,* complete the seam (*see note below*). Adjust the zipper tail out of the way of the stitching so you don't break the needle, *but do not pull on the zipper* tail or you might stitch a crooked seam with puckers at the end of the zipper. Backstitch when you begin or tie off the threads securely. Press the seam open.

end of zipper stitching

*Note:* As counterintuitive as it may seem, beginning the stitches just above and *slightly* to the left at the end of the zipper stitching ensures no gap in the finished seam. If you try to begin the seam precisely where the zipper stitching ends, you *will* create a gap or a pucker or both.

# Q How do I attach and finish the facing above an invisible zipper?

# A Here's what you do:

1. Assemble the facing following the pattern directions and trim any joining seams to ¼" wide; press open. Trim away the ⅝" seam allowance at each short end of the facing and finish the lower edge of the facing as desired (*see pages 261–263*).

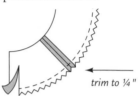

trim to ¼"

2. Unzip the zipper and place the facing and garment right sides together, with the trimmed short ends even with the zipper seam-allowance edge. Stitch ⅜" from the raw edges, using a zipper foot adjusted to the left of the needle to avoid the coil.

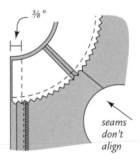

⅜"

seams don't align

3. With right sides facing, pin the facing to the garment edge, matching any seams. A fold will form as the zipper seam allowance wraps back over the zipper. Stitch the facing seam; trim, clip, grade, and turn right-side out. Understitch the facing as far as possible into the corners.

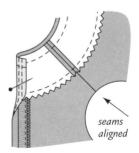

seams aligned

**Q** How do I shorten an invisible zipper?

**A** Bar-tack as for a conventional zipper (*see page 405*) or mark the desired length on the wrong side of each half of the zipper tape and stop stitching there. Backstitch.

---

**Q** Is there a way to anchor the lower end of an invisible zipper, so zipping is easier?

**A** Stitch the zipper tapes to the seam allowances only, *after* completing the seam below the zipper.

*stitch zipper tapes to seam allowance only, not to garment*

---

**Q** I'm having difficulty zipping the invisible zipper in my velvet dress. How can I correct this?

**A** Because the zipper coil forces the seam edges to roll to the center, thicker fabrics like velvet require stitching further from the coil than for medium- and lightweight fabrics. You can adjust the foot so the needle stitches farther from the coils. If you aren't sure how close to stitch in a heavy- or a very lightweight fabric, make a test sample on scraps, using machine-basting stitches so you can easily remove the zipper. You will need to baste about 3" of each half of the zipper and then test the zip. Adjust as needed, then remove the basting and insert the first half of the zipper at the new setting. Remember to adjust the foot or needle the same way for the other half of the zipper.

- - - - - - - - - - - - - - - - - - - - - - - - - - - - - -

**Q** I pressed the coil as directed, but the zipper tape shows after stitching. What's wrong?

**A** If the fabric is thin or lightweight, you probably didn't stitch close enough to the coils. Adjust the foot position so the needle will stitch a bit closer to the coils. If the zipper is already installed, simply adjust the foot and stitch a second time just inside the first stitching and closer to the coils.

- - - - - - - - - - - - - - - - - - - - - - - - - - - - - -

**Q** The pull tab on my invisible zipper is not a very good match for the fabric. Any quick fixes?

**A** Carefully apply a coat or two of nail polish to the pull tab and allow to dry thoroughly *before installing the zipper*. Paint for metal model cars works, too.

- - - - - - - - - - - - - - - - - - - - - - - - - - - - - -

**Q** How do I match stripes or plaids with an invisible zipper? And at waistline seams?

**A** Insert the first half of the zipper, close the zipper, and mark the design lines or waistline seamline on the unstitched half of the zipper tape. Unzip and position on the remaining half of the opening with lines matching. Hand-baste in place, zip the zipper to check the match, adjust if necessary, and then stitch permanently.

# Resources

Sewing books abound and sewing magazines keep you up to date on the newest fabrics, patterns, tools, notions, equipment, and software. In addition, sewing information abounds on the Internet. Just enter your question or subject matter in a search engine and you're on your way to lots of sewing fun, courtesy of the information highway.

Blogging about sewing is very popular; many sewing websites have a blog so that's a good place to start. Look for blogs at the websites of the major pattern companies and at those offered by the sewing machine companies for starters. Once you've found a blog, check out some of the blogger's favorite sites and you'll be amazed at what you can learn. When you find one you like, be sure to subscribe so you'll know when new content has been added.

# Suggested Reading

The lists that follow include the books in my library that I turn to again and again. Some are no longer in print but readily available at various used book sellers and from Internet sources. Also check at your local library. There are many more sewing books available on a variety of specific sewing techniques. Build a library of sewing books that reflect your interests and offer excellent instruction and inspiration.

## Sewing Basics

Bednar, Nancy, and JoAnn Pugh-Gannon. *Encyclopedia of Sewing Machine Techniques*. New York: Sterling Publishing, 2007.

Clotilde. *Clotilde's Sew Smart.* Big Sandy, TX: DRG, 2004.

Editors of Creative Publishing International. *The Complete Photo Guide to Sewing.* Minneapolis, MN: Creative Publishing International, 2009.

Editors of Reader's Digest. *New Complete Guide to Sewing.* Pleasantville, NY: Reader's Digest, 2002.

Editors of Singer Worldwide. *Singer Simple Home Décor Handbook.* Chanhassen, MN: Creative Publishing International, 2007.

————. *Singer Simple Sewing Guide.* Chanhassen, MN: Creative Publishing International, 2007.

Editors of the Singer Sewing Reference Library. *Sewing Essentials.* Minnetonka, MN: Cy DeCosse, 1996.

Editors of *Vogue Knitting* magazine. *Vogue Sewing.* Rev. ed. New York: Sixth and Spring, 2006.

Maresh, Jan Saunders. *Sewing for Dummies.* 2nd ed. Hoboken, NJ: Wiley Publishing, 2004.

Soto, Anne Marie and the staff of the Simplicity Pattern Co., eds. *Simplicity's Simply the Best Sewing Book.* Rev. ed. New York: Simplicity Pattern Co., 2001.

Simplicity Pattern Co. *Simplicity's Simply the Best Home Decorating.* New York: Simon & Schuster, 1993.

## Fabrics Facts

Betzina, Sandra. *Fabric Savvy.* Newtown, CT: Taunton Press, 1999.

———. *More Fabric Savvy.* Newtown, CT: Taunton Press, 2004.

Long, Connie. *Sewing with Knits: Classic, Stylish Garment from Swimsuits to Eveningwear.* Newtown, CT: Taunton Press, 2000.

## Fitting Techniques

Alto, Marta, Susan Neall, and Pati Palmer. *Jackets for Real People.* Portland, OR: Palmer/Pletsch, 2006.

Palmer, Pati, and Marta Alto. *Fit for Real People.* Portland, OR: Palmer/Pletsch, 1998.

———. *Pants for Real People.* Portland, OR: Palmer/Pletsch, 2003.

## Serging (Overlocking)

Baker, Naomi, Gail Brown, and Cindy Kacynski. *The Ultimate Serger Answer Guide.* Iola, WI: Krause Publications, 1999.

Bednar, Nancy, and Anne van der Kley. *Creative Serging: Innovative Applications to Get the Most from Your Serger.* Sterling Publishing, 2005.

Benton, Kitty. *Easy Guide to Serging Fine Fabrics.* Newtown, CT: Taunton Press, 1997.

Brown, Gail, and Pati Palmer. *Sewing with Sergers.* Portland, OR: Palmer/Pletsch, 2004.

Editors of the Singer Sewing Reference Library. *Sewing with an Overlock.* Minnetonka, MN: Cy DeCosse, 1989.

Griffin, Mary, Pam Hastings, Agnes Mercik, Linda Lee Vivian, and Barbara Weiland. *Serger Secrets.* Emmaus, PA: Rodale, 1998.

## Sewing Magazines

Some sewing magazines are available by subscription and on the newsstand — others are newsstand only. Here are a few favorites:

*Altered Couture,* www.stampington.com/html/altered_couture.html
*Sew News,* www.sewnews.com
*Sew Simple,* www.sewsimple.com
*Sew Stylish,* www.craftstylish.com/sewstylish
*Stitch,* http://quiltingarts.com/stitch
*Threads,* www.threadsmagazine.com

# Sewing Resources

## Pattern Company Websites

You can order patterns online at these sites and find free sewing information, education, and projects.

**Butterick Patterns,** *www.butterick.com*
**Independent Pattern Company Alliance,**
    *www.patterncompanies.com*
**McCall's Pattern Company,** *www.mccall.com*
**Simplicity Creative Group,** *www.simplicity.com*
**Vogue Patterns,** *www.voguepatterns.com*

## Sewing Machine Company Websites

Check these sites for sewing machine information as well as free projects, sewing education, and blogs.

**Baby Lock,** *www.babylock.com*
**BERNINA,** *www.berninausa.com*
**Brother International,** *www.brother.com*
**Elna International,** *www.elna.com*
**Husqvarna Viking,** *www.husqvarnaviking.com*
**Janome,** *www.janome.com*
**Pfaff,** *www.pfaff.com*
**Singer,** *www.singer.com*

## Sewing Supplies, Notions, and Other Accessories

**Clover Needlecraft,** *www.clover-usa.com*, metal pocket template and other notions
**Palmer/Pletsch,** *www. palmerpletsch.com*, pattern tracing paper and books

# Index

Page numbers in *italics* indicate illustrations.
Page numbers in **bold** indicate charts.

# Other Storey Titles You Will Enjoy

*One-Yard Wonders,* by Rebecca Yaker and Patricia Hoskins.
101 hip, contemporary projects, from baby items and plush toys to
pet beds and stylish bags, each made from just a single yard of fabric.
304 pages. Paper. ISBN 978-1-60342-449-3.

*The Quilting Answer Book,* by Barbara Weiland Tolbert.
Hundreds of solutions for every quilting quandary, guiding readers
through cutting, piecing, appliqué work, borders, and binding.
432 pages. Paper. ISBN 978-1-60342-144-7.

*Sew & Stow,* by Betty Oppenheimer.
Out with plastic bags and in with 30 practical and stylish totes of
all types!
192 pages. Paper. ISBN 978-1-60342-027-3.

*Sew What! Bags,* by Lexie Barnes.
Totes, messenger bags, drawstring sacks, and handbags — 18 pattern-
free projects that can be customized into all shapes and sizes.
152 pages. Hardcover with concealed wire-o. ISBN 978-1-60342-092-1.

*Sew What! Skirts,* by Francesca DenHartog &
Carole Ann Camp.
A fast, straightforward method to sewing a variety of inspired skirts
that fit your body perfectly, without relying on store-bought patterns.
128 pages. Hardcover with concealed wire-o. ISBN 978-1-58017-625-5.

These and other books from Storey Publishing are available
wherever quality books are sold or by calling 1-800-441-5700.
Visit us at *www.storey.com*.